Lara Pawson worked for the BBC World Service from 1998 to 2007, reporting from Mali, Ivory Coast and São Tomé and Príncipe. From 1998 to 2000, she was the BBC correspondent in Angola, covering the civil war, and has returned to the country several times since. She currently works as a freelance journalist and lives in London.

'With unflagging intelligence, fearlessness, and compassion, Pawson unfolds the human and political dimensions of this forgotten atrocity. She has done Angola a great service in writing this book, and all of us, Angolan or otherwise, do ourselves a great service in reading it.'

Teju Cole, author of *Open City*

'Pawson brings her sources to life like a novelist; her meetings are vivid and convincing. A simple, direct clarity of vision is brought to bear, and the reader begins to make some sense of the conspiracies and sub-conspiracies that led to the *vinte e sete*. By the end, Angola – along with some of its layered political complexity – is raw, vital, brutal and alive in front of us.'

M. John Harrison, author of *Climbers*

'In a highly readable investigation, Lara Pawson exposes not only a forgotten massacre but a cover-up, perpetrated by British journalists and historians blinded by ideology. Travelling from London to Lisbon and Luanda, she reveals new information about the role of Cuban forces in the killings, and shows how racism against black Africans lies at the heart of Angolan politics.'

Lindsey Hilsum, International Editor, Channel 4 News, and author of *Sandstorm: Libya in the Time of Revolution*

'Pawson is an investigative journalist and historical sleuth of rare candour. Her high ethical standards, probing questions, sharp critical gaze and keen observations make for a compelling text. She takes the reader in and along as she asks of herself and others difficult questions about painful times. While she had set out to discover "the unwritten truth", Pawson instead unveils a still more complex landscape of memory and history, mined with silence, and knit together with complicities, stories and the underside of ideals.'

Marissa Moorman, Associate Professor of African History, Indiana University and author of *Intonations: A Social History of Music and Nation in Luanda, Angola, from 1945 to Recent Times*

'Lara Pawson's account of trying to unravel the complex knots of memory, violence, identity and politics in post-independence Angola offers a richly detailed, nuanced and emotional psychogram of a nation simultaneously fixated on and forcefully repressing its unresolved past. She vividly evokes the difficulties of doing research in and on Angola, and brilliantly captures the everyday paranoia of life in Luanda, ranging from grandiose conspiracy theories to intimate recollections of loss and the broken promises of independence.'

Jon Schubert, Senior Africa Analyst, IHS Country Risk

'The work that Pawson has done here is long overdue. Her starting point is that although in Angola people refer to a certain "golpe" (coup d'état) to justify their political indifference, there is almost nothing written about the Twenty-seventh of May. Even many British journalists, who have chronicled the process of Angolan independence since 1975, have been complicit in its silencing. My impression is that by going through these layers of silence and complicity, Pawson is asking very deep and provocative questions about the relationship between past and present in Angolan politics. There is no way politics in contemporary Angola may be understood without an engagement with the causes and the consequences of the Twenty-seventh of May.'

António Tomás, Ray Pahl Fellow, University of Cape Town

IN THE NAME OF THE PEOPLE

ANGOLA'S FORGOTTEN MASSACRE

LARA PAWSON

I.B. TAURIS
LONDON · NEW YORK

Published in 2014 by I.B.Tauris & Co. Ltd
6 Salem Road, London W2 4BU
175 Fifth Avenue, New York NY 10010
www.ibtauris.com

Distributed in the United States and Canada
Exclusively by Palgrave Macmillan
175 Fifth Avenue, New York NY 10010

Copyright © 2014 Lara Pawson

The right of Lara Pawson to be identified as the author of
this work has been asserted by the author in accordance with
the Copyright, Designs and Patents Act 1988.

All rights reserved. Except for brief quotations in a review, this book, or any part
thereof, may not be reproduced, stored in or introduced into a retrieval system, or
transmitted, in any form or by any means, electronic, mechanical, photocopying,
recording or otherwise, without the prior written permission of the publisher.

ISBN: 978 1 78076 905 9
eISBN: 978 0 85773 470 9

A full CIP record for this book is available from the British Library
A full CIP record is available from the Library of Congress

Library of Congress Catalog Card Number: available

Text designed and typeset by Tetragon, London
Printed and bound in Sweden by ScandBook AB

*For two who cannot be named
but know who they are – thank you,
so very much, for everything.*

CONTENTS

GLOSSARY	ix
KEY POLITICAL FIGURES	xii
MAPS	xiii
A NOTE ON THE TEXT	xvi
INTRODUCTION	1

PART I

1	Meeting Maria	9
2	In the Shadow of DISA	19
3	The Saboteurs, the Parasites, the Opportunists	28
4	When Normal Things Don't Go Normally	39
5	Fascism Was Finished, Socialism Had Begun	46
6	Just Like the Movies	57
7	The Brother	64
8	Sounds of Microfiche	77
9	Never Meet Your Heroes	83
10	Sent to Cuba	88
11	Closing in on the Kill	97

PART II

12	So Many Dragonflies	113
13	Saved by a Poet	125
14	To Sambizanga	134

15	The Little Red Book	145
16	Kilometre Fourteen	154
17	Cold War Paradox	160
18	Appearances	171
19	A Death Camp	175
20	Metamorphoses of the Enemy	191
21	On the Beach	209
22	How Our Heads Are Formed	213

PART III

| 23 | Loose Ends | 225 |
| 24 | A Cuba Connection | 235 |

EPILOGUE	245
ACKNOWLEDGEMENTS	251
NOTES	255
BIBLIOGRAPHY	261
INDEX	265

GLOSSARY

assimilado   (lit. 'assimilated') A black or *mestiço* Angolan who, under colonial rule, met the criteria for Portuguese citizenship by speaking and writing Portuguese, having gainful employment, sleeping in a bed and adhering to Christianity. *Assimilados* constituted under 1 per cent of the population.

bairro   (lit. 'neighbourhood' or 'district') Often refers to poorer areas.

bizneiro   Slang for businessman.

bufo   (lit. 'wind') A spy, or informer, or someone who works for the secret police, DISA. The more metaphorical translation is a silent but deadly fart.

camarada   (lit. 'comrade') Usually signifies membership of or support for the MPLA.

candongueiro   A privately owned minibus. Such vehicles are used by the majority of Angolans as their day-to-day transport within and between cities.

DISA   Pronounced 'dee-zah'. Direcção de Informação e Segurança de Angola (Angolan Directorate for Information and Security).

FAPLA   Forças Armadas Populares de Libertação de Angola (Popular Armed Forces for the Liberation of Angola), the MPLA army.

FNLA   Frente Nacional de Libertação de Angola (National Front for the Liberation of Angola), one of three liberation movements that fought Portuguese colonialism, with backing from the CIA and Zaire's President Mobutu Sese Seko. It drew its support mostly from northern Angola.

golpista   (lit. 'coupist') A Nito Alves supporter, also called a *nitista* and a factionalist.

kizomba	Both a popular musical genre and style of dance, performed in pairs.
Kudibanguela	(lit. 'We will defend ourselves') A radio programme that was banned by the government for allegedly broadcasting factionalist propaganda.
Mbundu	Angolans from the north–central and coastal areas, who speak Kimbundu and from whom the MPLA drew much of its initial support.
mestiço	(lit. 'mixed') Someone who has African and European ancestry, combining a black- and a white-skinned parent, two *mestiço* parents, etc.
MPLA	Movimento Popular de Libertação de Angola (Popular Movement for the Liberation of Angola), the ruling party since independence in 1975. Initially a nationalist and socialist movement supported by the Soviet Union, East Germany and Cuba, it is now a petro-diamond-capitalist dictatorship led by President José Eduardo dos Santos.
musseque	Shanty town or slum.
netista	An MPLA member supporting President Agostinho Neto.
nitista	An MPLA member supporting Nito Alves.
OCA	Organização Comunista de Angola (Communist Organisation of Angola).
Ovimbundu	Angolans from the central highlands, who speak Umbundu and who provided UNITA with much of its initial support.
PADEPA	Partido de Apoio Democrático e Progresso de Angola (Angolan Party for Democratic Progress), a small political party that emerged in the 1990s.
PCP	Partido Comunista Português (Portuguese Communist Party).
PIDE	Pronounced 'peed'. Polícia Internacional e de Defesa do Estado (International Police for the Defence of the State), Portugal's vast network of secret police, established under Salazar's regime in 1945.

povo	(lit. 'people') The masses, the poor, the Angolan majority. Often given a capital letter by the MPLA in its slogans and literature.
SADF	South African Defence Force, the army of South Africa until 1994.
UNITA	União Nacional para a Independência Total de Angola (National Union for the Total Independence of Angola), one of three liberation movements that fought Portuguese colonialism. It was supported by the CIA and South Africa's white-minority regime, and led by Jonas Savimbi until his death in 2002.
vinte e sete	(lit. 'twenty-seventh') Refers to the Nito Alves uprising and the purge that followed.

KEY POLITICAL FIGURES

Nito Alves Minister of the interior until October 1976. Expelled from MPLA on 21 May 1977, charged with 'factionalism'. Led the uprising, or coup attempt, of the Twenty-seventh of May 1977. Executed later that year.

Iko Carreira Henrique Teles Carreira, minister of defence under Agostinho Neto.

Ludy Kissassunda Head of DISA, the political police.

Lúcio Lara MPLA founder, and its Secretary General at independence. Agostinho Neto's number two.

Saydi Mingas Finance minister. Killed in Sambizanga on the Twenty-seventh of May 1977.

Monstro Imortal Jacob João Caetano, known as 'Immortal Monster', a senior member of FAPLA and close confidant to Nito Alves.

Agostinho Neto President of Angola from independence until his death in 1979.

Onambwe Henrique de Carvalho Santos, deputy head of DISA, the political police.

Sita Valles Portuguese Marxist who went to work for the MPLA at independence. Zé Van Dúnem's lover, with whom she had a son. Charged with 'factionalism' and executed in 1977.

José 'Zé' Van Dúnem Political commissar in the MPLA's armed wing, FAPLA, until October 1976. Expelled from MPLA on 21 May 1977, charged with 'factionalism'. Executed in 1977.

Derived from a Wikimedia Commons image of Angola on the globe

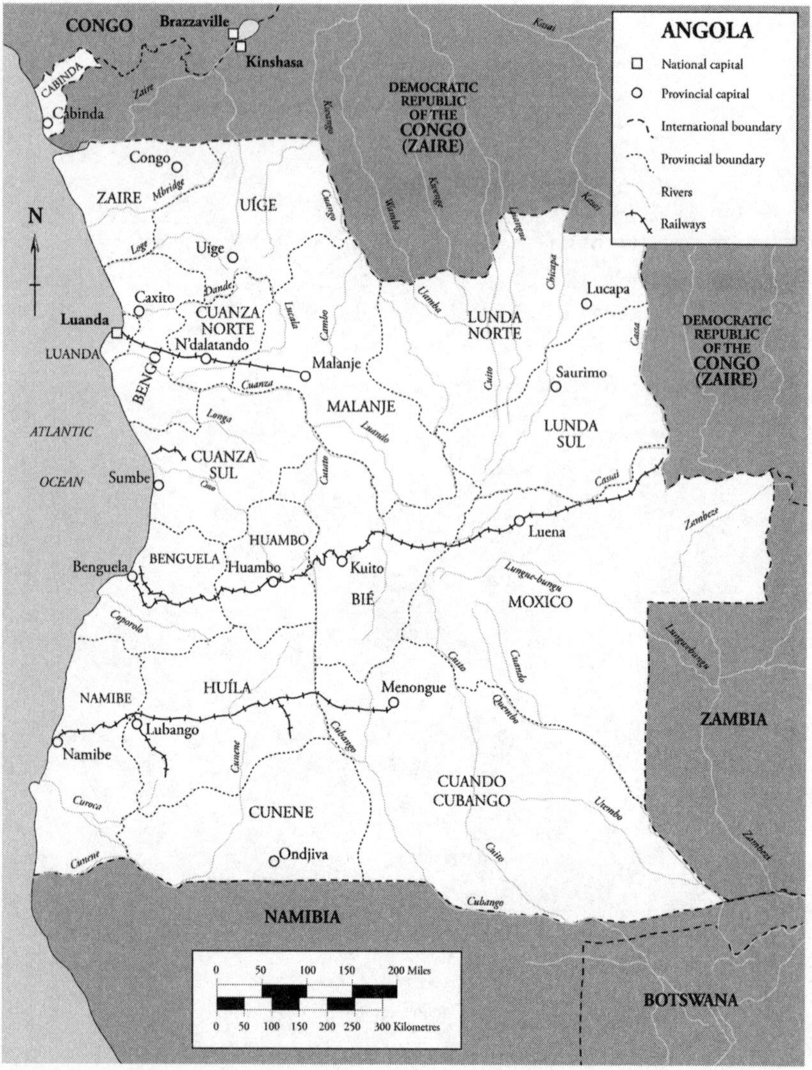

ANGOLA
National capital
Provincial capital
International boundary
Provincial boundary
Rivers
Railways
CONGO
Brazzaville
Kinshasa
CABINDA
Cabinda
DEMOCRATIC REPUBLIC OF THE CONGO (ZAIRE)
Congo
ZAIRE
UÍGE
Uíge
N
Caxito
Luanda
LUANDA
CUANZA NORTE
N'dalatando
BENGO
Malanje
MALANJE
LUNDA NORTE
Lucapa
Saurimo
LUNDA SUL
ATLANTIC
OCEAN
CUANZA SUL
Sumbe
Luena
HUAMBO
BENGUELA
Benguela
Huambo
Kuito
BIÉ
MOXICO
HUÍLA
Menongue
NAMIBE
Lubango
Namibe
CUANDO CUBANGO
CUNENE
Ondjiva
ZAMBIA
NAMIBIA
BOTSWANA
0 50 100 150 200 Miles
0 50 100 150 200 250 300 Kilometres

'Just remember, this is not your history. It's ours.'
Graça Francisco, an Angolan friend

'Real lives have no end. Real books have no end.'
J.M.G. Le Clézio, *The Book of Flights*

A NOTE ON THE TEXT

Because of the political climate in Angola, the names of some of the people in this book have been changed. In certain cases, other details about individuals have been either withheld or slightly altered in order to afford them some protection.

INTRODUCTION

One hot and sticky morning in February 2000, I stood waiting in a grassy square in front of a pale pink seventeenth-century Carmelite church in downtown Luanda. A few metres away, on Rua de Portugal, the traffic of the Angolan capital was heaving between broken gutters. An overweight *bizneiro* was talking into two cellphones inside his four-by-four, and a disappointed aid worker sat in a white Land Cruiser, its antenna pulled back like a giant antelope horn. Blue and white minibuses, the *candongueiros*, were pumping with people and the latest *kizomba* tunes as their drivers prised open the narrowest of spaces in the gridlock. At the junction, a policeman balancing on a rusting plinth was exploring odd angles with his elbows. He wore long white gloves that flashed like mirrors in his hands, and his fingers formed fleeting shapes in the starched heat. Miraculously avoiding death in the middle of all this was a dog with bulging testicles, trotting back and forth between the tyres and tonnes of metal.

Shortly before ten o'clock, a number of men began to gather between the trimmed hedges in the square. They were members of PADEPA, a young and feisty political party that stood for democracy and progress but was barely known beyond the borders of Luanda. When all were finally present, they sat down on the clipped lawn in pressed trousers, clean shirts and polished shoes and began a hunger strike in protest against a 1,500 per cent increase in the price of fuel.

Since I had arrived in Angola in October 1998, my work as the BBC correspondent had focused almost exclusively on the country's miserable civil war, which had begun a few months before independence in 1975 and had matured into one of the longest conflicts on the continent. One party – the Popular Movement for the Liberation of Angola (MPLA) – had been in power since the Portuguese colonial rulers left, and an act of political defiance, a protest like this, was rare. I was determined to witness it no matter how insignificant it might be to the rest of the world. I knew it was going to be difficult to persuade my bosses in London to give airtime to what was, by most standards, a tiny demonstration. But I persisted anyway, and pointed my microphone into the circle of fasting men. Within minutes, my recording equipment was picking up a loud and familiar sound. Two van-loads of armed police came sweeping into the centre of the square. Men holding large guns tumbled out and promptly arrested twelve of the protesters. As it turned out, this rapid response from the security apparatus is what sold the story: arrests make a more convincing headline than a half-hour hunger strike.

A few days later, another demonstration was organised outside the provincial governor's offices, just across the road from the church. It was smaller than the previous one, but that did not deter the police, who arrived shortly after the start and made more arrests.

The day after that, a third demonstration took place, this time back outside the church. Now, the focus had shifted away from price hikes to the previous days' arrests. The protestors included a few PADEPA supporters as well as other activists such as Francisco Filomeno Vieira Lopes, an austere but attractive economist known for his principled leadership of another small political party. I was in the middle of interviewing him when the police vans arrived. A small man belted up in blue pointed a Kalashnikov at us and shouted at me to hand over my recording equipment. I refused. He shouted louder. I shouted back, and then he turned on Vieira Lopes, swiftly handcuffing him and frogmarching him away.

Moments later, it was as though nothing out of the ordinary had ever happened. I found myself standing quite alone again, listening to the sounds of Rua de Portugal, feeling the furrows of sweat running from beneath my bra down over my stomach, and wondering how such a small act of dissent could have provoked such an excessive response.

During the days that followed, I kept reflecting on this rather curious sequence of resistance. I was struck by the paucity of protesters and even more by the absence of other journalists. Just one other reporter came to witness the demonstrations, and he was only there on the first day. When I asked my Angolan colleagues why they had not turned up, I was given a range of explanations. Some said that the protests were too small to bother with, that PADEPA was only interested in publicity stunts which would never lead to real change. Others blamed their lack of motivation on their editors, who had not paid them a living salary in months. One or two admitted that the fear of being arrested was what had deterred them.

But it was a slightly older journalist, a man in his early fifties, to whom I often went for advice, who told me something remarkable. What I had witnessed, he said, was Angola's *cultura do medo* – its culture of fear.

'The last time there was a proper protest in this country, they didn't just arrest everyone – they killed many of the protestors and then carried on killing for weeks.'

'When was this?' I asked.

'Nineteen seventy-seven,' he said. 'They killed thousands. People have been very afraid ever since.'

This was my introduction to the Twenty-seventh of May 1977,[1] and I was staggered. My journalist friend explained that, on this day, a faction of the ruling MPLA rose up against the party's leadership. He said that some people described it as a coup attempt, but he insisted it was just a demonstration that met with a brutal overreaction. He said he had been among those imprisoned without trial for several years and yet, like most of those killed and imprisoned, he had always supported the MPLA.

This story contrasted sharply with my understanding of the ruling party, certainly in its earlier incarnation under the leadership of the so-called father of the nation, Agostinho Neto. I believed it to have been a socialist movement that epitomised the heroism of African liberation. Unlike its right-wing, CIA-backed rivals, the National Front for the Liberation of Angola (FNLA) and the National Union for the Total Independence of Angola (UNITA), which allied itself with South Africa's white-minority regime, the MPLA had fought for the freedom and aspirations of all Angolan people, regardless of their ethnic origin, their place of birth or their skin colour. I had always understood that the greedy and dictatorial nature of the party that I encountered as a journalist had developed much later, under Neto's successor, the Soviet-trained petroleum engineer José Eduardo dos Santos, still president today. Perhaps because of my own political beliefs, I thought that the MPLA's ethics had not collapsed until 1990, after the fall of the Berlin Wall. Then the party abandoned Marxism–Leninism and embraced a market-driven economy, which rapidly morphed into a crony capitalism that enriched only a few families. I was even more dismayed when I heard that Cuba, the MPLA's loyal ally, which had defended Angola from a South African invasion at the moment of independence, had been responsible for a large number of the killings in 1977. More curious still, the whole episode of the Twenty-seventh of May had apparently pitted Cuba against the Soviet Union.

If this was all true, I wondered why it had remained so well hidden for so long. In a country whose people had endured 500 years of often bloody Portuguese colonialist expansion, including the horrors of the transatlantic slave trade, five decades of fascist dictatorship and nearly three of civil war, how could a relatively brief trauma during the earliest stages of independence continue to provoke such profound fear? How, in other words, could an internal party squabble trump 'a never-ending *process of brutalization*', as the political theorist Achille Mbembe describes colonialism?[2]

Were it not for the civil war between the MPLA and its main rival UNITA, and the amount of time I had to spend trying simply to stay abreast of it, I might have begun investigating this most potent of taboos there and then. But the daily struggle of unearthing the truth of the conflict was, let me simply say, extremely hard. A few days before Christmas 2000, feeling increasingly uneasy about my role as a foreign reporter, I left Angola and returned to London to take up a job on the Africa desk at the BBC World Service. Back home, I tried to push the country from my mind, and there were moments when I thought I'd almost succeeded. But I knew Angolans in London and, of course, we talked.

One afternoon in a pub, the topic of the Twenty-seventh of May 1977 came up. My friend Carla told me that two of her brothers had gone missing in the aftermath of what she called the *vinte e sete* (twenty-seventh). One had supported the governing faction of the MPLA, the other the uprising. Distraught, her mother searched high and low for her two sons, but as the weeks passed and no news came, she began to lose hope. She also started going blind. Then, one day, she learned that one of her sons had been found dead in Uíge, in the north-west. She travelled up there and, on being reunited with the body of her son, began to recover her sight.

Another friend, Rui, told me about his uncle, who had been a chauffeur for a government minister killed by a group of demonstrators on the Twenty-seventh of May. The authorities later accused the chauffeur of being 'a counter-revolutionary, a *nitista*', said Rui, and he too was killed. When I asked what a *nitista* was, Rui said that the leader of the *vinte e sete* protest was one Nito Alves, who had been a government minister until October 1976, when he fell out with the core leadership of the party. According to Rui, following the Twenty-seventh of May at least 30,000 people were accused of being *nitistas* and killed on President Neto's orders.

I found this new knowledge profoundly challenging. The events of the Twenty-seventh of May seemed to compare with Robert Mugabe's Matabeleland massacres in Zimbabwe during the early 1980s, and the thousands killed during General Augusto Pinochet's dictatorship in Chile. Yet both these cases are well known. Why has the *vinte e sete* remained such a well-kept secret? The question began to obsess me, and I started looking through my collection of Angola books, checking for references to Nito Alves. I found the odd sentence here and there, and in one case a few short paragraphs referring to 'the bloody events of May 1977', which 'finally enabled President Neto to eliminate his rivals and achieve uncontested supremacy within the MPLA'.[3] One British journalist, whose book *Death of Dignity* begins in 1974 and ends in the late 1990s, does not once mention the uprising, despite her narrative relying almost entirely on MPLA voices, largely from the elite. The author, Victoria Brittain, is the former associate foreign editor of the *Guardian*, a woman who fought hard to put news from Africa on the mainstream media map and whose example spurred my own ambitions to write the truth. I had long admired her courage and commitment to socialism, but this new discovery about Angola seemed to turn everything I thought I knew on its head. Even Basil Davidson, the respected British journalist and historian – whose work inspired many, including me, to try to understand the continent from an African perspective as opposed to a European one – seemed to have turned a blind eye to the many killings that followed the *vinte e sete*. His commitment to African national-liberation movements was so deep that, in the end, it seems he heard only the voices of their leaders and fell deaf to the calls from below. At least, that was how I felt when I finished reading his paper about the MPLA in a 1977 edition of *Race & Class*, one of the most influential English-language journals on racism and imperialism, and a home for radical scholars I myself had long sought to enter.

Nearly six years after I had first learned about it, I decided to try to uncover the unwritten truth behind the *vinte e sete*. Here is what I found out.

PART I

'More commonly, people who had incurred the displeasure of the Party simply disappeared and were never heard of again. One never had the smallest clue as to what happened to them. In some cases they might not even be dead. Perhaps thirty people personally known to Winston, not counting his parents, had disappeared at one time or another.'

George Orwell, *Nineteen Eighty-four*

1
◆
MEETING MARIA

Outside Lisbon's Cais do Sodré railway station, a bony woman with a moist cigarette hanging from her mouth rolls twelve anaemic carnations into a thick sheet of purple paper. I hand her a note which she stuffs into the pocket of an apron tied tight beneath the waistline of her jeans. As she digs for change she grins at me, yellow-toothed, and takes a long suck on the burning tobacco. '*Obrigada senhora.*' The cracked syllables float from her lips on curls of smoke.

Fingering the stems, I wonder why I'm buying flowers for a woman who is going to tell me about her husband's disappearance, a tale she has never even told their daughter, let alone a stranger. I think of polluted bouquets taped to London railings, the cellophane sculptures that mark the spot where someone has been stabbed to death or killed by a car, and wonder if my flowers will offend this seasoned widow, who has held her silence for almost thirty years.

Maria Reis has not spoken because she is afraid the authorities in Angola will come after her in Portugal and arrest her. For a long period, she was so terrified of being tracked down that if, on the Lisbon streets, she bumped into Angolans she knew, she would insist they had mistaken her for someone else. 'That can't be me,' she'd say, 'I'm from Mozambique.'

However, the first time we spoke, when I called her from London, Maria said she had begun to change her mind a little. She was still afraid of what she called 'the amount of power they have', but her daughter, Vânia, had started asking questions she felt obliged to answer. In fact it was Vânia who had found me. She'd heard about my research through a mutual friend and had asked if we could meet. When we did, she said she would ask her mother to talk to me. She hoped she might learn more about her father's death through my interview, that her mother might open up more easily to a stranger. To my surprise, Maria agreed. She had begun to consider the possibility that talking about the past might help her come to terms with the trauma she had tried so hard to bury – so hard, in fact, she was not sure she could remember the details.

'I do want to talk, I really do,' she told me over the telephone. 'It must all be down there, mustn't it? Somewhere in my subconscious?'

I took the gamble that it was and bought a flight to Lisbon.

A fortnight later, I'm sitting waiting for the train to depart to Cascais, a small seaside town a few miles east of the capital, popular among retired diplomats and surfers and girls wearing *fio dental* – dental floss, or thongs.

I watch as a grey-haired man and blonde woman slither between the sliding doors now closing for departure. Weak and clumsy, they walk down the carriage clasping each other like the front and back of a pantomime horse, dissolving into laughter when the train jerks forward, catapulting them onto the seat opposite. She picks at roasted chestnuts from a paper bag, cracking them between her teeth and spitting the skins to the floor. One piece of brown shell gets caught in a sling of saliva and swings from her mouth with the movement of the train. A few stops along the line, the man gets up to leave. He bends to kiss his friend goodbye but misses her cheek and crumples to the floor. She giggles as he scrambles from the carriage, but when we pull away her hands begin to twitch. The convulsions nudge up her arms and then to my memory of a Spaniard I once knew, so traumatised by the combined dictates of General Franco and the Catholic Church that he merged his adult life with smack. I want to blame religion and António de Oliveira Salazar for the state of this woman, but she's too young to have lived under the iron rule of Portugal's own fascist.

I turn away and plant my gaze beyond the window to the long, low Gothic monastery on our right. It is the sixteenth-century Mosteiro dos Jerónimos, built on the spot where Vasco da Gama spent an entire night in prayer before setting sail to India in 1497. The first time I visited Lisbon in 2002, I found myself an observer at a memorial service on the flat green lawns that stretch out in front of this monastery. The infamous UNITA leader, Jonas Malheiro Savimbi, the man who joined hands with the United States and South Africa's apartheid regime, had finally been killed in battle in eastern Angola. In a beautiful slip of irony, rumour has it that the CIA, and possibly Mossad, played a significant part in pinning him down. In the end, the Angolan army took all the credit, but his death seemed to underline the absurdity of all those years of conflict, of the hundreds of thousands of lives destroyed since 1975. At the memorial service, I watched with astonishment as Angolan and Portuguese men, black and white, howled in grief at their leader's death. One distraught man collapsed to the ground, prostrating himself in front of a large portrait of the late leader. It struck me as bizarre that Savimbi, who spent most of his adult life trying to gain power in an independent Angola, should be symbolically returned in death to the birthplace of Portuguese imperialism.

The train chugs on and my thoughts drift on this gentle journey that follows the Tagus River to its opening into the Atlantic. I think about Angola, about my time there as the BBC correspondent and about this investigation that has brought me back to Lisbon. I wonder what it is I'm really doing.

Maria Reis looks younger than I expected. A neat figure in a denim skirt at the end of the platform, she shifts her weight from one foot to the other, inspecting the human line moving towards her. For a brief moment I consider hiding. My nerves almost get the better of me, and I attempt to align my body behind a large metal pillar. But it's too late. Our eyes meet and I cannot disguise the recognition: I hear myself calling her name. She rushes up, opening her arms to embrace.

'Lara! *Bem-vinda. Está boa, minha querida?*'

I offer the flowers.

'*Que lindo!* How beautiful.' She hugs me and immediately begins a motherly chatter. 'I'm so glad the sun is shining. I told Vânia it would be good for you to feel the heat. Let me take your bags. You look tired. Perhaps you need to sit down. Take a coffee? At the beach?'

But I can't contemplate this conversation taking place in public, certainly not in the sand beside the sea, and suggest we go back to her home. Maria looks disappointed but agrees anyway and leads me out of the station. We weave through holidaymakers, passing women with caramel legs and young men in colourful shorts and open shirts that flap about waxed chests. A family wrapped in sunglasses walks eagerly towards a shopping mall, whose reflective glass walls might otherwise blind them, and cars bob by, lyrical music bouncing out of wound-down windows.

Maria beckons me to a large road junction. We cross and begin our steady ascent away from the centre of town. Every so often, she turns and looks at me quizzically.

'*Tudo bem?* Are you OK? Are your bags too heavy?'

'No, I'm fine,' I say, puffing heavily while she strides ahead, carnations swinging, charting an effortless path between the dog turds that decorate the mosaic pavement.

'I walk everywhere,' she announces over a shoulder, 'and sometimes I forget this can be hard work for other people who aren't as fit as me.'

Inside, her flat is mournful. She shows me to a neglected bathroom. I close the door and feel flattened by the stillness of the air. I wash my hands, splash water at my face and scoop a drink from the tap, then follow the narrow corridor back to a small lounge. Maria is sitting at the table, gazing into the room. I sit down beside her and scan the white space. A short leather sofa props up one wall, there is a shelving unit displaying ebony carvings, and an empty gas heater stands isolated on the floor. Crocheted curtains swirl gently in front of French windows that open onto a balcony. There is a framed photograph of a puppy and another of a young woman, Vânia. But what I am most aware of is the missing picture – of the man who was Maria's husband.

I turn to look at her. Tears are pushing down her cheeks and she is drawing long breaths, her chest heaving and tense. Quite abruptly, she stands up and rushes out of the room. I hear the twist of a tap. When she comes back, she pauses in the doorway and gulps down a glass of water. Then she goes back into the kitchen and fills the glass again, before returning to her chair, where she sits and quietens her breathing, nursing the glass between her hands.

For some time it feels as though each of us is waiting for the other to take the initiative, as though we might simply sit in the rising silence unable to say a word. And then Maria tries to begin. Her mouth opens, her head pitches forward, but nothing comes out. She lifts the glass to her lips and doesn't seem able to swallow. She leaves the table. I hear running water again. When she reappears, her face is blotchy, her eyes damp and pink.

'*Desculpa*,' she says. 'I'm sorry. These moments come with great force but they do pass.' Laced through her fingers is a paper tissue. She rips a shred from one end and dabs at her tears. 'When I came from Angola, I was filled with so much hatred that I tore everything up. I destroyed anything that had any link to the country.' She tugs at the tissue again, her fists tight, her voice frail. 'This is going to help me confront my hatred, so please, let us begin.'

And so she does, in short manageable sentences.

'Luena was a forgotten town. Even in colonial times. It was a town that only lived because of the train. My father worked there for a bit. On the railways.' Her voice is nasal, heavy with tears. 'No one could leave without a military escort. Even the train had to have a military escort.' The memory seems to perk her up a bit and she half smiles. 'Because of the war, we always had lots of soldiers coming and going. That gave it a certain liveliness, a certain spirit.'

Eight hundred kilometres east of Luanda, Luena lies deep in the heart of Moxico, a huge province that is only fractionally smaller than the whole of Great Britain. As remote as it was back then, it was not entirely forgotten, even by the Portuguese, who thought it was worthy of a branch of one of their largest banks, Banco Pinto e Sotto Mayor. And it was here, while working at the local branch, that twenty-five-year-old Maria met and fell in love with one of her colleagues, a young Portuguese man.

Victor Manuel Reis had been sent to Angola with the Portuguese army in the late 1960s when he was seventeen years old. He had been given a choice between two colonies: Guinea-Bissau or Angola. He plumped for Angola because it was said to be the safer option. The one, says Maria, with 'a slightly less intense war', the one which offered the best chance of returning home alive.

But by the time independence came in November 1975, the young soldier had, so the saying goes, drunk from the river Bengo. He had experienced a radical change of heart. 'He adored Angola,' says Maria. 'He adored the MPLA. He wanted to become an Angolan, to take Angolan nationality.' So, as hundreds of thousands of other Portuguese were fleeing the colony on the eve of its official release from colonialism, terrified of being murdered by the Africans they and their forefathers had exploited for 500 years, Victor was rejoicing. He embedded himself ever deeper into Angolan society, determined to live out a vision of freedom, equality and independence.

On the day he disappeared, Victor had been married to Maria for less than six months, and a father to Vânia for just twelve days. It was 27 May 1977, and it began much like any other.

He left the couple's small apartment on the top floor of Prédio Pinto Martins, a five-storey block, one of Luena's only high buildings, and made the short walk to work at the bank. Having recently given birth, Maria was not at work. She set about feeding the baby, cleaning the flat, preparing the dinner and all the other usual chores of the day. Towards the end of the morning, she was surprised to see Victor at the front door. He and his colleagues had been sent home early. They had been given no explanation why, and Victor had thought little of it. 'We knew from the radio,' says Maria, 'that something had gone on in Luanda, but we didn't have any idea what it was.' Victor certainly wasn't flustered. He decided to take advantage of the spare time and spent the afternoon reading and listening to music.

At the very end of the day, there was an aggressive banging at the door. Three armed men burst into the apartment. Maria slaps her hand down hard on the table. 'It was them!' she shouts. 'It was DISA.' It was, she means, Angola's political police, said by many to have been modelled closely on its Portuguese predecessor, PIDE. The three men rifled through everything the couple owned but found nothing worth taking. Nothing, that is, apart from Victor. As he was bustled out of their home, he called to his wife, reassuring her that he would answer their questions as quickly as possible then come straight back. 'I shouted out to him,' says Maria, raising a hand to her chest, 'I'm coming with you!' But it was too late. The door slammed shut. Victor vanished.

'I had never seen anything like it. I didn't understand what was happening. I never thought...' (she pauses to blow her nose) 'I never imagined for a moment that he could be involved with any uprising. And then he was gone, just gone.'

That night, Maria stayed up waiting for her husband to come home. At dawn, when there was still no word from him, she left the apartment with her baby, and set off to speak to Victor's friends. She assumed they would know what had happened because most of them were soldiers.

Arriving at the first house, she banged on the door and waited. No one answered. She banged again. Still, no one came. And again. Nothing. So she went to the next house. And then the next. And the next. Until she had been to every one of Victor's friends' homes. Not one of them was in.

'I was in complete confusion. Why would they take all of them? All those soldiers?'

Maria grew desperate. She wandered all over town, tears streaming down her face, looking for Victor. Anyone she saw, she asked for information. She even stopped a young boy. She remembers the child because he spoke, she says, like an old man.

'*Ah, camarada,*' he said, 'comrade, they have taken them all.'

Maria knew at least thirty men who disappeared that day, although now she can only remember two of them by name: a talented basketball player called Cada Vez (Each Time) and Gilberto, the brother of a police commander in Luanda.

'But it was a small city,' she explains. 'I knew they couldn't have gone far.'

The following morning, Maria headed out once again. This time, she walked to the prison, where she was certain Victor was being held, and demanded to speak to him.

'You can't!' said one of the guards. 'But you can bring him food, because we haven't got any.'

Relieved to have found him at last, she hurried home to prepare some lunch. An hour later, she returned to the prison and left a small parcel with the guards. The following day, she made another meal, which, as before, she handed over to the guards. The day after that, she did the same, and every day for the following week. The guards always took the food, but they never gave her any information about Victor.

'I became frantic with worry,' she says, pulling a clump of hair off her face and training it back behind one of her ears. 'I pleaded with them to tell me if Victor was ill but they insisted he was fine.'

Maria didn't believe a word.

'If he's fine then he can write me a note,' she told them. 'It doesn't have to be something significant – his signature is enough for me.' But the guards said they did not have a pen. Then they said they did not have any paper. Then they said it was not permitted. No matter how distraught she became, they always had an excuse. They always said no.

One day – Maria cannot remember exactly when – a young girl appeared at the front door. She said she had a message.

'There is no point going every day to the prison with food for Victor,' announced the child. 'He is dead. He has been killed.'

From the balcony, a bird breaks into song. Maria looks up, distracted by the interruption. Then her body collapses, as though her spine has given way, and she is sobbing, her face hidden behind her fingers, her hair hanging like a veil over her head.

'I never believed it was true. Never! They just shot them all the next day, 28 May, and left them there. This is what I discovered. All that time I had carried on hoping he was alive, I had carried on visiting him. They even told me to bring clothes for him, to bring blankets.'

But even after the little girl's visit, Maria could not accept that Victor was dead. Clawing obsessively at a packet of tissues, she says, 'When these sorts of things happen, the person they are happening to does not believe they are really happening.' She was sure her husband had done nothing wrong and could see no reason why the authorities would kill him. She never saw or heard anything that might have suggested he was involved in any sort of political factionalism. 'I'm not politically minded but I'm not stupid either. I'm not!' She is certain she would have noticed if he was involved in 'all this Nito Alves stuff'. Throughout her pregnancy with Vânia, she had suffered many complications and had taken almost nine months' leave. 'In all that period I saw nothing. Nothing! I would have known if they were up to something. I would!'

Over and over, Maria told herself that Victor could not have been killed, and eventually she succeeded in pushing the message the child had delivered right out of her mind. The next day – 'Or was it the day after? I cannot remember those dreadful days' – she returned to the prison to confront the guards. She told them she was not going to come any more, that there was no point if they would not let her see her husband. Their response was simply to laugh at her, and then announce that Victor had been taken to Luanda. 'He went this very morning,' said one.

Maria was sure this was a lie. In those days, the most secure way in and out of Luena was by air – and even flying was risky. The planes spiralled tightly in and out of the airport, descending and ascending in steep screws to avoid being hit by UNITA anti-aircraft fire. Because the runway was close to the town centre, Luena residents could always hear when planes were coming in and taking off. On this particular day, Maria had heard nothing. She was certain Victor could not have been sent to Luanda. But she decided to go there anyway.

It took her several days to acquire the necessary authorisation to leave Luena. 'You have to remember,' she says, irritably, 'that everyone was under curfew.' While she waited, she began to consider the reason for her trip. 'All the time I was thinking, "What will I do there? Where will I go? Who will I talk to?"' And then she remembered, as if this fact could have been anything less than essential, that Victor was Portuguese. In fact, it was Maria who had insisted he keep his nationality when he was so keen to change it. 'I told him a long time before the whole *vinte e sete*: "Victor, it's not worth becoming Angolan because if things get much worse here, we will need to be able to get out."' The 'things' she believed could get worse were the war. It had never occurred to her that they might leave Angola because of a conflict *within* the MPLA.

Nevertheless, she went to Luanda filled with hope that the Portuguese embassy would find her husband. 'I left my home in Luena thinking that I was going to the capital to resolve Victor's problems. I had already decided what I would do if he was in prison. I would come straight back to Luena to sort things out, then I would return once more to Luanda and settle myself, in order to be near him.'

She rubs the back of one hand across her forehead. Her voice drops to a patter. 'But of course I never got back home. I never saw Luena again.'

A dog which has been barking on and off for the past two hours opens its lungs and releases a long howl. Maria shakes her head: she's heard this performance before. She walks to the French windows and slams them shut. The handle falls to the floor. Cursing, she pushes it impatiently back into the hole. She's drained. Her golden face has become dappled with grey, her eyes are red and sore. Is this sudden plunge into her past too much? I suggest pausing, taking a break. 'I can always come back,' I say rather disingenuously: I am in Lisbon for four days only. But Maria isn't having any of it anyway.

'No!' she protests. 'You must go on. Your questions are helping me remember what I thought had gone forever.'

◆

Her memories of Luanda are vague. She recalls arriving at the airport and feeling as though everyone was treating her with suspicion. She glances up at the ceiling, searching the white paint for the right words. 'It was as though... as though I myself was a *golpista*, as though I myself was guilty of something.' Travelling into the city centre, she noticed that people were not speaking to each other. 'They seemed too afraid even to share eye contact with one another.' But somehow, Maria held her nerve. 'I was optimistic and headed straight to the Portuguese embassy.'

Fighting more tears, she pushes back her chair and leaves the room, muttering about something she's lost. I listen to her footsteps hurrying over the tiled floor of the flat. When she returns she's speaking with an awkward, breathy enthusiasm. 'I found them. Here we are,' she says, trying to buoy herself or me, I'm not quite sure. She looks into my eyes and it strikes me this is the first time we have looked at each other since the interview began. 'I hoped I could help you with more documentation but all I have left, after ripping up so much of it, are these.' She tips the contents of a large envelope onto the table: her wedding certificate, Vânia's birth certificate, and some official letters. She points to one of them. 'You see? I wanted to leave the country with Vânia but in order to do so, I had to have the authorisation of the father.' She looks down at her lap, crossing her arms, rubbing her hands over her elbows.

When Maria first arrived at the Portuguese embassy, the staff had told her, yes, they had heard there had been 'a bit of trouble' and promised to look into Victor's case. Then they ushered her out. So she went and found the police commissioner, whom she knew to be the brother of Gilberto, Victor's friend from Luena. What he had to say was a turning point for Maria, 'the moment when I finally began to accept that Victor was dead'. Many young men had been killed across the country, and Victor and Gilberto had been among them. The police commissioner begged her to leave Angola as soon as she could.

2

IN THE SHADOW OF DISA

In order to go to Portugal, Maria needed to show that Vânia was the child of a Portuguese man. 'I had to go through the formal process to prove he was dead.' She pushes one of the letters towards me. 'I had to prove they had killed him.'

The letter is from the embassy of Portugal in Luanda to the Ministry of Finance in Lisbon, dated 27 July 1977. Maria leans over the table, her finger tapping on the paper, egging me on. 'Look at it! Look here, Lara. Look!'

In the top right-hand corner, in a tight scrawl, someone has penned '944 Golpe Estado' (944 *coup d'état*). 'The fact they have written those words must mean they knew perfectly well what was going on, don't you think?' But I'm not sure. I'm still trying to read the rest of the letter:

> Victor Manuel Reis, the local manager of Banco Pinto e Sotto Mayor, and Almeida Fernandes were summarily executed by the son of the commander known as 'Dangereux' once he knew that his father had been killed in the plot of the Twenty-seventh of May.

A little further down, it explains that despite the perseverance of the Portuguese diplomatic staff to clarify the details of these deaths, 'they had not had any response.'

Now Maria is holding another letter in front of me, shaking it under my chin. 'Look at this! This one is from the Portuguese Foreign Ministry to the authorities here in Cascais. Look at what it says at the bottom.' She lets the sheet fall to the table. 'Do you see what it says? Do you see that?'

Before I realise which bit it is she wants me to read, she is telling me: '*It has not been possible up until now to obtain a death certificate.* You see? Their words! It is clear that they killed my husband without any sort of trial. They can't give me a death certificate because they killed him in the open air, without any record. Can you see now?'

But I'm still not sure. I don't know who she thinks killed her husband, or why. And I don't understand what she thinks the Portuguese had to do with it.

Her voice softens as she tries to explain. 'It is clear that the Portuguese knew he was dead, otherwise they couldn't have sent these letters and they wouldn't have got me a job here. This bit. Look. Here.' I follow her finger as it runs along wobbly lines of type:

> The widow of the man cut off in his prime, Manuel Reis, Senhora Maria Irene Reis, also an employee of the same Bank, finds herself understandably too profoundly traumatised to be able to continue in Angola.

The letter requests that she be transferred to Portugal to continue her work for the Cascais branch of Banco Pinto e Sotto Mayor.

In September 1977, Maria arrived in Lisbon with a four-month-old baby in her arms. She was a wreck.

'I came here with so much hatred. I hated my mother, I hated my father, I even hated myself for being Angolan.' She swallows hard and more words come spluttering out between bursts of tears. 'I kept it all to myself, I kept it all secret, to save my daughter, and yet sometimes I remembered so much.'

Caught up in memories of memories, she pauses. When she speaks again her voice is hollowed out. 'Someone who carries hatred like the devil every day of their life cannot love anyone.'

During the first few years in Portugal, there were times when Maria considered ending her life. Had it not been for her job at the bank, her suicidal thoughts might have developed into an attempt. But the work and its routines kept her going. She recalls how, every lunchtime, she would go out walking for the entire two-hour break. 'I'd walk and walk and walk. Often I walked without knowing where I was going, so sometimes I got lost and wouldn't return to work until late in the afternoon. And I still walk,' she says.

At the end of each working day, she would sit and stare in stillness for hours, unable to do anything, even to care for Vânia. Often it was her mother or aunt who looked after the baby, feeding and changing her. Yet despite their practical support, Maria's family – nearly all of whom were living in Portugal at the time – never once spoke to her about what had happened. Nor did Victor's. Not even his parents. They went to their own graves having never asked Maria a single question about their son's death. I suggest that maybe they couldn't face it, the details of his disappearance. Maria shakes her head. She thinks it was partly because they were afraid of making her relive such horrific experiences, but also because the *vinte e sete* became such a taboo.

'You simply did not discuss it,' she says. 'Absolutely everybody kept quiet.'

Even today Maria lives with what she describes as 'a certain fear'. She knows many people who fled to Lisbon and remain so badly affected by the events of 1977 that they still won't talk about it. Even though she accepts that Portugal does offer some protection, she still worries for the safety of her relatives who live in Angola, including a sister who returned to Luanda after several years in Portugal because her husband, a Portuguese man who grew up in Angola, could not readjust to life in Lisbon.

'Many of us are still scared because the MPLA sent police here to pick people up, people who were alleged to have been involved. It was done in a brutal undercover way, beginning in 1977 and continuing throughout 1978 and 1979. Innocent men and women were taken back to Angola and thrown in prison. You don't forget.'

In the lull that follows, I become aware of the sound of a violin. It must be one of the neighbours. Have they been listening to us? Is this some kind of signal that we're being watched? Suddenly I doubt Maria. Is this whole thing a set-up? Have I fallen into a trap, just as I did when I was invited by the MPLA to interview one of Jonas Savimbi's so-called sons in 1999? It turned out that he was not one of the rebel leader's offspring, but a fix, a plant, a fact of which every journalist in Angola seemed to be aware apart from me.

I listen to the violin, its music so full of despair, and wonder whether Maria has even heard it. She seems determined to keep talking.

'What I want you to understand,' she says, raising her voice to get my full attention, 'is that in those days, DISA was very powerful. It was modelled on the system that existed in Portugal when it was a police state. People suffered so much in the Portuguese prisons because of PIDE. And in Angola, it was the same. Everyone was frightened because DISA had all the power. If you went to them and said that your neighbour was against the MPLA, or was a wrongdoer, a culprit, or anything, they would come and take that person away.'

Maria is certain this is what happened to Victor – and I am swept with guilt for having just doubted her.

'There was this man,' she says ominously, 'the principal cause of his death.'

'The son of Dangereux, you mean? The one mentioned in the letter?'

'No, I don't mean him.'

She means Baltazar Rodrigues da Silva, a colleague at the bank in Luena. He was a senior employee who had once offered Maria a promotion, which she had turned down. She did not want to feel obliged to a man she neither trusted nor liked, a man she was sure was 'a party man', a man from the MPLA, 'who spent too much time with the *comissário*', the regional commissar. When she refused the post, he became angry, telling her that it was an honour and that she had no choice other than to do as he said. But Maria insisted: she did not want the job. Her relationship with Baltazar worsened when he discovered that she was in love with Victor. He could not bear the fact that she, a *mestiça*, had chosen a white Portuguese man over him, a black Angolan, and taunted her with threatening tales. 'He'll run back to Portugal and leave you behind,' he would say, 'because that's what all the white men do.' But in Victor's case, Baltazar was wrong. The former soldier had no intention of going anywhere and when Maria became pregnant, he suggested they get married. When Baltazar found out, he was livid.

'Things that I thought were insignificant became very significant,' says Maria, trying to explain Baltazar's point of view. 'People had old and very deep rivalries. Everything mattered. There was a great deal to be lost. Baltazar was so jealous that I was with Victor. I know he was the one to blame, the one who instigated everything.'

She thinks he used his position of authority and his relationship with the local police to exact revenge on Victor, whom he saw as a professional and political rival. 'And the other thing,' she adds, 'is that Victor was light-skinned. After the *vinte e sete* a lot of the people who were killed were light-skinned. Many people felt that the Portuguese were still in charge, which was a problem.'

You can hardly blame Angolans for resenting the Portuguese. From the end of the fifteenth century until halfway through the nineteenth, Portugal enslaved hundreds of thousands of Angolans. Throughout the twentieth century until independence, the colonisers coerced so many Angolans into forced labour that even in the 1950s it was said that only the dead were exempt. And during the liberation war from 1961 until 1974, the Portuguese used napalm to bomb and kill tens of thousands. The resentment was, frankly, appropriate. But Maria is quick to correct me when I ask her if she means that the *vinte e sete* was an uprising against the continued presence of the Portuguese in Angola. 'No!' she shouts. 'Remember that even the president, Agostinho Neto, had a white wife. She was Portuguese.'

In fact, if Maria blames anyone for the killings that followed the *vinte e sete*, it is Neto – and she shouts it at the top of her voice. 'He was the father of the nation! It was him who said there should be no pardons. Of course he knew what would happen! He was an educated man. A poet! He knew there were many uneducated people. And he knew it was not a democracy. When he said that no time should be wasted on the guilty, it was like shaking a bottle of fizzy drink and pulling off the lid. It was obviously going to make a lot of mess.'

She is adamant that the clampdown which followed the protest led by Nito Alves on the Twenty-seventh of May gave people an excuse to revenge themselves on those they disliked, whatever the reason. She is sure this was the case with Baltazar, who decided it was payback time for Victor.

But if she is right, and Baltazar was responsible for Victor's death, why does the letter from the Portuguese embassy in Luanda state that Victor was killed by the son of Comandante Dangereux?

'That was tribal,' comes Maria's bald response. Comandante Paulo da Silva Mungungo Dangereux, to give him his full name, was a senior commander from FAPLA, the MPLA's armed wing, and came from Luena. During the liberation struggle, he held positions of high responsibility, including overseeing the transfer of Soviet weapons into the country. He was, if you like, one of the heroes of the young nation. So when, on the Twenty-seventh of May, news came through that he had been killed in Sambizanga, a poor Luanda neighbourhood, by a group of *nitistas*, it was only a matter of time before repercussions would be felt. In Maria's analysis, this explains why so many of the people who were killed in Luena came from Luanda: they were blamed for the death of Dangereux. And it was his son, she thinks, who was sent out to kill people in revenge for the murder of his father. Or at least, Maria thinks that is what she thinks. She's not completely sure, and admits that until she read the embassy's letter, she never even knew whether Comandante Dangereux had a son or not. 'And Luena,' she says to emphasise, 'was awfully small.'

Which leaves me more muddled. I want to persist with more questions but I don't want to cross-examine Maria. So I keep my mouth shut and wait for her to continue. To my surprise, she begins talking about her daughter.

One of her greatest fears is that Vânia, now a strikingly beautiful woman, will fall in love with an Angolan man. 'Imagine how I would feel if I discovered that my grandson, Vânia's child, was also the grandson of someone who harmed my husband. Imagine that!'

I try to console her, reminding her that since Vânia does not live in Angola the chances of her falling in love with a man who happens to be Angolan are probably quite slim. But my attempts are a failure. She leans into her hands, fat tears rolling down her cheeks, despairing of the trap into which her life seems to have fallen.

'The problem, Lara, is how would I ever know? There has been no tribunal. We don't know who is who, or who did what, or who is linked to who. No one has ever said sorry for all these years full of suffering and pain. I don't want compensation – there is no compensation – but the point is that many innocent people were killed. They weren't even given a trial.' She stops. Her voice drops, suddenly deeper and slower. 'And what I want to know is why didn't they kill me? Why? Why didn't they kill me too?'

Maria has cried so much now that I wonder whether it is possible to become dehydrated from crying. I seem unable to calm or comfort her, and feel a growing desire to recoil from all my questions that have triggered this avalanche of unbearable memories.

'Sometimes I think it's a nightmare,' she says from behind her hands, 'that one day I will wake up and it won't be like this. I've even thought of going to see a psychiatrist to find out if I'm mad.'

I suggest that surely the real question is how she has managed to stay sane given what she's been through.

'What has given me strength is my daughter,' she says. 'She's been my guardian angel. Without her, they would probably have killed me. It was only because I had a baby that they spared me.'

She also kept going, she says, because she knew that she was all Vânia had. When Victor died, she wore black, not out of any obligation but because she couldn't be bothered to wear anything else. Then one day a friend told her to take off the black. She warned Maria that her daughter would develop into a sad child. Maria thought about this, and went out and bought a colourful dress. 'And my little daughter, she must have been about two or three by then, she told me I was beautiful.' Maria struggles to smile. 'This was my reward.'

On the table in front of her, between her open hands, is a pile of shredded, sodden tissue. Maria looks at it, surprised, as if she is not sure how it got there. Then she looks to the window, to the sunshine coming in behind the white curtain. 'Why don't we go out?' she says. 'We are losing the beautiful day.'

I do want to go – I'm desperate to get out of this flat – but there is one last question I want to ask. Does she have any pictures of Victor? 'We have been talking about this man for several hours now and I have no sense of what he looks like.'

Maria leaves the room and when she returns she's holding a large photo album, like an offering to the gods. 'I never went back to Luena,' she says. 'Our home was taken over, occupied you might say, by other people. They threw our things onto the street. A friend of mine rescued some of it, including these pictures.'

A skinny young man, tanned, dark haired and with a thick moustache, is standing on a beach with another, slightly paler man. Both of them are beaming. Huge smiles. 'This one is in Luanda,' says Maria, 'on the Ilha, I think.' She turns the page. Victor is standing next to a woman and a child, all three of them screwing up their eyes in the sun. 'He's on a rooftop, I'm not sure where, with some friends.' She turns some more pages. 'I don't have many of him. Most of them were abandoned in Luena.' She pushes the album further towards me. 'But look at these.' In one, Victor is standing upright beside a poster of Mao Zedong, which he is looking at proudly. In another, he is in front of a photograph of Che Guevara. 'He was a revolutionary,' says Maria. 'If he was guilty of anything, it was trying to change Angola for the better. And they killed him.'

The terrible irony is to see Victor's obvious admiration for Che Guevara and to know that Maria blames the Cubans, in part, for his death. She looks at me, fighting her tiredness but desperate to make me understand the basics before we finish. 'Lives could have been saved, you know, innocent people who shouldn't have been killed. Those who are guilty must be judged, including the Cubans and the Soviet Union.'

She leans back and looks at me firmly. 'Now,' she announces, 'we go to the beach.'

Our fingers move between a plate of prawns, our lips and a bowl of chips. The table is beside the sea, our toes almost touching the sand. The breeze blows Maria's thick black hair across her face. She sits upright, strong and smiling. I noticed, as we walked along the beachfront deciding where to eat, her smooth and muscular calves. Not a single blemish. And only now do I observe the pinkness of her lips and the silver crucifix that hangs from a silver chain around her neck, still slender and firm beneath her chin. You would never imagine, looking at her today, here, outside in the light, the grief she is supporting within.

And what is there to say? We agreed when we left the flat that the interview had ended. Yet, sitting here, beneath a hot blue sky, audience to a theatre of athletic bodies balancing on waves that come bowling up to the shore, our conversation might never have happened. I feel the day slipping between the cracks of the earth. Someone has told me a story. Why do I believe it? Will anyone else? I just want to stay very still, to let the heat fill me up, and to know that Maria is there beside me, that we are together, sewn into each other's skin by an immense effort to visit the past. Before I met her today, I believed that cultivating the memory was an obligation: now I'm beginning to understand that it's also an art.

Then I hear myself asking her one more question, as if the rhythm we have established won't let up. 'Will you ever go back, Maria?'

She picks up the thread immediately.

'I want to go back. My heart is there. It's my country. But I don't know how long I'd be able to endure Angola today. I don't want to give up my Portuguese nationality, to go back and become an Angolan. I don't know if I could readjust.' She pauses and looks out to the sea, inhaling the air and the view, the smell of suncream and young flesh. 'Nowadays, the beaches there are filthy. There's rubbish everywhere. The poverty is the same. The degradation is the same. For Angola to change, the entire elite will have to disappear. All of them. Their children are also a problem. They don't want to lose the privileges of their parents. But do you know what I worry about most of all?'

'What?' I ask.

'The doctors. I have tension in my irises and need medicines to control it. Angola doesn't have proper doctors and it's hard to find proper medicine.'

The waitress interrupts us. She wants to know whether we'd like *sobremesa* (pudding) and coffee. I tell her I'll just have coffee.

'I won't have pudding either,' says Maria. 'And I don't drink coffee.'

'Not even a small espresso?' asks the waitress.

Maria shakes her head. 'I've suffered from hypertension for years,' she says, her voice so light it vanishes on the wind.

Lisbon at dusk and the giants are playing with dry ice. The Tagus has disappeared. Even the lights at the top of the 25 de Abril bridge are smothered under a curling carpet of cold air.

I'm sipping whisky by a kiosk in the clouds. Around me, young couples are entwined on benches and gathered in groups at tables, and the homeless are huddling into hedges – their bedrooms for the night. Sitting, watching, alone and tired, I notice a hole widening inside the white drift. The clouds part and Christ the King appears from across the river, huge and overbearing. A fleeting glimpse and the clouds close on Salazar's statue. I suck the last of the whisky and leave my table.

I follow the narrow cobbled streets back through the low-slung Baixa (downtown), tracing a path up a steep rise of steps to the *pensão* where I'm lodged. I collapse onto the large white bed that fills the white room and slip into sleep filled with music and chattering from the street below.

Later, I wake with the dregs of a dream. I'm in a dusty marketplace watching the man I love disappear in the grip of two soldiers. Further and further he's taken away, melting into the scorched heat, slipping, slipping, smaller and smaller, until all I can see is a shiny black sliver on the horizon. I lie in the dark, tears streaming, thinking of Maria, lost in her story, and how I might ever retell it.

3

THE SABOTEURS, THE PARASITES, THE OPPORTUNISTS

Back in London, I'm trying to be optimistic. I'm in the heart of Westminster, walking down Dorset Street, to where the Angolan flag is flapping. If I'm to get to the bottom of the *vinte e sete*, I will need to get back into the country. But that's never easy. The government dislikes foreign journalists at the best of times, and I've never had a very fruitful relationship with the embassy. If they get wind of my research, I might not see a visa for a long time. So I brace myself as I approach the elegant Georgian house. Steps at the back lead to what would once have been the servants' entrance. Now it's the door to the consular office, a small, pale room decorated with a pot plant and a portrait of President José Eduardo dos Santos. I take a ticket and prop myself up against the wall. When my turn comes round, the young, suited man behind the glass panelling tries to be reassuring. 'The system has really improved. It shouldn't take more than a few weeks,' he says, and I swear I see him wink.

The following day, I'm listening to what London Underground call their 'safety advice' in the depths of Russell Square Tube station. 'Ladies and gentlemen,' says a piped male voice from the foot of the stairwell, 'there are 175 steps to street level, which is the equivalent of a fifteen-storey building. Please wait for the next available lift.' I think of my old flat in Luanda, on the tenth floor of Prédio Limpo (the Clean Block). The lift stopped working in 1976 – that's what the neighbours told me – so there was no option but to trudge up and down the stairs. Sometimes I'd pass children, buckets of water on their heads, taking one wobbly step after another. And here I am in London, with just a satchel.

At the top, panting desperately, I walk west, passing the neat gardens of Russell Square towards my old college, the School of Oriental and African Studies. The library has excellent material from and on Africa, although the 'Africa section' only appeared in the 1960s when Western scholars finally began to consider that the continent might have a history of its own after all – never mind that *Homo sapiens* actually evolved there.

In front of the main entrance, a scarlet-faced woman, her hair flattened beneath a rustic headscarf, is selling copies of the *Big Issue*. Behind a wooden table marked 'Student Union', a pair of younger women are half dancing to a Manu Chao song about immigration that's leaking from a CD player on the wall behind them. A bald man tries to sell me a copy of *Socialist Worker*. Another hands me a leaflet for a meeting on Marxism. 'Resistance, revolution,' he mumbles as I weave between a sprawl of smokers up the steps.

Inside, I head straight to the library, to Floor C, where squares of turquoise carpet lead me along a row of shelves with labels like 'Buddhist Art', 'Numismatics' and 'Lacquer + Wood'. At the very end, beyond 'Christian and Byzantine Art', I arrive in 'Africa'. I turn the corner to find a pale young woman, pearls at her neck, fiddling with the knot in the sarong around her hips. She looks up. She blushes. We exchange awkward smiles and I dive right.

I'm not entirely sure what I'm looking for, but I start scanning the shelves anyway, occasionally pulling out a book I can't resist. *Angola: Secret Government Documents on Counter-Subversion*, published in 1974, shows just how far the Portuguese were prepared to go to cling to the colonies.[4] The chapters give it away with headings like, 'Control of the population by means of identity cards', 'Factors which promote rebellion' and 'Secret police and militia'. Other collections include a volume of Portuguese documents on Central Africa and Mozambique from 1497 to 1840, and there's a pile of ethnography with titles to repel even the most enthusiastic student. A 1949 study by the US missionary Gladwyn Murray Childs, *Umbundu Kinship and Culture: Being a Description of the Social Structure and Individual Development of the Ovimbundu of Angola, with Observations Concerning the Bearing on the Enterprise of Christian Missions of Certain Phases of Life and Culture Described*, is a case in point.

Horrified, I scoot to the next stack and am drawn suddenly to a familiar set of colours on a lower shelf. I pull out a slim book and lay it in my palm. The cover is divided horizontally, half red, half black, with a large yellow star folded around the spine. It's the MPLA flag. The word 'ANGOLA' is printed across the top, and beneath, in white, the title: *A tentativa de golpe de estado de 27 de maio de 77* (The attempted *coup d'état* of 27 May 1977).[5] I open the book and find that the loan slip has been stamped only twice, once in 1984 and again in 1996. Am I really only the third person to look at this in a quarter of a century? I note the hammer and sickle wrapped around the publisher's name, Edições Avante!, the publications arm of the Portuguese Communist Party. Beneath that, Lenin is quoted: 'Study, study, always study'. Over the page, it's Marx and Engels: 'Workers of the world, unite!' Amazed by what I think I've found, I flick frantically through the book, skimming the section headings all the way to the final sentence, which is printed in letters so large it fills the whole page:

> WE WILL APPLY
> THE
> DEMOCRATIC REVOLUTIONARY
> DICTATORSHIP
> IN ORDER TO FINISH, ONCE AND FOR ALL,
> WITH THE SABOTEURS,
> WITH THE PARASITES,
> WITH THE OPPORTUNISTS.
>
> THE MPLA POLITICAL BUREAU – 12/7/1977

It's the official MPLA account of the *vinte e sete de maio*. I never imagined such a thing existing, least of all in a London library. I feel a twinge of delirium. 'So it really did happen,' I mutter to myself, 'it really did.' I feel vindicated. I hurry to the issuing desk, where a man with a dusting of sky-blue eyeshadow stamps the little text for the third time in its lonely life.

Back at home, I begin the peculiar task of trying to distinguish propaganda from fact. Barely two pages in and I'm feeling weirdly nostalgic.

The self-righteousness, verbosity and bizarre claims about the wants and wishes of 'the People' sound familiar: it reads just like the government rhetoric I was fed as a correspondent, day after day, as the country limped its way through civil war.

The book begins its account on 21 May 1977, six days before the uprising. The MPLA Central Committee knew trouble was coming, because it passed a resolution that acknowledged the existence of 'factionalism'. It claims that this phenomenon, or abstract concept, or idea – it is hard to tell exactly what factionalism is – 'presents itself with an apparently revolutionary cloak but really seeks to divide the MPLA and to distract the People from their true objectives'. Two men are named as its leaders: Alves Bernardo Baptista and José Jacinto da Silva Vieira Dias Van Dúnem, better known as Nito Alves and Zé Van Dúnem. They were both senior MPLA members who had been on the Central Committee until that January. Apparently they had made a three-year plan to seize power.

First came the 'phase of infiltration'. Alves and Van Dúnem pushed their supporters into every part of the MPLA, 'infecting' department after department with factionalists whose minds had been filled with 'erroneous ideas'. Page after page details the Soviet-sounding structures: the centres of revolutionary instruction with names like 'Blood of the People' and 'Certainty', the government ministries, the provincial and municipal commissions, the department for the organisation of the masses – which, as I write it, makes me think of sheep – as well as the People's neighbourhood committees, the action committees, the national workers' union, the youth wing, the women's wing and even the children's wing, whose official name was the Organisation for Angolan Pioneers. In each case, we're told that Alves and Van Dúnem installed supporters to promote their ideas, such as alleging that the MPLA leadership was 'Maoist' and 'right-wing', not Marxist–Leninist and left-wing.

Apparently Alves also began cultivating his personal support base. So he became president of Progresso do Sambizanga, a popular football club in the Luanda slum of the same name. Then, when he became minister of interior administration at independence in November 1975, he placed his followers in key posts: one became the director of Rádio Nacional, another editor-in-chief of the newspaper *Diário de Luanda*. Van Dúnem, too, promoted his friends and at least seven close relatives to senior positions such that, at the very heart of the MPLA, a 'little factionalist island' grew.

At the start of 1976, we're told that the pair unleashed phase two of their plot, 'the phase of deliberate sabotage and the discrediting of the existing structures'. Across the country, their activists worked tirelessly to promote Alves' name while whipping up distrust in the existing MPLA leadership. This, claims the Politburo in an increasingly paranoid tone, led to the 'strangulation of the entire economy' as factionalists blocked the circulation of goods and peasants' produce and sabotaged the state-run shops, while blaming the government for the shortfall in supplies.

As the authority of the MPLA weakened, the army spiralled into crisis. The chief of staff had to suspend a large number of officials for 'flagrant violations of military discipline' and morale was further eroded when soldiers' salaries started disappearing, allegedly siphoned into the safes and bank accounts of corrupt factionalists. If we believe the Politburo, this was all part of an elaborate scheme conjured up to create discontent and confusion and, ultimately, to provoke an uprising. Indeed, it even claims that the factionalists wiggled their way into the state intelligence services – into DISA.

Despite its density, its listing of so many different individuals, the endless acronyms for myriad committees, and the alleged conspiracies and sub-conspiracies, I find this little book really compelling. It provides a superb insight into the MPLA of the 1970s and the mentality of its leadership, even though it is also quite contradictory. For example, the Politburo claims that the factionalists got into every crevice of the MPLA, yet it never fully explains how they managed to gain so much support in the first place. We're not told that Alves and Van Dúnem pressured or bribed anyone. So how did they become so popular? Was Alves simply a supreme manipulator able to brainwash a slice of the population? Moreover, if we are to believe what we're told – that President Neto's wing of the MPLA was in fact the most popular – then how did much younger and less powerful comrades come to occupy that space so easily? Whatever the answer, the meticulous detailing of the vast network of factionalists makes conspicuous its absent counterpart: information about those who were killed in the aftermath of the *vinte e sete*, who I've been told were in the tens of thousands. If the leadership really believed they had so many enemies, they may well have wanted to destroy the threat. It wouldn't surprise me, however, if President

Neto's wing exaggerated the extent of factionalism in order to justify the violence it would later unleash.

Honest MPLA militants, says the text, were substituted in meetings at the last minute by 'more and more fanatic' factionalists. Abusive rhetoric was used to discredit the MPLA leadership as 'anti-Soviet' and 'anti-communist'. Sometimes Nito Alves graced these gatherings in person, but he rarely stayed for more than 'a few scanty minutes'. Meanwhile, some schoolteachers began telling their pupils that Alves was an intellectual, 'a philosopher and a poet'. In the Politburo's view, this was utterly false: he and his fellow factionalists are denounced as 'pseudo-Marxists', 'elitists' and 'abusers of the good faith of the People'. They consumed 'an unstoppable flow of revolutionary literature' while suffering from 'ideological indecision': one moment they gained inspiration from the Albanian leader Enver Hoxha, the next they preferred the lectures of Mao, then Lenin became leader of choice.

Apparently, they were just as fickle about their supporters. Despite Alves and Van Dúnem's alleged racism towards non-blacks – we're told they criticised the number of whites and *mestiços* in senior MPLA positions – we're also expected to believe that they hypocritically welcomed support from whites on the right, some of whom had served with the colonial secret police and certain white urban militia groups. Most of their support, however, is said to have come from 'the Luandan lumpen' and a chunk of the petite bourgeoisie, who merely pretended to be 'guardians of a "pure Marxist–Leninist line"'.

For the fact of the matter is, claims the Politburo, the factionalist leaders were 'utterly incapable of identifying with the independent Angolan people or with the militants'. It diagnoses their condition as some sort of superiority complex, their 'factionalist intellect' being 'incapable of disentangling itself from the mentality inherited during colonial times, unconsciously carrying a certain ideological paternalism that often assumed the form of neo-colonial intellectualism'. On top of that, they are accused of hypocrisy, of being people who 'used ultra-Marxist vocabulary while leading private lives and militant practice that left much to be desired'.

The irony is stark. Ever since its inception, the MPLA had been characterised by this very problem: the class and cultural gulf between its leaders and the mass of Angolan people it sought to make its followers. Founders of the movement had long acknowledged the need to close the gap between their *assimilado* selves and those sometimes referred as *preto boçal*, literally the 'untamed black'. Referring to the MPLA leadership, the British journalist Basil Davidson, an admirer of the movement and friend of Neto's, wrote that

> the gulf between themselves and the *preto boçal* was [...] wider, since they were the products of Portuguese higher education. They were the very pillars of Portuguese Africa's educated élite [...] They were a million miles from the backland villages. They had even forgotten their mother tongues.[6]

These early leaders believed they had a duty to 'de-Portugalise' and then 're-Africanise' themselves.[7] Indeed, a whole literary movement was born out of the desire to shed '*portugalidade*' and to embrace what was coined '*angolanidade*', as an African national consciousness.

Whether these efforts led to any real bridging of the gap with the much-vaunted *Povo* is questionable. To this day, many senior MPLA figures do not understand Kimbundu, the language spoken by the bulk of their traditional supporters. I've even heard that a proportion of Luanda's elite have asked to be described on their identity cards as *mestiço* rather than black – even if they are, by common-sense definition, black. Others deny they are African at all, as I discovered one morning in 1999 during an interaction with the then vice minister of health, Teresa Cohen. We were standing in a Luanda slum beside the remains of a cargo plane that had crashed into the neighbourhood hours earlier, killing twenty-eight people. Cohen had ordered the police to use gunfire to push back the crowds. When I asked her why, she replied, 'They are not like us,' explaining that she was, like me, 'a European'.

In contrast to the many senior MPLA figures who came from privileged *assimilado* families in Luanda, Nito Alves grew up in a rural village, without running water, electricity or the relative comforts of urban living. Unlike Neto and his number two, the MPLA Secretary General Lúcio Lara, who was the son of a wealthy *mestiço* sugar-cane planter, Alves had never left the country nor benefitted from an education in Lisbon. He remained in Angola throughout the liberation struggle, fighting for his life and the survival of the MPLA, in the bush for the best part of eight years. Undoubtedly, he would have been able to identify far more closely with ordinary Angolans than many of his erstwhile comrades.

The Politburo itself seems to recognise this. By January 1977, it says, Alves had become so popular that there appeared to be two MPLAs: one led by Neto, the other by Nito, as Alves was commonly known. The Central Committee suspended Alves and Van Dúnem that month. It also announced an inquiry into what it called 'factionalist activity', to be led by José Eduardo dos Santos, then minister for foreign affairs.

Up to this point in the text, the Politburo gives the impression that Alves and Van Dúnem were a well-organised pair with vast support. Now the tone changes. No longer factionalists, they are now called 'the *golpistas*'. We are told that they were so disorganised, with such poor communication and apathy among their followers, that they did not attempt a coup just once, but three times. The first attempt was on 20 May when the Central Committee was due to meet, but when the venue of the meeting changed at the last minute the *golpistas* were thrown into disarray. The second attempt was on 25 May, but did not get off the ground because the section of the army supposedly committed to Alves failed to turn up. So a third attempt was hatched.

It started quite well. On Friday, 27 May, at four o'clock in the morning, a few 'anarchical shots' were fired in Luanda. Lots of prisoners were freed and a few factionalists started running through the streets. Rádio Nacional was taken over and 'strange factionalist phraseology' broadcast. But these early successes did not endure. According to the Politburo, a 'liquidation mission' was launched under the command of DISA's feared deputy, Henrique de Carvalho Santos, known as 'Onambwe'. It began at the radio station, where, so we're told, 'the childishness of the *golpistas* had already caused a dozen deaths', and progressed to the barracks of the 9th Brigade, where several senior MPLA figures were believed to have been captured. Rapidly, the factionalists' supporters melted away and the coup attempt collapsed. Earlier ambitions to kidnap President Neto and kill his inner circle were abandoned and, by dusk, Alves and Van Dúnem – who had hoped to be president and prime minister respectively – were running for their lives.

Meanwhile, the burned bodies of six prominent MPLA figures were found inside a car in Sambizanga, together with the remains of two less well-known people. Miraculously, a ninth person had managed to escape and stagger to the port, at least a kilometre away, where he raised the alarm. Two names of the dead strike me. One is Comandante Dangereux, whose son was named by the Portuguese foreign-affairs ministry as being responsible for the death of Maria Reis' late husband. The other is Saydi Mingas, the finance minister: his chauffeur was the uncle of a friend of mine and was killed after the *vinte e sete*.

Despite the abject failure of the alleged coup attempt, the government's response did not soften. Such was the extent of 'vile treason', we are told that 'all the People demanded that this ambitious band of adventurers and traitors, who committed these abominable crimes, be punished with the greatest severity, without pardon'. In order to satisfy the so-called 'national sentiment', a special military tribunal was established. And it is here, towards the end of this extraordinary little book, at the moment of announcing what is clearly to be the death penalty, that the Politburo makes a far more wide-reaching set of allegations against the factionalists. They were, we learn, not simply a domestic threat from within the movement and within the country. Apparently they were also part of an international, imperialist strategy to destroy the MPLA. The Politburo wrote:

> It cannot have escaped anyone's notice that during the days running up to the coup, our borders to the north, the south and the east were subjected to serious provocations, violations and even an increase in the concentration of Zairean and South African troops [...] The whole world heard the declarations of the president of Zaire saying he was in favour of the coup, and of Nito Alves.

It claims that the factionalists were also chummy with Angolan rebel leader Jonas Savimbi, who, it alleges, not only supported the coup but had prior knowledge that it was going to occur.

The references to foreign threats cannot be dismissed. In 1977, just one month before the alleged coup attempt, Neto said that President Mobutu Sese Seko of neighbouring Zaire had launched an invasion into Angola to overthrow him. It was no secret that Mobutu distrusted the socialist MPLA, and would have preferred either of its opponents, UNITA or the FNLA, in government: like him, they had the backing of the CIA. In this Cold War context, Neto was certain that foreign mercenaries had participated in the mission with the backing of the United States. Mobutu countered these accusations with his own claims that the MPLA, in March, had supported an invasion of Zaire's southern Shaba province. He also alleged that Cuban soldiers had supported the invasion.[8]

That may be true. Fidel Castro had visited Luanda in March 1977. During his trip he said that the withdrawal of 36,000 Cuban soldiers, sent to Angola in 1975 and 1976 to fight for the MPLA, had begun. But in April, the withdrawal was stopped on the grounds that Egypt and Morocco had started sending troops to Zaire, with logistical support from France. Castro told a US journalist, 'We have reasons to believe that behind all this there may be a further plan to attack Angola.' Confusingly, he insisted that Cuban soldiers had 'neither trained, nor armed, nor had anything to do with that question of Zaire, because it is strictly an internal question.'[9] To twist the Cold War screw a little further, this point is disputed by a Cuban pilot who operated in Angola in 1975 and 1976. 'We received orders from Havana to plan bombings of the Inga hydroelectric plant, Zaire's "Kitona" airbase near the mouth of the Congo River, and Mobutu's palace in Kinshasa,' he said.[10]

Certainly, there had been very real hostility towards the MPLA from Zaire for many years. In 1975, up to 11,000 Zairean troops carried out incursions into northern Angola. Other neighbours also threatened the MPLA. That same year, South Africa sent as many as 6,000 soldiers into Angola in its effort to unseat the MPLA, which Pretoria claimed was a communist threat. Behind South Africa stood the United States, which had long tolerated the late Portuguese dictator, Salazar, an old MPLA enemy. So it is not difficult to understand why Neto might have been paranoid about reactionary forces and imperialist interests. But are we really supposed to believe that men like Nito Alves, who had risked their lives fighting for the MPLA, would suddenly turn heel and team up with Mobutu and the National Party of South Africa? The MPLA's foreign enemies might well have tried to take advantage of the movement's fracturing, but that would not mean that the factionalists were obsequiously in their service.

At the end, I'm left disappointed at the hypocrisy that seemed to characterise the MPLA so early on. The attacks on the 'pseudoleftism' of the factionalists could be applied, quite appropriately, to the elite that ruled Angola then and ever since. Likewise, the claims that the factionalists set up 'a network of spies' across the country only reminds me that, today, there are spies everywhere, some less official than others, so that you worry you are being watched and overheard even when you are not. Gazing at the hail of blustering propaganda and exclamation marks that forms the penultimate page, I wonder who wrote this call to kill and how it must have sounded in the minds of those who heard it:

LONG LIVE THE UNITY OF THE NATION!
DEATH TO THE FACTIONALISTS!
FORWARD TO THE CONGRESS!
THE FIGHT CONTINUES!
VICTORY IS CERTAIN!

Luanda, 12 July 1977
The Political Bureau of the Central Committee of the MPLA

4
◆

WHEN NORMAL THINGS DON'T GO NORMALLY

At a square and slightly unstable table in the British Library café, I'm waiting to meet one of Angola's most respected social scientists. I'm anxious. We agreed on half past three and it's already twenty to four. I know this hardly qualifies as late, but I've been given strict instructions to take up no more than fifteen minutes of her time.

Luiza Silva Mendes is in London to complete her doctorate. One of her advisers is a very affable professor, a man I always picture in tweed and Hush Puppies, who has devoted at least fifty years of his life to exploring mainly Angolan and Portuguese history. When he suggested I meet the woman he referred to as 'Lu', he did so on one condition: 'I've told her she must write a thousand words a day, so you must promise not to disturb her for long.' I gave him my word.

As the minutes tick by, my slot slims into negative time. I try busying myself with a pamphlet full of statistics about this huge public building. Like worry-origami, I fold and unfold the paper, pondering the 13 million books stored on 200 miles of shelving, when my academic appears.

Almost immediately, I get the sense she is not someone to discuss Angola, or anything else for that matter, in a hurry. Attempting to loosen us both a bit, I ask how she is enjoying London. Her dark eyes lock onto mine as she considers a response, examining me carefully for several drawn-out seconds.

'At least here I can work without any distractions,' she says in a long, slow voice. 'In Angola, as you must know, it is almost impossible to write because there is always so much to do. Everything takes so long, whereas here, daily life is easy. There is water in the tap so I do not have to fetch it. There is electricity. I do not have to read in the dark. There are computers, the internet. Everything works all the time.'

She stops quite abruptly, and looks at me as though waiting for my next question. It occurs to me she might like to stay on after her PhD. 'Perhaps to teach on a more long-term basis?'

'Why would I want to do that?' she asks, a certain amazement scratched into her words. 'I'm Angolan. I will stay in Angola. Why would I want to leave and live here?'

The question makes me feel foolish. I wasn't trying to suggest it's somehow better here than there. 'Just that it might be an interesting experience; it might allow you to write more. Of course,' I add, back-pedalling feebly, 'London is terribly expensive.'

But again she challenges me. 'Not really. There's so much you can see and do for free.'

Mendes is a handsome woman. A thick sweep of steel hair pushes back over her head, away from the solemnity of a face that seems shaped by a despair in her olive skin. She is elegantly dressed. Reading spectacles perch on the bridge of her nose and a light, feminine scarf dresses her shoulders. Sketching over some of the details of her life, she becomes wistful remembering the long drives with her parents to the south, to Huambo, Benguela and Lobito.

'Freedom for Angolans, freedom for us is about being able to move,' she says. 'Always, the war was judged in terms of movement. Can we get through? That was always the first question. When we cannot travel, it is the worst thing that can possibly happen.'

Her words, at once poetic and dramatic, are heavy, as though Angola's history, and the years she has spent reflecting upon it, resonate in every syllable and breath.

'The roads,' she says, sighing, 'there are so many accidents. You hear of people being killed all the time just because the drivers don't drive properly and because they all drink so much.' Her voice thickens to a concentrated seriousness that provokes in me a certain guilt. 'We talk about going to the provinces as if Luanda, the city, is not itself in a province. And in the provinces, people talk about the provincial capital as if it is the entire province, and the municipalities as if they are the bush. What is this urban bias which exists all over the world?' Her voice trails off, her attention briefly distracted by a man brushing past our table, and when she turns back, it is to caution me, as if everything else she has said up to this point forms the backdrop, the preparation, for her next statement.

'It is very important that you read our history if you really want to understand Angola, if you really want to understand us fully.'

I nod, 'Of course, of course,' and she proceeds to talk me through some of that vast history, beginning in the late seventeenth century with Dona Beatriz Kimpa Vita. Born to Kongo aristocracy in 1684, at the age of twenty Kimpa Vita believed she was possessed by St Anthony. She insisted that Jesus was Kongolese and became deeply critical of the Italian Capuchin missionaries for refusing to support black saints. The period through which she lived was one marked by many wars. The majority of those captured in battle were exchanged with Europeans for muskets and gunpowder. In the early years of the eighteenth century, approximately 7,000 people were sold into slavery each year from Kongo. Kimpa Vita sought to end these conflicts, and led a popular if short-lived peace movement. In 1706, just two years after her 'awakening', she was burned at the stake for heresy and witchcraft at the instigation of the missionaries in São Salvador, as M'banza Kongo in the north-west corner of Angola was then known.

'Even today,' Mendes explains, 'there are people who think they are the reincarnation of Kimpa Vita.'

Her list of dates and events continues, moving across centuries and space. I scribble into my pad as she talks, feeling increasingly inadequate and wondering if she's forgotten what I'd said in my email about the *vinte e sete*, or whether she really does believe that to write about the end of the twentieth century I must have studied the previous four. She names John Thornton, 'a brilliant US professor', who wrote *The Kongolese Saint Anthony*, a book devoted to understanding Kimpa Vita. She advises me to track down Jill Dias, a historian and anthropologist based in Lisbon who 'knows a huge amount' about nineteenth-century Angola. 'She's English,' she says, perhaps trying to encourage me, 'but married a Portuguese.' The list goes on, and my sense of being out of my depth deepens, so when she suggests emailing me a reading list to save time, I welcome the idea and fall silent.

Mendes stoops a little, leaning into the table and looking over her glasses again. I feel as if I am being read, as if her gaze alone is enough to expose my ignorance.

'What I do not fully understand,' she says, 'is why you want to study this subject. What is it about the *vinte e sete de maio* that interests you so much?'

The tone of her voice feels disapproving. I put my pencil down and sit back in the chair. I want to try to find the right response.

I begin by telling her about the demonstrations in 2000 and how I had first learned about the *vinte e sete* and Angola's culture of fear. I admit to feeling betrayed, however misplaced that feeling might be, by those writers and journalists I had always admired on the political left. 'Either they didn't write about the *vinte e sete* at all, or if they did, like Basil Davidson, they only told the story from the official MPLA point of view. They don't say a word about all those deaths. Thousands of them!' I can feel myself becoming angry, which I don't want her to see. I mention Mugabe's Matabeleland massacres and the thousands killed under Pinochet. 'Why should the MPLA be accorded secrets that others are not?'

Mendes says nothing. She simply listens and looks, which makes me talk more to fill the silence. I tell her about Maria Reis and her husband's disappearance. Then I talk about my Angolan friends, here in London, who say their relatives were killed in the aftermath of the uprising, or coup, or whatever it was. 'They say it is still taboo, that no one is supposed to discuss it, that their families are still afraid.' Still, she says nothing. So on I go, repeating the snippets I have picked up here and there.

'Apparently the Cubans helped with the killings, but the Soviets supported Nito Alves. That's what I've heard. I don't know if it's true, and that's what intrigues me,' I say, hearing my voice filling with passion again, 'all the secrecy, the misinformation, and the fear, yet so little has been published about it, particularly in English.'

Mendes is still observing silently, making me increasingly paranoid. 'I want to find out what happened,' I say. 'I want to write the truth about this great tragedy, that's all.' As those last words fall from my lips I realise how naive they must sound. Toning it down a little, I say, 'I'd like to make a contribution to knowledge if I can.'

Now she is shaking her head. 'You must be very cautious of those who say it is the greatest tragedy in Angola's recent history. That makes me very angry.' She pauses, checking for my full attention. 'The *vinte e sete de maio* came from within the MPLA. It grew beyond that, sure, but it is essentially about the MPLA. It is not a UNITA experience. So we must be cautious.' She rubs a finger over the table. 'You cannot have a monopoly on suffering,' she says sharply, 'it's egoistic.' She pushes her empty cup of coffee to the far side of the table and folds her arms into the space between us.

'If you want to understand what happened in the aftermath of the uprising, you have to try to consider what happens in a revolutionary process. Everyone was in this communist, Stalinist frame of mind. Everyone was in their twenties, such young radicals. At that age you look at everything as a question of life or death. I myself look back and ask, how was this possible?'

A waiter appears and removes our cups. He wipes the table. My eyes follow his hands as they swirl over the damp surface. Mendes' voice softens. 'I know people who don't know if they are a widow or not. They don't have bodies,' she says quietly, 'or even papers to say their relatives and friends are dead. So they do not know for absolute certain what happened. It is a terrible thing of terrible suffering.'

Another waiter is stacking brown trays into a pillar, slamming them down on top of each other before swinging back into the room, whirling in and out of the tables, turning chairs upside down, scheming his way through the end of the day. I look at my watch. We have long ago exceeded the fifteen minutes permitted. But Mendes shows no signs of stopping. On the contrary, I now feel as though I am having a private lecture.

'You need to understand that there were revolutionary trials,' she says. 'It was revolutionary justice. You could decide to kill someone simply because "the People" agree. You know what Neto said, don't you?'

I think I do.

'"We are not going to rely on normal procedures; we will do what we want in the name of the People."' She looks at me firmly. 'Revolution is this, Lara: it is when normal things don't go normally.' She pauses. 'The question that needs to be asked is not how the government could have done what it did, but how we, as Angolans, could have accepted it?' Her voice tightens now. 'It is the same with the argument that Angola was the victim of the Cold War. Yes, we were exploited by outside powers, but they were not responsible for our fighting and our warring. We were.'

One of the waiters approaches. 'We are closing, ladies.' He smiles at us and Mendes smiles back, nodding as if to say she's understood and could he now leave? 'Five minutes,' he says, 'and we're closing.'

She continues. 'The difficulty we have is that Angolans do talk about the *vinte e sete de maio*, but not in any detail. This is why the young get so confused. Sometimes they hear that it was a fight for representative democracy, but it wasn't. It was about people power.'

'But isn't that precisely what people power is?' I say. 'Democracy.'

She shakes her head. 'The meaning of people, here, is different. It is a very vague concept.'[11] She pulls her hands apart. 'The MPLA went from one end of the spectrum to the other.' She waves her fingers to indicate the leap. 'And it never looked back with a critical review.' Now she moves her hands even further apart. 'How can you go from here,' she raises her left hand, 'all the way to here,' up goes the right, 'without once looking back?'

I assume she's referring to the party's journey from national-liberation movement to government, and then dictatorship: 'Are you suggesting some sort of tribunal to bring the guilty to justice?'

She's shaking her head again, but I'm not sure whether it is in disagreement or frustration. 'We are not South Africa, Lara. The Protestants have a tradition of confessing publicly but it's completely different among Catholics. In Angola, there is no history of public confession. And anyway, we do not know if truth and reconciliation even go together. We know that South Africa went through the process, but do we know whether it worked?'

The waiters are watching us from the counter. It's gone six o'clock. Her professor will be cross: I share with Mendes the promise I made him and she laughs lightly.

We walk from the building into the greyness of London's King's Cross. She asks where I am going next and smiles when I tell her about the 'Stop the War' rally. She promises to email me various bits of information, her bibliographies and a chronology of Angola's history. She's much more generous than most. I thank her, and we part.

An hour later, I'm squeezing into the back of a packed church hall, cradled in wooden beams. At the front, a stout Scot is speaking brilliantly about the US and British war in Iraq. Expelled from the Labour Party for his candid attacks on our prime minister, Tony Blair, in 2005, George Galloway became the first MP for Britain's socialist Respect Party. Such was my outrage about the invasion, I set aside some of my misgivings about Galloway and joined Respect. This evening, I'm here with hundreds of other supporters, all applauding and cheering this polished political performer. Galloway has that gift of rhetorical rhythm that provokes people to clap even though they're not entirely sure why.

'Hassan Nasrallah is the real leader of the Arab people!' Applause. 'Hugo Chávez is the real leader of the Arab people!' Applause. 'Fidel Castro is the real leader of the Arab people!' Applause.

My hands remain firmly on my lap. A wave of cynicism sweeps over me as I look around the hall, wondering whether any of us really knows what this means. Then Galloway is back to Blair, jogging our memories with the tale of Walter Wolfgang, an eighty-two-year-old Labour Party member who was forcibly removed from the party's annual conference for shouting 'Nonsense!' at the Foreign Secretary, Jack Straw, during his speech on the Iraq war. As Galloway recounts the story, a grey-haired man enters the back of the hall just a few feet from where I'm sitting. He pushes into the crowd and shouts, 'Fascist!' Immediately, two large men pull him back and shove him outside to localised cheers. Galloway carries on speaking.

I think of Mendes and her belief that whatever happened during the *vinte e sete*, one cannot simply blame the politicians: it was the people, she said, who allowed it to happen. Listening to Galloway now and watching the crowd around me, I wonder how long it would take for a purge to be unleashed in London, given the right conditions. The feelings of anger about the war in Iraq are so strong among some of us, I don't doubt we, too, could kill for our views.

At the end of the speech, I raise my hand. I suggest to Galloway that we in Respect should not behave in the same way as our opponents, and that he should have stopped the ejection of the man. A few people clap approvingly, but the majority toe the line behind Galloway and for a very brief moment, I feel a peculiar sense of fear.

A few days later, Mendes' email arrives with its gift of attached files. She has highlighted several books and advises me to track down one author in particular, a Portuguese lawyer by the name of Ildeberto Teixeira. Then she signs off, short and to the point.

'If you don't give up, I wish you good luck. You are going to need it.'

5

◆

FASCISM WAS FINISHED, SOCIALISM HAD BEGUN

A pale pink lump of liver fat is collapsing on a saucer.

'I'm afraid it's duck,' says my host, 'not goose.'

We take turns slicing the foie gras, slapping it like soft cement onto thick pieces of toast. I feel flattered by the delicacy, and a little guilty. All I've brought is a gingerbread man wearing a pointy hat and holding a broomstick.

It's Hallowe'en and I'm sinking awkwardly into a spongy sofa in the central London home of Michael Wolfers. Well schooled and well spoken, he has an air of the chaotic professor about him: a rare delight, who is more concerned with intellectual content than outward appearance. A flop of grey hair distorts his broad crown and a blanket of whiskers softens his cheeks. His belly strains against tiny buttons defiantly holding his shirt together. His humble house is higgledy-piggledy too. Cardboard boxes of books and papers and stacks of notes are piled up in the front room, filling at least half of it.

'Sorry about the mess,' he says. 'It's my Thomas Hodgkin biography.'

It comes as little surprise to learn that Wolfers is working on a book about the respected Marxist scholar. After an education within the most elitist of establishments, Hodgkin rejected an early career choice at the Colonial Office in the 1930s to devote himself to the critical study of British imperialism and, later, African nationalism. Impressive for a British man of such privilege, his work brought him into contact with two of the most remarkable revolutionaries of the twentieth century, Che Guevara and the

Martiniquan psychiatrist Frantz Fanon. Together with Basil Davidson, Hodgkin's commitment to Africa posed a formidable challenge to colonial and enlightenment narratives about the continent, earning them high praise from Edward Said in his 1993 book *Culture and Imperialism*.

Wolfers' friendship with Davidson and Hodgkin is an indication of where his own political sympathies lie. He too has spent a lifetime on the left, writing about Africa for a spread of publications, including the *Morning Star*, the London-based *West Africa* magazine and *The Times*, during a spell as its Africa correspondent. He has also translated the writing of some of Africa's most prominent political figures, including Guinea-Bissau's foremost Marxist, Amílcar Cabral, and Mozambique's first president, Samora Machel. Wolfers' work has introduced readers of the English language to a number of leading Angolan novelists and poets, such as Pepetela and José Luandino Vieira. He has also translated books by the Egyptian Marxist economist Samir Amin.

In essence, then, Wolfers is a radical man of letters, an intellectual of the left. But the first time I met him, my impression was quite different – and, as it turned out, entirely wrong. We were facing each other across an expanse of polished wood in a private room at Chatham House in London's Piccadilly. This eighteenth-century building, the former home of three British prime ministers, today houses a think tank for international affairs. Wolfers and I were attending a round-table discussion about the possibility of peaceful elections in Angola. The event had been organised by the Angola Forum, whose sponsors – BP, Exxon, Chevron, De Beers, Marathon Oil, Statoil, Standard Chartered Bank, Banco Africano de Investimentos and occasionally Angola's state oil company, Sonangol – are a good indicator of its overriding interests. On this particular occasion, a handful of us were listening patiently to an Angolan minister who sat at the head of the table making monotonous pronouncements about the main opposition party, UNITA. Afterwards, I watched Wolfers speaking to the minister, and wondered if he was like the many British men I had met in Luanda, usually involved in diamonds or security or both. Or was he one of those former civil servants who cashes in on the many contacts he has collected for a more lucrative role in the petroleum industry? The former British ambassador to Angola, John Flynn, who became an adviser to Chevron, is just one example. I was mulling this over when a voice whispered into my ear.

'He was *actually* there!'
'Where?' I mouthed.
'In Luanda. When the coup happened. You must talk to him.'

A fortnight later, I'm following my nose into a network of narrow streets, an enclave of late-Georgian terraced houses with undulating roofs that scallop the skyline. What was once a public estate for artisan workers, developed on marshland by a gold refiner in the 1820s, is now a conservation area less than a minute's walk from Waterloo station. I count my way up the street and knock on Wolfers' front door. Smiling uneasily, he beckons me in.

'I'd only intended to stay for a couple of days,' he begins, recalling his arrival in Angola in 1975. 'I just wanted to be part of the celebrations for Independence Day. I arrived two days before, I think, on 9 November.' Wolfers speaks with his tongue resting on the inside of his lower lip, just over his teeth, almost a lisp. 'It was a marvellous time. The MPLA had won the war of liberation and the Portuguese had left.' A broad smile opens his face. 'Fascism was finished. Socialism had begun.'

After the celebrations, Wolfers was invited by the MPLA to stay on in Luanda and train journalists at Rádio Nacional. He was a trusted figure. He had met Agostinho Neto at a meeting in Sudan in 1969, and another senior MPLA figure, Saydi Mingas, in Oxford in 1974. His southern-Africa credentials were also solid. He was close friends with eight members of the Politburo of Mozambique's socialist government, which had celebrated independence a few months before Angola, on 25 June 1975. He also knew Frene Ginwala, a respected comrade in the African National Congress who had lived in exile since 1960. Indeed, it was she who recommended he visit Angola.

So he accepted the invitation and became part of a privileged group of sympathetic Europeans working within the higher echelons of the movement. He says his ideological beliefs were part of the reason he went to Angola, but insists he kept his journalistic head. 'I was objective,' he says, 'until the occasion when I was asked to give blood for FAPLA soldiers on the frontline. At that moment, I jumped ship. I went on writing, but I was writing from a different perspective than when I had been working for *The Times*. I was there because I'd been involved in supporting the MPLA. It was our victory.'

Wolfers' support for the movement is evident in the 1983 book *Angola in the Frontline*, which he wrote with Jane Bergerol, another British journalist, the *Financial Times* stringer in Luanda. Theirs is one of the very few books to include, in depth, an account of the *vinte e sete*. They devote two whole chapters to the subject. However, what struck me when I read it was the extent to which the official MPLA version of events seems to be adhered to. Perhaps I should not have been surprised. Bergerol's former editor, Bridget Bloom, has spoken about the shortcomings of her raw copy, which required a lot of editing: 'it was virtually propaganda for the MPLA [...] it was not the sort of thing we could have published in the *Financial Times* without losing out completely on objectivity.'[12] In Bergerol and Wolfers' book, the so-called factionalists are given no space to defend their point of view; however, one of the conclusions they make suggests they acknowledge the long-term impact of the violence meted out on the protesters, or *golpistas*.

I take a deep breath. 'What interests me,' I say in as soft a voice as I can muster, 'is that towards the end of your chapter "The Alves coup", you state that its long-term effect "was to sow doubt about the wisdom of getting involved in politics". I wondered what exactly you meant by that.'

'Did I say that?' comes his response, almost jovial. 'Gosh! I'm not sure why.'

'You definitely wrote it,' I say, trying to be firm.

'Never been back since. Apart from a trip to the border with Namibia. Of course I see Angolans almost on a daily basis. I'm in touch with people from that period...'

He stalls, leaving all the non sequiturs hanging, and we look at each other expectantly.

'Oh gosh,' he says, 'I suppose... well... I'm now doing *ex post facto* reasoning.'

I nod, holding his gaze, urging him on.

'You see, what you'd had in the year before the Nito Alves coup... I was aware of the problem... I had been watching the thing fester, the unease in the political process. Basil [Davidson] thought I was just a whingeing foreigner. When it actually happened, he rang me to apologise. You see, he had dismissed the thing.'

This is the second time he has implied Davidson's inferior knowledge of Angola. The first was at the end of the Chatham House meeting, when

I asked him what he thought of Davidson's work. The trouble with Basil, he'd said, was that he never stayed in Angola for more than a few days or at most a few weeks. Apparently, he didn't speak Portuguese either.

'What you'd got,' Wolfers continues now, 'was all kinds of anomalous activity. For example, these radio programmes like *Kudibanguela*. They were broadcast through the state radio mechanism by sectarian groups, which had somehow escaped the normative process. There wasn't censorship, but there was a normative environment.'

I wonder what he means by the word 'normative': it sounds so unrevolutionary. I'd like to unpick it a bit, but I'm not quick enough and his voice washes over mine.

'One had a sense of what was proper: this was improper.' He catches his breath. 'I am convinced that I saw this truck with Nito Alves in it. I knew him. I had breakfasted with him.' He takes a quick pant between sentences. 'You do not expect to see a senior member of the leadership driving a truck. I may have been mistaken, but I do not think I was. I knew the man well.'

He's lost me. So Alves was driving a truck. So what? In a newly independent and socialist country where people greeted each other as comrades, I would have thought this was a positive step, a sign that a member of the Central Committee was not above menial work.

'The point,' says Wolfers, 'is that the norms are being broken.'

By way of illustration, he tells me the tale of the electric stove. A friend had promised to give him his spare, so long as Wolfers came to collect it. So Wolfers set off to his friend's house, but on the way there he got lost. He ended up outside the house of another comrade, Anselmo Mesquita 'Sianuk', who was discovered, later, to be a factionalist. 'I went in to Sianuk's house. And there he was with a range of people, ostensibly listening to an important funeral on the radio. But this was not a family gathering. It was a particular mix.'

Wolfers continues, recounting another, similar experience at the house of Virgílio Frutuoso, the editor of *Diário de Luanda*, who – like Sianuk – turned out to be a factionalist. 'There again, this gathering of clearly disparate people. It looked like a cell. Puzzlement,' says Wolfers, his quizzical brow hanging on to the word. 'Then you realised why. When you saw this was a plot. These clusters of people.'

I'm not sure how this answers my initial question, but I think I'm beginning to settle into his stream of thought.

'It was like those bizarre things at the Cidadela,' he says, referring to the main sports stadium in Luanda, which was often used for political rallies. 'I went to them out of curiosity. One did. We were swept along.'

'By what? By Nito Alves, you mean? By his charisma?'

'No! Alves was not a charismatic man. It was the message. He was nice-looking in a slightly twisted way. He was nugly.'

It must be clear from the expression on my face that I don't have the faintest idea what he means. 'Nugly?'

'A word we had as schoolboys,' he says, smilingly. 'Nice–ugly. Nito was nugly. He was personable but not film-star good-looking.'

This nostalgic reference is touching – I try to picture Wolfers as a young boy – but he's on a roll, and switches to Zé Van Dúnem.

'Now,' he says, 'he was rather ominous-looking.'

I'd love to explore these aesthetical observations further, but it feels like Wolfers is avoiding my question. I try to nudge him forwards. 'You said something about Nito's message?' I say.

'Yes,' he says, 'this thing about white men sweeping roads. I was there for that. I thought it was silly. But if you were an underpaid African worker in Luanda, that could have quite an appeal.'

Famously, Alves said that there would only be true equality in Angola when white people were seen sweeping the streets alongside blacks. I've always found this a very compelling idea – that equality should involve the loss of power and status by the dominant group, not simply the taking of power by the oppressed – and I put it to Wolfers that this quest was far from silly.

Apparently I've misunderstood.

'It was reverse racism. If you were in the Citadela back then, this hypnotic line was being peddled, but the doors were guarded. You could not leave. Normally you could walk in and out as you liked. But with Nito, there was an element of physical control, of menace. You were inside a trap. That message was a way of being racist.'

'Do you mean that you felt trapped as a white man among so many blacks?' I ask.

'It had nothing to do with being white,' he shoots back. 'An Angolan would also have been prevented from leaving. I didn't feel white. When I am in Africa, I do not feel white. In the Congo, I...'

He mutters something that I don't catch.

'In Africa, I feel a human being,' he goes on. 'I would never think about being black or white. It does not occur to me to separate out.'

For a moment, I'm puzzled. I cannot imagine how a white European man with such a radical intellectual background could live in Angola in the 1970s – a country whose population had only just escaped centuries of racially stratified rule – and be unaware of the resonance of skin colour. I wonder if I have misunderstood him.

'So Alves' statement about street cleaners, you mean, had no bearing on reality?'

'It was about mobilisation,' he says, 'about playing the race card. As often happens. It is always the number twos who are attracted, you see. They think they can replace the number ones. It was the second-raters.'

But I'm not sure it's quite so straightforward, particularly where class, race and colonialism are concerned.

Wolfers continues, 'Neto said at one point that the Valles family had failed to make a revolution in Portugal so they came to make one in our country.'

He is referring to Sita Valles, the woman who arrived in Angola from Lisbon in June 1975 to give her support to the MPLA, just as Wolfers did five months later. However, unlike Wolfers and other British socialists, Valles was actually born in Angola, in Cabinda, in 1951. Contrary to the Politburo's claim that she was white, Valles' father was from another Portuguese colony, Portuguese India, now known as Goa. So her genetic roots were in Asia. In Lisbon, she had been a leading radical figure, just like many members of the MPLA elite, and was active in the communist students' union, even representing them in Moscow. Later, she and Zé Van Dúnem fell in love and had a child. But the point is, if Valles was guilty of trying to make up for Portugal's failed revolution, what about the many British socialists, who, it might similarly be argued, went to southern Africa for exactly the same reason? At least Valles had an authentic claim to the continent. I know I ought to put this point to Wolfers, but something stops me and I listen instead as he throws another dart at Nito Alves.

'He was very influenced by the Valles family, you see, so he was influenced by the Portuguese. It was not organic, it was not part of Angola.'

But you could say the same of the MPLA's entire socialist project: that it was not organic to Angola. Although arguments continue over whether Neto was a member of the Portuguese Communist Party (PCP) or not, there is no doubt that he and several other senior members of the MPLA were influenced considerably by the Portuguese, not least during the years they spent in Lisbon. You only to have to turn to Basil Davidson's book, *In the Eye of the Storm*, to find support for this view. Davidson wrote that although the 'deeply clandestine and hunted Portuguese communist party' was not as powerful as its French and British equivalents, 'it seems to have been far better than nothing.' Davidson then quotes Neto as saying in 1970: 'We learned from the sharp conflicts that existed in Portugal. They provided us with useful lessons.' Davidson adds, 'In this way [the MPLA] approached the ideas of Marxism, and these became a powerful strand in the developing fabric of their post-reformist and therefore revolutionary ideas.'[13] It is worth remembering, moreover, that Neto married a Portuguese woman.

I try to be tactful, but when I make the point to Wolfers he takes off in another direction. 'There was this business of flooding the Lello bookshop [in Luanda] with Nito Alves' poems, of creating an image of a person who writes poetry.'

Again, I seem only to hear the flaws in this argument. 'But isn't that what happened with Agostinho Neto, too? This image of the great poet who liberated "the People"? In fact,' I add, 'isn't it valid to question whether Neto's poetry was really good art at all?'

I may have hit a nerve.

'Look,' he says, 'Neto was a distinguished poet long before he was a president. Long before there was ever any moment of struggle, there was a cultural renaissance. The whole nucleus of the MPLA leadership was in Lisbon, in the Casa, the Casa...' I want to finish the sentence for him – he means the Casa dos Estudantes do Império, which was a cultural and political centre for Africans in Lisbon – but he starts again. 'The point is that you can trace Neto's work. I did the anthology of poets and you can trace all of their careers. But when a book just appears in a bookshop by someone who is not previously known to have written a single word of poetry, it is suspicious. Neto and Nito, you see, they were trying to create an alter-Neto. Nito as the alter-Neto.'

Wolfers may well be right, but I'm beginning to get worried about running out of time, and he's still not answered my first question. So I remind him once more: 'This statement you made in your book, the one I referred to earlier, it seems to mirror what several Angolans have told me – that the long-term effect of the *vinte e sete de maio* was to stop people from participating in politics, from protesting, from voicing their opposition to the MPLA – what you refer to as "getting involved".'

At last, he relents.

'I would say that the system broke down,' he says. 'During the period of 1975 and 1976, there was immense local participation. It was exhilarating and promising. But once it turned out that the department of the organisation of the masses had been infiltrated, and the political department, and that all these positive structures, some of which were the holy grail of FAPLA, had been turned on their heads, corrupted from within... If you could no longer trust these structures, then what could you trust? I think that's what people felt.'

'You mean it poisoned their hopes?' I say.

'I'm not in a position to judge. I think people became less confident of what they could rely on. Maybe that's what you have been hearing.' But he refutes the idea that lots of Angolans were killed for supporting Alves. 'I go to these meetings and I hear people saying that x thousand were killed after the coup. It cannot be true because people I know, who have been mentioned as dead, are still alive. I go to friends' houses, Angolan friends, and I see photographs of people who I was told were dead. And yet, there they are, in a recent photograph, alive. There cannot have been mass executions.'

I am not in a position to argue about this. Beyond the MPLA's claims in its document, I have not seen any solid data detailing the number of people who were killed during the entire episode of the *vinte e sete*. All I have is the word of a few Angolans who have urged me to investigate, and Maria Reis' testimony of her husband's disappearance.

'What makes me cross,' Wolfers adds, 'is that I was actually there. I know what went on. The people who invent these figures were not there. I was.'

He makes an important point. But I have spoken to other people who were also there – people who always supported the MPLA – and their accounts differ quite radically from his.

'Are you saying that no one was killed on Neto's orders?' I ask him.

'Nito Alves and Zé Van Dúnem were shot,' he concedes, 'and Sita was also bumped off. However, most of the Portuguese who got involved were allowed to go home.' He stops to think and then he says, 'It is true, though, that a list was never published.'

There is just one last question which has been puzzling me since reading his book. In discussing the ambitions of the factionalists, he and Bergerol assert that, 'The demonstrators would call for Alves and Van Dúnem to be reintegrated into the government and for changes in the government and MPLA leadership.' I find it surprising that that is all they wanted. And I'm more surprised by Wolfers' answer.

'They didn't want much,' he confirms. 'They wanted the *nitistas* in the big jobs. But basically, it was to be a reshuffle.'

Clearly, a reshuffle is not the same as an attempted coup. So if this is true, why were the factionalist leaders executed? What serious threat did they pose to the regime?

The answer, for Wolfers, is obvious. 'If they hadn't murdered those senior figures in Sambizanga, they would not have been killed. They would simply have been dismissed.'

From here, our conversation fizzles to what feels like a rather unsatisfactory end. Wolfers tries chomping his way through the gingerbread man's plastic broomstick, and looks surprised when it won't break between his teeth. For myself, I can't help but feel a bit disappointed by this encounter – I think it's his loyalty to Neto that I find frustrating. And yet I admire Wolfers enormously for seizing the opportunity to commit to a socialist revolution at the height of the Cold War. When I went to Angola in 1998, I had also hoped, ignorantly I admit, to contribute to some sort of anti-imperialist MPLA project. But I was twenty years too late. The Marxists had long gone, and far from making friends with the regime, I found myself quite unpopular.

So perhaps I envy Wolfers too. His relationship with the MPLA has given him access to people I have never got close to. He was even offered an Angolan passport by the ambassador to London – he says he did not accept it – but as I leave his house, all I can think about is my own longed-for visa. It's been weeks since I made my application, and right now I'd give up an awful lot to get back into the country.

Feeling mildly anxious about my own predicament, I wander into the herb-filled gardens of St John's Church at the end of Wolfers' street. I tread the gravel path around the lawns, listening to the drone of traffic, to the trains going in and out of Waterloo station, and the seagulls that season the sound of this city. The church itself is curious, a Christian building with a design based on pre-Christian architecture. From the front, it looks just like the

Parthenon, complete with an entasis in each of its six columns. But in the fourth century BC, there would not have been a white van parked at its front gates, offering free food and company to ex-servicemen, our otherwise forgotten 'homeless heroes', according to the volunteers' T-shirts. I stand on the church steps and watch the miserable queue of drunk and jobless men.

According to an inscription inside the church, St John's was originally built in 1824, 'by a grateful nation in thanksgiving for the victory of Waterloo'. This was the British Empire charging towards its zenith, soon to have a hegemony on world trade. I think about my country's history, the way we expanded across the world to control almost a quarter of its land mass as well as half a billion people. We were experts at bloating ourselves on the blood of others, including millions of Africans bought and sold for slavery, many of whom came from Angola. I think of my doubts about this research, and those who have questioned my interest in the bloody episode of the Twenty-seventh of May. Why don't I dig up dirt on Britain, they ask? Aren't British crimes proportionately far worse than any of Angola's?

Looking at the scene before me now, I wonder if I should indeed be writing about *our* wars and *our* homeless, traumatised fighters. Of course Britain's rulers have far more blood on their hands than Angola's. The history of this church, spanning the height of empire through to two world wars, tells part of that tale. But in 1940, St John's was struck by a high-explosive bomb and 'shuddered to her depths'. Five years later, as World War II ended, Britain was virtually bankrupt and the empire was in decline. Meanwhile, across Africa, national-liberation movements were rising up to demand freedom. Angola's independence would come later than most, but it would come eventually.

So why, I ask myself now, am I so interested in such a dark but apparently minor moment in Angola's contemporary history? What am I trying to prove? I'm still not sure I know.

6

◆

JUST LIKE THE MOVIES

Wolfers' generosity went beyond foie gras. During our conversation, he handed me a copy of a nine-page letter that he had typed in Luanda on 2 June 1977. It was initially sent to Polly Gaster, another British Marxist, who, like him, had left London to support the socialist revolutions taking place in Africa, only she was working for the Mozambican government in Maputo. Thomas Hodgkin also received the letter, a slightly extended version, five months later. When Wolfers gave me my copy, he tried to persuade me to read it there and then, but I thought it better to use that time for talking, and told him I would look at it later – which I do, the moment I am home. It tells an interesting tale.

When he awoke at half past six on the morning of 27 May, Wolfers was not sure whether he was actually awake or dreaming. He thought he could hear gunfire and lay still for several minutes, trying to distinguish the imaginary from the real. Then he thought of the radio beside his bed. He switched it on. The usual transmissions were being broadcast. So he got out of bed and went to the window. From his ninth-floor apartment, he could see an armoured vehicle patrolling the streets. He could also see ordinary people walking to work. So he washed and dressed and drank a cup of coffee, and set out from his flat fractionally earlier than normal.

Downstairs, he bumped into the porter, who warned him that shots were being fired close by. Wolfers was undeterred. An important statement by Neto's second-in-command Lúcio Lara was due to be broadcast that day, an exposition of the tactics of the factionalists. Worried that an attempt would be made to interrupt the transmission, he bid the porter goodbye and began walking towards the radio station, just a few minutes away.

Now he heard the shooting himself. Then he saw people running. Although he cannot be sure – his watch was a little fast – he estimates that it was about twenty to eight. He considered turning back, but such was his sense of loyalty to the MPLA, 'to the genuine struggle waged by the comrades', he continued. Moreover, he thought it unlikely that the factionalists – he calls them 'a few empty-headed people' – were capable of doing any real damage. So on he went, as calmly as possible.

By the time he reached the back gate into the grounds of Rádio Nacional, the streets had emptied completely. Wolfers was not alone, however. There was a soldier in the bushes, who called out to him, 'Where are you going?'

'To work!' responded Wolfers, flashing his staff pass.

The soldier let him continue, and he entered the building and made his way to the library. There, he was greeted by his boss, Ilda Carreira, sister of defence minister Iko, and her assistant Pedro. He told them about the shooting outside, but Carreira rebuffed him, insisting it was further away, in the *bairros* on the outskirts of town. So they walked together to the studio to listen to Lara's recording, and to begin the translations for the daily news bulletins. In a corridor, they noticed two soldiers with a portable military communications set and a field telephone. They thought little of it. The men seemed calm, they were probably doing routine security work.

Up to this point, everything appeared quite normal.

Shortly after eight o'clock, another person entered the studio and went straight to Carreira to tell her that a member of staff was trying to stop transmissions 'in the name of the revolution'. The man in question had not said on whose orders he was acting, but Wolfers knew him. Rui Malaquias was 'very young and silly' and 'quite capable of getting confused and over-enthusiastic and taking some silly idea of his own, or some idiotic initiative'. Luckily, the presenter on duty that morning was experienced, 'one of our best comrades', observes Wolfers. He ignored the 'hothead' and continued to broadcast.

On receiving this information, Carreira immediately called the Department of Revolutionary Orientation, which had replaced the Ministry of Information, to explain what was happening. However, the response she received was rather vague. She was about to seek further advice when

Malaquias made another attempt to interrupt transmissions, this time with the support of three soldiers.

It was during the next two to three minutes that the factionalists took over the entire radio station. Among them, Wolfers recognised several members of staff. Each one had paired up with a soldier to control key points of the building – the studio control centre, the technical centre, the cabins, the recording studio, the door and the switchboard. Through the network of loudspeakers, Malaquias could be heard broadcasting a message. Wolfers describes it as 'rubbish', and was convinced 'it would only be a brief moment of false glory while these idiots ranted over the radio'.

By now, Wolfers and Carreira were under armed guard. They had been ordered not to touch any machinery or make any calls. However, as the time passed, the atmosphere in the studio became calmer, even 'tedious', writes Wolfers. He managed to hide the tape of Lara's speech, which he was sure the factionalists would want to destroy, and he and Carreira were allowed to go and make a cup of coffee. Later, he went to the library to choose some books, which he had 'the vague idea of carrying [...] to prison if we were rounded up'. He chose a collection of Shakespeare plays and a book about art nouveau, commenting disdainfully, 'Over the months I had worked in the "library" and I had seen there were virtually no books of great interest.'

By mid morning, 'a small crowd' had gathered in front of the radio buildings. Wolfers believes this was in response to the appeal that had been made on the radio, and what he calls 'some bullying' in the *bairros*. Still remarkably calm, he and Carreira 'drifted back to the library' with two other 'loyal comrades' and waited for 'liberation'. From inside the radio station they watched as a growing number of soldiers appeared outside, as well as six armoured cars, or possibly tanks, Wolfers could not tell. As the tension increased, he and Carreira decided to employ a technique they had learned watching American films: they opened the library doors, just in case a group of armed men should suddenly burst in and open fire. It was, writes Wolfers, 'Just like the movies!!!'

At about a quarter past eleven, 'a large number of soldiers' who were 'well armed' and 'dynamic' did indeed appear in the library. Wolfers was relieved to see them and could tell immediately that they were government troops loyal to Neto. He and Carreira and the other two staff members were ordered to leave swiftly, and to move towards the front entrance of the building. Meanwhile, another group of 'liberators', including two Cubans, took over the broadcasting. Writes Wolfers, 'the first loyal voice one heard if one was listening to the transmission outside was a Cuban, but this was almost chance.' Apparently the Cuban was not aware that his voice was being broadcast across the entire country. All he was doing, Wolfers insists, was asking an Angolan comrade to make a broadcast.

It was at this stage – just when it seemed that the uprising might be over – that the real trouble began. About forty members of radio staff, including Wolfers, were escorted out of the building. As they exited the main doors they found themselves heading towards factionalist demonstrators, some of whom were armed. Wolfers and his colleagues were in a vulnerable position, sandwiched between what he refers to as their 'liberators' and their enemies. Fearful that a shoot-out might erupt at any minute, some of the staff immediately sat down and others lay flat on the ground. Then they all began crawling back into the building on their bellies, 'a moving human carpet'. The moment they were safely inside again, they made their way down into the basement of the building. As they did, shooting broke out behind them and some of the women became hysterical. The firing lasted about twenty minutes. When it ended, the forces loyal to Neto had regained control.

Wolfers walked home. He informed some of his neighbours 'that they should expect an official announcement very soon'. Then he entered his little flat, where he made some lunch and answered a series of telephone calls from friends and colleagues, including Basil Davidson. After that, he sat down to write what he calls his 'aide-memoire' so that he would be able to separate the fact from the gossip which would, he was certain, inevitably follow.

Given the dearth of published information about the *vinte e sete*, this letter is an important piece of historical documentary evidence. Not only does it detail the sequence of events, but Wolfers' language and personal opinions offer useful insights into 1970s European socialist thought. His fidelity to the MPLA, for example, is overwhelming; his devotion almost cultish. He states that he was 'absolutely prepared to be killed' for the movement and praises the leadership for what he calls its 'passionate reasonableness'. 'I had a duty,' he writes, 'to maintain a conscientious level of work

[...] provided that it is work for the MPLA and to the genuine struggle waged by the comrades who are loyal to the MPLA.' He describes those who support Neto's leadership of the movement as 'comrades' and 'honest and loyal friends'. The factionalists, to contrast, are 'villains' and 'tawdry people', both 'surly and obstructive' and 'empty headed'. As if watching a bad film, he divides the Angolans he encounters into goodies and baddies, whom he is either for or against. While reading, I find myself thinking of Stuart Hall, the cultural theorist who wrote in 1987 of 'the doubling' of 'fear and desire' in which the black subject is constructed as 'noble savage and violent avenger'.[14]

Woven into Wolfers' letter are his own observations on the racial and class composition of the factionalists. 'I was sad to see that there was a clear division on race lines,' he tells Polly Gaster. The factionalists at the radio station, he explains, were 'all black' and had 'clearly excluded from their plotting any whites or *mestiços*'. They included those who showed 'least diligence as workers and were the most obstructive'. Wolfers attributes their involvement less to 'coordinated activity' than to 'social problems', especially in the public service, which was 'a noticeably bourgeois and "idle" sector'. Nito Alves, he asserts, played on 'the anxieties of the inadequate and insecure' and 'forces which were present among the lumpen'. At the radio station, certain individuals 'showed signs of being unsympathetic to the MPLA, while being nominally militant' – a defect that Wolfers ascribes in part to 'psychological factors'. Some were 'in jobs which they could not cope with'. Many, he writes, 'should have been sacked purely on the basis of the failure to work to a modest let alone a good standard'.

I find Wolfers' letter a little unnerving. His writing seems to loop unwittingly into Frantz Fanon's critical gaze. For Fanon observed in 1952 that the colonial machine creates, among the colonised, a feeling 'that one is a Negro to the degree to which one is wicked, sloppy, malicious, instinctual'. Having internalised the world view of the white colonial oppressor, the black man thus 'enslaves himself' – and the idea that 'black = ugliness, sin, darkness, immorality' becomes the collective unconscious.[15] Yet Wolfers, at least in his letter, seems unaware of this dynamic. Empathy is lacking.

Despite his deep knowledge of African history and sincere passion for its liberation, the social and cultural formations that had developed over hundreds of years in Angola seem to pass him by. He writes as though colonialism – 'an immense project to break the will of the colonised people'[16] – could be overcome overnight; as though centuries of slave-trading should have vanished without a trace from the Angolan psyche; as though the policy of *assimilação*, which had attempted to transform a minority of Angolans into honorary Portuguese whites – prohibiting them from speaking indigenous languages, eating traditional foods and much more – could simply dissolve without consequence in a liberated Angola. It is as if Wolfers believes that when revolutions occur, they usher in entirely new worlds, wiping the slate of history clean, emptying the minds of the people. But of course there is always continuity with the past, with what went before. It cannot be blasted away.

What we seem to get from Wolfers is anger at the factionalists for disputing the MPLA's 'basic aim', as he calls it, 'of a non-racialist socialist society'. But the plan to transform Angola so rapidly from a highly racially stratified society into a 'non-racialist' one was utopian at best. Portuguese colonial rule had inculcated a racialised hierarchy comprising five categories, which are still used in common parlance today: the *negro*, born of black parents; the *cafuso*, born of a black and a *mestiço* parent; the *mestiço*, born of one black and one white parent; the *cabrito*, which translates as 'goat', born of a *mestiço* and a white parent; and the *branco*, born of two white parents. Given that race was the paradigm through which the everyday was experienced – in many ways, it still is – Wolfers' gripe about the factionalists' exclusivity 'on race lines', as he puts it, seems an inadequate response, one that attempts to wash over the nasty and brutal business of racial exploitation that had rooted itself deep down in the minds of so many.

What I also find interesting is how Wolfers situates himself. In his letter, he says he is 'an ordinary worker'. It is hard to fathom how an Oxbridge-educated, white British male, living in Luanda in the mid 1970s, could have perceived himself to be ordinary. This is someone who was present for Angola's independence day, having met the future president in another African state a few years earlier. Wolfers was such good friends with the finance minister, Saydi Mingas, that they spent Christmas together. He worked alongside the defence minister's sister, as a trainer and supervisor at the radio station, and he regularly lunched with other Europeans and senior members of government. This was not the sort of social life enjoyed by ordinary Angolan workers.

Despite these shortcomings, Wolfers' work on the *vinte e sete* has gone unchallenged by writers, academics and journalists working on southern

Africa. To this day, the two chapters that focus on this episode in his and Bergerol's book are widely cited as the most reliable published narrative there is, especially among those who only read English.

Considering this now, I feel all of a sudden rather alone and, potentially, quite foolish. I'm worried about how my research will be received by friends on the political left. Several have already voiced their concerns, warning me not to play into the hands of the right – the implication being that any attempt to disrupt the established narrative on the *vinte e sete* will do precisely that. I feel torn between the search for truth and my political beliefs, which I'm beginning to think, in itself, is rather a luxury.

7

♦

THE BROTHER

João Vieira Dias Van Dúnem's lips are pursed, as though poised to whistle, but instead what shoots from his mouth is unabashed vitriol.

'If Neto was alive today, I would kill him three times. And if he came back to life, I'd kill him again as if it were the first time.' Pointing at my notepad, he adds, 'I want you to write that down and quote it.'

I'm recording the conversation, but I make a note of his feelings towards Angola's first president anyway, and scribble a star in the space next to it.

'That man was a massive criminal,' he continues. 'It was him who gave the green light to kill all those young Angolans. It was him who created this empire of thieves, this kleptocracy that is Angola today. It was him.'

João stands up and paces the room. He looks to the window, where the branches of old plane trees are barely swaying above the traffic of London's Strand. We're in his office, which is tucked away in a cramped corner of the north-east wing of Bush House, home of the BBC World Service. João is the editor of the Portuguese for Africa section, a complicated department staffed by part-time poets, ex-DJs, former freedom fighters and die-hard journalists from Angola, Guinea-Bissau, Mozambique, Cape Verde, São Tomé and Príncipe, and Portugal. Most give the impression they loathe this organ of the British establishment and would rather return home to their beloved countries of birth. João, certainly, is one.

Tall, elegant and gently handsome, he has an air of patrician privilege. Once, I heard him describe himself as 'Angolan aristocracy'. He is probably a descendant of a white Dutchman, Balthasar Van Dúnem,[17] who arrived in Luanda in the 1630s and became a successful slave-trade contract manager.[18] Balthasar was nearly thrown out of Angola when the Portuguese, with thudding hypocrisy, began expelling immigrants. Insisting he was German, not Dutch, he managed to convince them to let him stay and soon afterwards became a Portuguese citizen.

Today, the Van Dúnems are one of the most powerful families in the country. If you run down a list of the political and social elite, the name pops up a lot. Yet, stripped of power and even the right to work, João left Angola in 1979, two years after Zé Van Dúnem, his older brother, had been executed for his part in the *vinte e sete*. João was, himself, imprisoned for two years, before being freed and allowed to leave the country. First, he went to Portugal; then to London, to join the BBC, which is how we met, much later, in 2001.

'You must understand,' he says urgently, 'that there is not an Angolan family that escaped the Twenty-seventh of May. Every single one has a friend or a relative who was killed. And the MPLA used it as an excuse to kill their enemies too, so people from UNITA also disappeared. At least 25,000 were killed, Lara! If you don't believe me,' he says, now standing before me, 'ask Filipe.' He turns and points through the glass wall that separates him from the rest of the office, to a man, probably in his early fifties, wearing a peaked hat and glasses, and gazing into a computer screen. João knocks at the window, signalling at Filipe to join us. His colleague stands up and walks over, slightly wobbly, with a stick. The moment the door opens, João is talking at him, explaining what has been said.

'I told her that every single family has been affected by the *vinte e sete*.'

Filipe agrees vociferously. 'It's true, it's true,' he says. 'They went around, house to house, in these lorries, picking people up.'

'Many were intellectuals we could ill afford to lose,' adds João.

'That's why development has been so slow,' says Filipe, 'because the brightest people in the country were wiped out.'

I'm curious as to what they mean by 'intellectual'. Not so long ago, I was told by an Angolan sociologist that when his compatriots use the term, they are referring to anyone who remained in school until the age of sixteen.

'I'm talking about the leaders of the MPLA,' says João, 'and the entire youth wing. Not a single member of the JMPLA was left. Not even those in Luanda managed to escape. They were all killed. Executed! And those who were members of committees and the leaders of the unions were also killed, or imprisoned.' He runs through a list of names. 'José Agostinho,

Luís Kitumba, Paulito... and many others. All of them killed. It was indescribable, Lara. Indescribable.'

Filipe is shaking his head, muttering soft agreements at the awfulness of it all. 'It's all true,' he says quietly. He puts a hand on João's shoulder and then he leaves the room. As the door closes softly behind him, I offer an opinion, admitting that I find it implausible – in the midst of civil war, at the height of the Cold War, whilst facing perpetual threats from its northern and southern borders – that the MPLA could have devoted so much time and energy to wiping out piles of its own militants. It doesn't make sense.

'It makes perfect sense!' says João, spitting laughter. 'Neto had always planned to clean out the opposition. It started in the 1960s.' He blames the international media attention that Neto received when he was imprisoned in Portugal. 'It turned him into something of a cause célèbre. He was one of the reasons Amnesty International came about.' Indeed, Neto was one of six prisoners of conscience whose cases were taken up by Peter Benenson, the British man who founded the now world-famous human-rights organisation.[19] His name became known far beyond Angola, as a symbol of the struggle for freedom. 'Among Portuguese communists, he was treated as a hero,' says João, 'but those of us who were fighting didn't like him. We lost respect for him because he lived abroad. He never fought as we did.'

I'm not sure this is entirely true. In Basil Davidson's book, there is a delightful black-and-white photograph of the author with Neto, deep in the Angolan bush. It is June 1970. Neto is balancing a Kalashnikov casually on his left shoulder. Both men are smiling.

But João is laughing at me. Apparently the pictures in the book were taken in Congo-Brazzaville, not Angola. 'You shouldn't believe everything you read,' he says a little scornfully. 'Neto had no military experience at all. He didn't even know how to use a gun.' João believes that one of the worst things about Neto was that he was not in the country during the most brutal battles with the Portuguese, in the late 1960s and early 1970s. 'Operation Sirocco was particularly harsh,' he says. 'They used helicopters, defoliants, dogs and anything else they could to destroy the enemy. We didn't stand a chance.'

It almost sounds as if he blames Neto for the severity of the liberation war, but he insists he's merely wishing to impress upon me how detached the man was from the struggle. 'If you want further proof,' he says defensively, 'let me tell you this: when Neto returned to Luanda for the first time in years, in February 1975, he didn't even recognise the city as he flew over it to land! He turned to those who were with him, and asked, "Where is this? Where is this?"'

This sounds like *fofoca* to me – rumour, or gossip. 'How do you know that?' I ask.

'I give you my word of honour,' he retorts, insisting he was told the story by Dr Eduardo Macedo dos Santos, a founder of the MPLA and the man so trusted by Neto he became his personal physician. 'And do you know what else, Lara?'

'What?'

'When he landed in Luanda, he told Eduardo that he was horrified by how well organised the MPLA of the interior was. You see, he could see how well structured we were, despite the fact our army had been almost destroyed.' João pauses. He comes and sits next to me. His face softens. He pulls his spectacles from the end of his nose and takes a deep breath. 'It was at this very point that Neto made up his mind to destroy those [in the MPLA] from the interior. You see, Lara, it was he who wanted to defeat the so-called *nitistas*, not the other way around.' He puts his glasses back on, stands up and steps to his desk, turns and sits on it, so that now he's looking down at me. It is only in this moment that I notice how he's dressed, smoothly, casually. He wears suede shoes and a dark-blue jacket made of cotton or possibly linen, with matching trousers loose around his legs. He looks at me thoughtfully, intelligently, and I feel suddenly self-conscious. I'm touched by his sadness, his appearance of calm and the softness of his voice. Yet as he speaks, at times almost with a tremor because he's so livid, the word that keeps coming back to me is 'bitterness'. How does he manage to suppress it all, I wonder?

'Our very huge mistake,' he continues, 'was at the Inter-Regional Conference in Moxico in 1974. We should never have let Neto take over. The trouble was the movement: it was in threads. People had even begun to call it *a retrosaria*.'

'The what?' I ask. 'I don't know that word.'

'*A retrosaria*,' he says again, then, in English, 'the haberdashery!' Another burst of laughter, but his face is tight with anger.

Our conversation edges forward with João sometimes standing, sometimes sitting, sometimes moving about, a combination that makes me edgy.

I tell him I've read the MPLA document on the *vinte e sete*. 'It makes a number of accusations about the factionalists.'

He looks at me sternly. 'You mustn't use that word,' he says. 'They called my brother a factionalist. The term implies that Zé wanted to break from the MPLA, which is completely wrong. If you want, call them *nitistas*.'

'OK,' I say, continuing, 'well, it claims that they held back food supplies and stole money from the army as part of a plan to provoke a rebellion.'

Now he looks ready to implode. 'You were in Angola in the late 1990s, weren't you?' I nod. 'Was there food in Angola then?' Not much: the UN's World Food Programme was there, distributing to hundreds of thousands of Angolans. 'And there weren't factionalists then, were there?' I shake my head again: there weren't. 'There wasn't food though, either, was there!' I'm still shaking my head: certainly there were massive shortages. 'So this idea of a food crisis has nothing to do with any sabotage. It's a structural crisis, an absence of production.'

He is probably quite right. Angola's food crisis in the mid to late 1970s probably resulted from a collapse in agricultural production, transport infrastructure and food distribution.[20] After Lisbon's Carnation Revolution in 1974, many of the whites who had been managing Angola's northern plantations for years, sometimes generations, were terrified by the prospect of black African rule and fled the colony for the metropole. This alone was damaging enough, but in 1975, when the so-called second war of liberation erupted between the three competing movements (the MPLA, the FNLA and UNITA), labour also diminished. The majority of workers were Ovimbundu men from the central highlands, and as insecurity increased, they were less and less tempted to migrate north, away from their homelands and the communities they trusted. The impact on the coffee industry, by then Angola's second-largest foreign-exchange earner, was severe. In the 1977 to 1978 season, for example, 90,000 workers picked 80,000 tonnes of coffee,[21] less than half the amount produced under colonial rule. Although the new government had tried to build up agricultural brigades to work on the plantations, over half of the new workers were young, inexperienced and unmotivated – they resented being forced from their urban homes to endure the hardship of rural obscurity. Steadily, the squeeze on foreign exchange tightened. The situation worsened further when Angolan maize farmers pushed for a reduction in the heavy taxes they had endured under the Portuguese. It was simply not politic for the new government to ignore this pressure – so it dropped taxes and unwittingly provoked a decline in overall production. Before long, Angola was using its shrinking foreign-exchange budget to buy expensive imports of maize and other emergency food supplies.

As well as the fall in production, continued conflict in 1975 and 1976 damaged the transport and distribution systems. Only small sections of the Benguela railway were still functioning, many bridges had been blown up, and many of the trucks used to transport had been either burned during fighting or driven over the border by the Portuguese who were abandoning Angola. Compounding all of this was the departure of white petit bourgeois entrepreneurs, who had owned and managed nearly all of the trading posts where food was sold. The resulting retail vacuum was the final nail in the coffin of food production, and contributed to widespread discontent. Political opposition grew and the government became too ashamed – and perhaps too panicked by the rise in support for Nito Alves – to admit the truth. Instead, it accused one of its own ministers of stockpiling food supplies in order to provoke an uprising against Neto. This failure to acknowledge the political and economic reality was disastrous – and João argues that it was made even worse by the government's response to the Twenty-seventh of May.

'We could have increased the national production with the skilled people we had,' he says. 'But because of the repression, the killing of all the *quadros nacionais*, the experts, we no longer had the ability to correct the problem.'

Building his case against President Neto and his defence of the *nitistas*, João tells me about a conversation between his brother, Zé, and their first cousin, the finance minister, Saydi Mingas, who was later killed in Sambizanga. 'Do you know what Saydi said? He said, "Look, we're cousins, we're brothers, and you are with Nito." He then tried to dissuade my brother from hanging out with Nito, who he called a "*pé descalço*", a barefoot, a sans-culotte from the street. Then he told my brother this, "I know you guys have got power, but the day you do something, we'll open the gates of the food warehouses and get the food to the people."' João is looking at me, a smugness in his lips. 'Can you see, Lara? Do you understand? There was a plan, on the part of Neto. It was obviously a set-up.'

I'm finding the layers of conspiracy a little muddling. Not that I want to ignore them. I learned, working in Angola, just how much both sides would lie about each other simply to strengthen their own case. I had witnessed horrendous ambushes that were carried out by the Angolan army but were reported in *Jornal de Angola* as the work of UNITA – and which the rebels also claimed was their doing. Anything was possible. But the suggestion that Neto wanted to force Nito into attempting a coup stretches my political imagination a bit too far, particularly when the evidence is third-hand. My doubt seems to irritate João.

'We [the *nitistas*] didn't want a coup,' he says impatiently. 'The Cubans had promised my brother that they would not intervene. So it was a condition *sine qua non* that there would not be a coup. But my brother was the humanist. He didn't want a bloodbath. And, anyway, a *coup d'état* is anti-Marxist so it couldn't be a *coup d'état*.'

I'm not sure it's that simple. I can't help thinking about Portugal's Carnation Revolution. That was a Marxist military coup and the very catalyst that led to Angola's independence. But perhaps I'm taking him too literally.

'There were discussions,' he continues, 'long discussions, about what to do and how to do it. Guerrillas like Nito Alves and Monstro Imortal defended the idea of a coup. But Zé's idea was to have a demonstration, which would force the president to make changes.'

I'm wondering what sort of changes his brother wanted. 'Earlier, you said Neto created an empire of thieves. Do you mean that he was, personally, corrupt?'

To my surprise, João is quite taken aback by this question. 'Neto? No! Nor was Lúcio Lara, at least, not materially corrupt. Lara was morally corrupt: he never said anything to your face, he always spoke behind your back.' But the core problem, at least in João's opinion, was Iko, the defence minister. 'Now he was materially corrupt.' João alleges that he ran a business out of Portugal that sold military uniforms to both the MPLA and UNITA. He also alleges that Iko – who died in 2000 at the age of sixty-six, after living for thirteen years with severe paralysis from a stroke – made a lot of money from stolen diamonds. I have seen no hard evidence to support this, but a Russian who worked in Angola's diamond regions during the 1980s has made similar allegations.[22]

João believes that Iko was also responsible for the deaths of the leading *nitistas*, including his brother. At the end of one particular Central Committee meeting, the defence minister threatened Zé Van Dúnem.

João imitates him, word for word, as if he, too, had been there: '"Camarada Zé speaks too much when he should be keeping quiet. If he doesn't keep quiet, I'm going to shut him up my own way."' He says that the defence minister was intent on building 'a state within a state', and was constantly trying to loosen Neto's hold on power in order to tighten his own. In the aftermath of the *vinte e sete*, says João, 'Iko killed all the people around the president and replaced them with others he trusted, whilst building an army more to his own liking as well.'

The focus on Iko, the son of Portuguese and Italian parents, is intriguing. I only wish he were still alive to answer. What's more, I'm still confused about the coup that was not a coup.

'If it was the case,' I say, 'that your brother persuaded the others not to conduct a coup, why was there an attack on the prison of São Paulo and why was the radio station taken?'

'Look,' says João, 'the armed forces were out with tanks and they took the prison and took the radio. It was a strategy of the armed forces.'

'Maybe, but they were soldiers who supported Nito Alves and they entered the prison by force. That's not what you do during a demonstration, is it?'

'Look,' he says, repeating himself, 'it was the armed forces who decided to liberate their cousins, their friends and their comrades who'd been imprisoned.'

'And the radio? Why did they decide to take control of the radio?'

'They didn't,' he says firmly. 'They used it.'

'I see,' I say, trying not to smile.

'It was the only way to mobilise the people, to incite them to go to the palace. But it was not taken. This is misinformation. Everyone who worked at the radio, those at the top, they were all Marxist factionalists. So there never was any taking over of the radio. They just used it.'

I'm not convinced. What about Wolfers' boss, Ilda Carreira? She was senior and she was not a factionalist. Moreover, Wolfers said that each factionalist member of staff that day was accompanied by an armed soldier. But even if, for the sake of argument, I accept João's claim, we are still left with the killings in Sambizanga. I put the question to him, and a long silence extends between us. When, finally, he responds, his voice is melancholy. 'I don't know,' he says simply, 'I really don't know. I think there was a lack of coordination. My brother thought those killings were done in order to incriminate the *nitistas*. You need to understand that there was a lot of confusion.' Thinking the matter through further, he says, 'But if it had been a coup, they would have got rid of the president. You have to go for the head in a coup. And yet Monstro Imortal was with Neto that day – he was right next to him, by his side; he could have killed him.'

But he didn't. I've heard this story before – that senior military man, Jacob João Caetano, otherwise known as 'Immortal Monster', and one of Nito Alves' closest confidants, couldn't bring himself to kill the president. In trying to help me understand why not, a friend explained to me that Neto was too much of a father figure to all these young men: 'Deep down, Monstro Imortal loved Neto.' But João believes that it is thanks to his brother, Zé Van Dúnem, who knew that Neto symbolised Angolan independence, not only domestically but for the outside world too. 'He had to be preserved,' says João. 'And looking back now, I think that was their biggest mistake. It was the error of my brother. He didn't kill Neto and instead, he was killed.'

On 12 June 1977, Zé Van Dúnem was captured. He was taken to the Fortaleza de São Miguel, an ancient military fortress built in 1576 on the top of a small hill overlooking the bay of Luanda. Once the heart of seventeenth-century colonial administration, it had been a key holding point for slaves before they were forced onto ships and transported across the Atlantic. Centuries later, under Salazar's rule, the fortress became the headquarters for the Portuguese army; at independence, the MPLA turned it into a prison.

Zé, says João, was held in a *n'guelelo*: his ankles and wrists were tied behind him for hours on end; if he struggled, the rope tightened, causing tremendous pain. Even during torture, he questioned everything and gained the admiration of the guards. 'I will say this to you frankly,' João tells me proudly. 'Nito Alves may have been the populist figure, but he was not the thinker. My brother was the thinker. Sometimes people called him "the little philosopher".'

He thinks this is one of the reasons the leadership were so afraid of Zé: his intelligence. He blames Lara, in particular, for pushing his brother out of the central power structure. 'It's important you understand this. We should really minimise the role of Nito.' João argues that Alves was used by the MPLA to fight extreme-leftist groups, such as the Amílcar Cabral Committee and the Henda Committee, and later groups like the Communist Organisation of Angola (OCA). 'But he didn't represent anything, socially speaking,' João boasts. 'He didn't have pedigree like my family, a very powerful landowning family in Luanda. We had too many seats on the Politburo – that's why they couldn't kill all of us.' Apparently tickled by his own snobbery, he lets out a short peal of giggles that completely throws me. I find his class complex confusing. This is a man who, so I had thought, was a radical, a man who dreamed of a socialist revolution. Once, he asked me to help him frame a set of photographs of Che Guevara. I agreed, assuming, because of his history, that he would have his own personal collection. Instead, he asked me to buy a set of the ubiquitous black-and-white gift cards that have stripped the late Argentinian hero of all his ideological fervour, transforming him into a bland consumer product, diluted with good wishes, happy birthdays and vague notes of friendship. Listening to João now, preening himself on his breeding, I feel foolish and gullible. Whether he notices my irritation or not, I can't tell, but my feelings subside as he continues talking of his brother.

When Zé was captured, people walked to the Van Dúnem family home in Luanda, chanting, '*Viva! Viva! Viva!*' João's mother was there. She opened the window, and seeing the crowds, knew that something terrible had happened to her eldest son. 'When the whole thing was over,' João tells me, 'she had a nervous breakdown.'

Hearing this sad detail, I almost regret asking him any questions about his mother. But what follows sends me spinning back into doubt about the authenticity of his account so far. He tells me that at the time he had no idea of his mother's torment, nor of his brother's arrest. In fact, he knew nothing about what was happening at all – he was in Havana. He'd been there since 6 October 1975. 'I was called by the party,' he says. 'I was there for the MPLA.'

João was one of several hundred Angolans sent to Cuba for military training. They were expected to become an elite force that would protect Angola from invading South African and Zairean forces, as well as the internal enemies UNITA and the FNLA. 'I did not know about the Twenty-seventh of May for many, many months,' he says. There was only one very short story in *Granma*, the Cuban Communist Party newspaper. Communications in both countries were also very poor, making it hard to get through to Angola. On top of this, João recalls, 'the Cubans controlled the amount of communication I could make.'

It was not until July 1977, when Neto visited Cuba, that João began to get a sense that something had gone wrong. The president was there to thank Fidel Castro for 'defending the revolution', as João puts it. He came with a large delegation, including DISA's number two, Onambwe. During the trip, a meeting was held for all the Angolans in Cuba. 'I remember it well,' says João, 'because my leg was in plaster.' Neto stood up and spoke of a group of opportunists who had tried to take power by force in Luanda. He said they had been repelled and destroyed, and that none of them would see justice. João says he can remember Neto's very words: '"There won't be judicial processes. There will just be death sentences."' It seems odd, to me, that Neto would have admitted this so publicly, but João insists he did, and when the talk ended, he raised his hand to ask the president a question. 'All I wanted was to know what had happened in Luanda. I wanted to know what was going on.' But Neto refused to hear him, and told Onambwe to talk to João instead.

'And do you know what he said?' says João, almost shouting. 'He told me I was very lucky. He told me that people were being buried. And then he said, "Soon, we will be sending you to your grave too." That's what he said, Lara!'

On 19 November, João was ordered to return home. He still knew nothing of what had gone on in his absence. Now, looking despairingly around his office, he says, sarcastically, 'The only information they had in *Granma* was about the success of the glorious Angolan revolution of Agostinho Neto.' Many of the Cubans he had trusted had lied to him. They told him that the reason he was returning home was to attend the MPLA First Party Congress, when it would officially adopt Marxism–Leninism and transform from a movement to a party. The congress did indeed take place in December – the MPLA was rechristened the MPLA-PT, meaning the MPLA-Workers' Party – but this was not the reason João had been sent for.

'It was a lie,' he says, his long elegant fingers playing with his spectacles, 'and they knew it.' In an unpleasant twist of history, João travelled back across the Atlantic in the belly of a Cuban ship. 'From the moment we boarded, I knew we were prisoners.'

Arriving in Luanda, he was taken immediately to the Casa de Reclusão. This was one of the prisons that had been attacked by Angolan liberation fighters in 1961, marking the start of the war against colonialism. For the next two years, he was detained in a number of different places. He was tortured and lost his hearing in one ear, the result of a mock execution. But perhaps what haunts him most are his memories of those he met, such as Manuel Peres. 'He was always well turned out, in white linen trousers, white shoes, and his hair kept very short and neat,' says João. He had been a cook for São José Lopes, the former director of PIDE, but he had nothing to do with factionalism, nor any political movement. One day, a guard named Pitorro told Peres that he was going to die. The following day, another guard, Guabi, whom João describes as 'the head of the killings', as good as admitted he had killed Peres. 'I can still remember his words,' says João. '"You can see in my eyes that I'm smoking a lot today because we're killing a lot."' As Guabi spoke, João noticed he was wearing Manuel's shoes and Manuel's trousers. They were covered in blood.

By the time João was freed in 1979, his mother had already left the country. She had taken with her João's young nephew, whom he calls 'my son, Che'. João Ernesto Vieira Dias Van Dúnem was born in February 1977 to Sita Valles and Zé Van Dúnem. Contrary to the claim made by the Politburo, Valles was not in a relationship with Alves. She was with Zé. When the couple were killed, their child, Che, as his family call him, was due to be sent to a special children's camp. According to João, these were revolutionary centres devoted to re-educating the sons and daughters of factionalists and making them loyal to the revolution. Thanks to the Van Dúnems' standing in society and the bravery of a number of friends, João's parents managed to leave Angola with baby Che.

This was a terrible period in Angola's post-colonial life. People were going about their day-to-day lives in shame and humiliation. 'Everyone was asking everyone else for favours, like beggars,' João recalls. He knows because he was among them. He had applied for a visa to leave the country, but it was rejected. In the end, he was helped by a blind old aunt, Domingas Vieira Dias. She owned a large house, for years frequented by her young relatives and godchildren. Among them, José Eduardo dos Santos had often spent time there, playing the guitar, flirting and having fun with the girls. But the young stud was now president of Angola. He had succeeded Neto, who died in Moscow in September 1979 – more likely, says João, from Chivas Regal, 'the cheap whisky Americans sell to Africans to kill themselves on', than any Soviet plot. However he died, Neto's passing gave Tia Domingas a direct line to the presidency. She told João she would phone dos Santos and ask for help. 'This bastard in power is your cousin,' she said. 'He can resolve this.'

The old lady was right. Once she had called the new president, her nephew received his visa and, shortly after, left Angola, his heart and spirit shattered.

8

◆

SOUNDS OF MICROFICHE

Several weeks pass in which I become increasingly exasperated with the visa situation. I call the embassy again and find myself being passed between staff, none of whom is able to help and all of whom promise I have nothing to worry about. 'Lara needs to stay calm,' seems to be the general advice. Truly I'm trying hard to do exactly that, but it's been six months since my application went in and my optimism is sinking.

Determined not to give up quite yet, I explore other ways forward. I send off a pile of emails to people I would like to meet, including Ildeberto Teixeira, the Portuguese lawyer Luiza Mendes told me about. But days go by, and no one writes back, and I begin to wonder whether this book will ever come to life.

I take a train to Barnet, one of London's more miserable boroughs, and certainly not a place to visit if you're feeling glum. Over eight miles from the city's throbbing centre, London Underground's Northern Line emerges in daylight somewhere close to Golders Green. Here, we near the more hellish reaches of British suburban life: row upon row of postwar semis divvied up with high-rise hedges, empty washing lines and front gardens that have been covered in concrete for cars. Looking up at the tiled roofs, I see shabby dormer windows tacked on to every other house, as if it were a directive from the state.

We rattle north and the passengers thin out, until only I and a man opposite are left in the carriage. He has a tremor in his right hand, which he keeps moving between his cheek, his chin and his knee, in serial attempts to set it still. We smile at each other as we pass the police training centre, noticing, simultaneously, a blue Tardis by the fence. 'Doctor Who!' he says a bit too loudly, in an accent I think might be Greek, and we both start laughing. At the next stop, when I stand up to leave, all I see are his jelly fingers in a farewell wave.

This is Colindale, and I have come here for one reason alone: the British Library's newspaper repository. Less than a minute's walk from the station, this functional red-brick building is, to the inquisitive researcher, what Clapham Junction is to the trainspotter. Here you can find newspapers from all over the world, including Angola's state-owned daily, *Jornal de Angola*, from as far back as 1975.

I leave my belongings with a pair of security guards so busy boasting to each other about their parachuting abilities – 'You're still at static-free-fall stage,' says the elder of the two – that they barely notice me. Upstairs, I fill out a small white form listing the issues of the newspaper I would like to read. 'It'll be about twenty minutes,' says a pleasantly plump man in a lime lambswool V-neck, 'so you might as well find yourself a seat.' I follow his directions to a windowless room, its four walls and ceiling painted black. Running down each side are five cubicles that might have been built by a brothel owner, or a set designer for a David Lynch film. Inside each cubicle is a large wooden box with a high-quality lens looking down from above to magnify reels of microfilm. I choose the one furthest from the entrance, sit down in the dark and wait. For nearly half an hour, I listen quite happily to the other readers whirring and spinning their way through reams of cellulose acetate, until a young woman appears. She slips a piece of paper before me. 'Your order is ready.'

For the next few hours, I am engrossed. Early MPLA government propaganda may be predictable, but it is surprisingly moreish. There is a seemingly endless supply of copy on Agostinho Neto's travels, particularly his meetings with Fidel Castro, beside whom Angola's president looks awfully bookish. The pair are pictured vigorously striding out together in all sorts of places, making pacts and reading speeches to vast, cheering crowds. Often they are attending meetings with other leaders from across Africa, pictured in awkward line-ups, waving resolutely into the middle distance. In a number of editions, column after column is devoted to speeches by Lenin, or excerpts from some of Marx's finest works. Black-and-white photographs from the Soviet Union pop up quite regularly too, images of Moscow monuments and huge statues of revolutionary leaders, with senior figures from the MPLA and the Communist Party standing side by side in the foreground, wrapped snug in heavy coats and hats. There are pages and pages of speeches by MPLA leaders, more often than not Lúcio Lara, explaining one policy or another in language so prolix it's painful to read. I come across one short and relatively punchy speech from March 1976: it is the work of Nito Alves, and is an attack on the communist organisation OCA. What occurs to me is the similarity between his criticisms and those the Politburo would make of him and his fellow *nitistas* over a year later – that the petite bourgeoisie are the real problem.

But reading through these issues of *Jornal de Angola*, from 1976 and 1977, I find two trends intriguing. First, the entire newspaper appears to be a performance of concern for the much-vaunted, ever-capitalised *Povo* – also referred to as 'the workers and the peasants' – while always defending the political elite. Secondly, it strongly implies that racial prejudice – as opposed to the stark inequality between rich and poor, urban and rural – was the most pressing matter of the day. On the front page of several editions, the message, '*Abaixo o racismo*' (Down with racism), is set into a colourful, eye-catching box, often reprinted in other strategic places further in. I lose count of the number of times a news report, or an opinion piece, or yet another speech, refers to racism and calls on the *Povo* to look out for the 'lizards', the 'divisionists' and the 'factionalists' who are promoting racist ideas. What makes this so interesting is that the implicit reference, made mostly through juxtaposition, is to racism against whites and *mestiços*, not blacks. On 15 May 1977, beneath the title 'The racism of the lizards', staunch criticism is made of those promoting 'unequalled racism' and making personal attacks on individuals in government, senior members of the movement, and staff at *Jornal de Angola* too. The following week, the paper publishes a lengthy speech by Neto in which he states that 'The idea of class has nothing to do with the problem of skin colour. There are white workers. There are *mestiço* workers. There are black workers. And, also, there are bourgeois blacks.' This seems a little disingenuous. Of course, there were always exceptions to the rule – it is certainly true that *mestiços* had lost many of their earlier privileges during the later years of colonialism, as Salazar had encouraged more and more whites to emigrate to Angola; and it is also true that there were a few whites at the bottom of the proverbial pile, more due to downward slippage than any structural racial equalising – but the president's insistence that there was no link between class and colour is remarkable. While Portuguese colonialism may have lacked the degree of overt racial discrimination evident in, say, nearby South Africa, racialised inequalities had characterised Angola for centuries and certainly during Salazar's reign in the twentieth century.

In his groundbreaking 1978 book, *Angola under the Portuguese*, Gerald Bender remarks,

> rigid educational standards and Draconian class barriers effectively precluded Africans in Angola from seriously threatening the white bastions of exclusivity (e.g. jobs, neighbourhoods, private schools, social clubs). These conventional and technically non-racial mechanisms were, in fact, so effective that they obviated the necessity (after 1961) to adopt explicitly racial legislation or to develop segregated institutions in order to guarantee the preservation of white superiority and domination.[23]

Turning Neto's comment on its head, in other words, the 'problem of skin colour' had everything to do with class.

This is not to deny his genuine reasons for wanting to dilute racial tensions in Angola. On a personal level, he had married a white Portuguese woman, Maria Eugénia, in Lisbon in 1958. Together, they had three children. What is extraordinary, however, is that just months after independence, Neto and *Jornal de Angola* seem determinedly in denial about the legacy of Portuguese race relations, presenting the country as though, overnight, it had become a place of two equal halves. In the issue of 9 April 1976, I spot a photograph of a large MPLA poster erected somewhere in Luanda, showing a huge white arm interlocking with a huge black one, the fists clasped together. Beside the painted poster is another popular MPLA slogan, still used to this day, '*um só povo, uma só nação*' (only one people, only one nation). Nearly three weeks later, another photograph promotes the same message. This time, we see Neto dancing with his wife and, beneath, the caption: 'This gesture completely symbolises the programme of National Unity. Only one people, only one nation.' The following week, in May 1976, another speech by Neto is printed, in which he goes to some lengths to reassure 'the People' that they are not racially disempowered and need not harbour racial resentment. In a neat rhetorical triptych, and following several references to racism, he says, 'Power is in the hands of whom? Of the People. And who is in charge? It is the People. And who is the People? It is the MPLA.'

The binding of power and 'People' into party and, eventually, president, tightens as the months pass. Under the headline 'National unity', a leader piece published on 8 May 1977 claims preposterously, 'The Angolan People are the MPLA. The MPLA are the Angolan People.' It continues, 'This is real unity, true and revolutionary, in which there is no space for camouflaged manoeuvres with doomed objectives.' In a bizarre twist that reads like revolutionary parody, it ends by tossing aside the party and 'the People', and raising the president alone to the heavens. 'To defend Neto is to defend the Revolution,' it claims. 'To defend Neto is to defend national unity!'

The difficulties with these statements – and believe me, there are many similar examples to choose from – are so numerous, it is hard to know where to begin. A herd of questions stampede around my head, and I only wish Neto was there to answer them. If the Angolan people 'are' the MPLA, then who, or what, are the people who support the FNLA or UNITA, or who don't support any party at all? Are they non-people? Are they non-Angolans? Where do they belong? It seems as if the MPLA has every single angle covered: there are even 'militants', we're told, who aren't really militants at all. They are, believe it or not, 'camouflaged "militants"', whose only goal is to undermine the movement. And since when did one man come to represent national unity? Since when did he become the entire Angolan revolution? What is this man? Is he no longer human? Is he, in fact, God? For this is how it seems to me, just as Frantz Fanon wrote in his classic text *The Wretched of the Earth*:

> Since the proclamation of independence the party no longer helps the people to set out its demands, to become more aware of its needs and better able to establish its power. Today, the party's mission is to deliver to the people the instructions which issue from the summit.[24]

That is it. A dictatorship, not of the people, but of the leader at the top to the masses at the bottom.

Ill-tempered, I turn the knob to rewind and watch the roll of microfilm spinning rapidly clockwise, wrapping this extraordinary history back into itself. I pack away my pencils and my notebook, now full of angry lead markings and exclamation marks, and stare into the dark, miserable and ashamed. Why didn't I do this research before I ever set foot in Angola? Why didn't I inform myself properly? Who on earth did I think I was, turning up in a country to report on its civil war, knowing so little about its recent past? I think of Maria Reis and of João Van Dúnem, and the terrible losses they have suffered. I think of Basil Davidson, then of Michael Wolfers, and feel a surge of frustration at these British intellectuals. Why did they allow ideology to override justice?

9

NEVER MEET YOUR HEROES

Talk to Basil Davidson. That was the plan. If I could just meet him in person and discuss, face to face, the *vinte e sete*, perhaps I could gain more empathy for the position he and other Marxist writers took. Perhaps he could give me a sense of what it was like to be writing about Angola at such a pivotal point in the country's history, at the height of the Cold War. Had I been a journalist then, I probably would have taken the same line, and defended Neto's leadership above all else. I'd love to share these discussions with Davidson, whom I have long admired, but it is not to be. His wife has responded to my request with some sad news. The mind of this once brilliant man is failing – an interview is out of the question.

So I decide, instead, to try for the journalist Victoria Brittain. A close friend of Davidson's – I've often thought of her as his protégé – her entry into Angola benefitted hugely from his earlier connections. In her book *Death of Dignity* she mentions a letter of introduction written by Davidson to Lúcio Lara. Thanks to this, during her visits to Luanda between 1984 and 1996, Brittain stayed with Lara and his German wife, Ruth, and gained superb access to the MPLA old guard.

Published in 1998, her book came out just before I went to live and work in Angola for the first time. I read it, cover to cover, and was heavily influenced by the author's insights. Unlike some readers, I had no difficulty in accepting her admission on the very first page that this was a partisan piece of work, heavily biased towards the MPLA and without a single UNITA interview. 'It was a time of secrets,' she wrote in her defence, 'a time of polarisation and taking sides, with no middle way for impartial observers.' Back then, I agreed entirely. In fact, I rather envied her flattering accounts of the men I would never get close to. Of Lara, she wrote, 'tall, spare, aesthetic, with a heavy Latin moustache [...] who epitomised the heroic Angola'; of Iko, by then the former defence minister, 'a hero of the liberation war and a friend of one of my friends [...] Sophisticated, amusing and extremely good looking, Iko was immediately friendly.'[25] It was only after I began living in Angola that I started to see the flaws in such an approach: I began doubting the authority of someone who had relied so heavily on a particular slice of the elite for her information. By the time I found out about the Twenty-seventh of May, I felt strangely betrayed by Brittain. I wanted to understand why and how an intelligent and committed journalist could have turned her back on such an important story.

'I'm not sure how I can help you,' was how she responded when we spoke briefly on the telephone. Nevertheless, she agreed to meet and suggested a café in Belsize Park, one of London's wealthier neighbourhoods.

Arriving at the Chamomile on England's Lane, I clock four women sitting at separate tables, who all appear to be in their fifties or sixties. Then I notice the one seated furthest away tentatively raising a hand.

'Victoria?' I call across the room.

She nods – she looks uneasy – and I hurry over to join her.

'Hello,' I say, panting lightly, 'have you been here long?'

She shakes her head and I think I hear her say 'No'.

'I've come from Hampstead Heath station,' I explain. 'It took slightly longer than I'd expected.'

'If I'd known that,' she says, already irritable, 'I'd have suggested meeting near there because it's much closer to where I live.'

Oh dear. This isn't going to be easy. She's avoiding any eye contact, she's speaking curtly, and her arms are folded firmly and defensively around her waist.

A young waitress passes our table. Brittain stretches out a hand, signalling to her, 'A latte please. Decaffeinated.' Her tone suggests the order is complete, and the waitress strides off towards the counter.

'Can I have one too?' I say, calling out. 'Make mine caffeinated, please.'

The waitress barely stops. She turns and looks over a shoulder, signalling she's understood. But I'm more surprised by Brittain. She looks so polite, so well groomed and, if I'm honest, so posh. She wears a sleeveless bodywarmer over a polo-necked sweater. Light-framed spectacles offer a certain seriousness, offset by her blonded grey hair falling in dainty waves around her face. She's bright-eyed and attractive.

For all my reservations about her book, I admire Brittain on many other levels and am longing to compliment her. She made it all the way up to associate foreign editor at the *Guardian*, an impressive climb in itself, but she did it at a time when British foreign journalism was even more male-dominated than it is today. For this alone, I salute her. She also toiled to get African stories published when many others were happy to ignore them, and she did a fine job exposing the damage caused by the IMF and World Bank across the continent. I know, too, from friends, that she has been very supportive of young black journalists, helping them get a foot on the very white media ladder. More recently, she has switched her attention from Africa to the Middle East, and has devoted herself to exposing British and US atrocities in the wars in Iraq and Afghanistan. In 2004, she co-wrote *Guantanamo: Honor Bound to Defend Freedom*, a documentary drama portraying the lives of detainees in Guantánamo Bay. Originally performed in London, the play crossed the Atlantic and won critical acclaim in the United States. Hoping to appease her a little, I offer my congratulations.

'I'm only sorry I missed it,' I say sincerely.

But Brittain doesn't respond, which makes me nervous, and I follow up this first statement with a second. I mention another play that I have seen.

'It was called *Talking to Terrorists*,' I say keenly. 'A bit like yours, the script worked directly from dialogue with real people.'

'Oh, it's not at all like that,' she says. 'But let's get on with it, shall we? Why don't you ask me what it is you want to know?'

I take a deep breath. 'Well, I suppose what I really wanted to understand is why, in *Death of Dignity*, you didn't mention the Twenty-seventh of May 1977?'

As quick as you like, she comes back at me. 'I wasn't covering that period,' she says.

But this isn't true. The book spans the period from just before independence to the mid to late 1990s.

'Oh it does,' I say. 'Your first chapter starts in 1975.'

Apparently she hasn't heard me. 'The eighties were a difficult period. People had a lot more on their minds than that. It just wasn't that important.'

'You mean the Twenty-seventh of May?'

'Well, some of the people I knew made the odd joke about it, but it wasn't something we discussed in depth.'

I'm a bit taken aback. 'People made the odd joke about what? The alleged coup attempt, or what followed it?'

I notice a fraction of hesitation. 'About it all,' she says, rushing her words.

Now I'm the one hesitating. I tell her that for some Angolans, the Twenty-seventh of May was the day everything went wrong, the beginning of the end, if you like. 'Even MPLA supporters, including those who are close to the elite, know that it was not a joke,' I say. 'Perhaps 20,000 or more were killed. That's not a joke, is it?'

'Anyone who says that what happened after the Twenty-seventh of May was more important than what was going on in the 1980s in Huambo and Malanje... well,' she says firmly, 'they're just not telling the truth.'

Certainly, during the mid 1980s, there was horrific violence in Angola, fuelled in part by increased US support for UNITA. Significantly, in July 1985, Congress voted to repeal the infamous Clark Amendment. This was a major victory for conservatives and the New Right in Ronald Reagan's America, and more so for Jonas Savimbi, who would now be able to benefit from a massive injection of US military assistance, including TOW and Stinger anti-aircraft missiles, anti-tank weapons, rifles, ammunition and fuel. Between 1981 and 1988, it is estimated that at least 500,000 Angolans died due to the war, at least two-thirds of whom were children. Tens of thousands lost their legs to anti-personnel landmines, which were laid across the country by both sides. Brittain is right when she states that much of the suffering was concentrated in the central highland province of Huambo, but Bié, Moxico and Huíla were also affected. The town of Malanje, known for its MPLA support, was also targeted by UNITA rebels. Many were killed in these areas, not only in the mid 1980s, but also in the 1990s, with some of the worst violence taking place during my time as correspondent from 1998 through to the end of 2000. And it continued through to April 2002, when the war finally ended. By then, several million Angolans had fled their homes for the relative safety of Luanda, which partly explains why the capital developed such vast and sprawling slums. So I would not dream of dismissing that which took place during the war, not only in the 1980s as Brittain seeks to emphasise, but at many other points too. The fact is, however, that some Angolans still see the *vinte e sete* as one of the most traumatic moments in their recent history – the moment when the MPLA turned on its own. None of this is to deny the war, but it cannot be passed off as some kind of joke. Trying to reinforce my point, I mention my interview with João Van Dúnem.

Brittain rises in her seat a little. 'Of course,' she says smoothly, 'the exiles would think it's the worst thing that ever happened because they don't know any better.'

This throws me. Surely she doesn't really believe that, as a foreigner, she's more informed than Angolans who grew up in the country, who endured the war against colonialism and who have family members still living there?

'And what about the non-exiles?' I say. 'When I first heard about the *vinte e sete*, it was from a journalist who has never lived outside Angola, a man who is from within the MPLA, who began his career working for *Jornal de Angola*. He too believes that the purge was one of the worst episodes his country has endured. But he also knows full well the horrors of the war.'

For a few seconds, Brittain doesn't say anything. She looks at the table, then her coffee, then at me. 'Look, I'm not feeling well. I wasn't going to come today at all. But now I feel very unwell. I need to go.'

She stands up and marches straight out of the café. I can hardly believe my eyes. I call the waitress and pay as quickly as I can. Then I run out into the street looking for Brittain. She's crossing the road at an angle, heading towards the pharmacy. I rush after her.

'Victoria, please don't go!'

But it's pointless. She walks off, leaving me standing in the middle of the road, perplexed and disappointed.

I'm not sure what to do now, or where to go. I'm cross with myself and cross with her, and Belsize Park isn't helping. A lady totters past me, her face covered in powder; prancing at her heels on the end of a red thread, a pair of pooches. I cross to the other side of the street, itching to get away. This parade of shops is a hotspot for yummy mummies with offspring weaned from breast to babyccino in a matter of weeks. It's a part of London where bankers do yoga and teenagers rebel by cutting holes in their Diesel jeans, where a two-bedroom flat costs the best part of a million pounds and residents simply have to have a Range Rover Vogue to negotiate smooth tarmac. I think of Luanda, where potholes swallow cars and even trucks, and rain turns roads into rivers. At least there the rich have some justification for owning a four-wheel-drive.

10

◆

SENT TO CUBA

Clifford Chance, 'the world's first global law firm'. That's where we met. It was hosting a one-day conference at its Canary Wharf offices titled 'Courting justice – Rule of law and reform in Africa'. Angola's then deputy prime minister, Aguinaldo Jaime, was on the panel. A short, rounding figure, he gave an absurd speech about the lack of patronage and clientelism in Angola, insisting that foreign businessmen and -women would find only transparency if they sought contracts there. His talk was followed by coffee and biscuits. We were told there would be time for questions afterwards. But when we returned to our seats, the Excelentíssimo Senhor Jaime was nowhere to be seen. Instead, we were invited to throw questions into the air, as though venting opinion could be just as useful as holding a politician to account. One woman did stand up, however, not to ask a question but to inform the rest of the room about her beloved country. She spoke excellent English.

'The Angolan government has been destroying us since 1977,' she said. 'They have always been concerned with themselves. Angolan people are still living in poverty. In M'banza Kongo, next to Soyo, where all that oil is being exploited, there is terrible suffering. People can barely feed themselves.' She continued speaking for several minutes, offering examples of the great wealth gap in her country, until, seeming to run out of energy, or realising the pointlessness of the exercise, she slumped back into her seat. After the meeting, I approached her to ask if she had been referring to the Twenty-seventh of May. '*Absolutamente!*' came the irate response. 'They killed my husband and sent me to prison.'

◆

SENT TO CUBA

A few months later, I'm in Bond Street Underground station, the black hole of British shopping. A pair of policemen in stab-resistant vests are standing on the other side of the barriers from me. Patiently, they offer advice to streams of frantic consumers fighting their way up to ground level and the scrum of Oxford Street like sperm racing to the uterus. I check my watch, worried that the woman I am due to meet will have changed her mind, but the anxiety lifts when I see her solemn figure in one of the tunnels, walking steadily towards me. She lifts the fingers of one hand in a shy wave and I return with a symmetrical signal of recognition. She is shorter than I had remembered and perhaps a little older, maybe in her mid fifties. She's dressed smartly in a dark jacket and trousers, with a neat handbag and tidy hair curled away from her face. She greets me generously, rubbing one of my arms and smiling, but her voice is ribbed with tension and her eyes are elsewhere.

'Let's get to Debenhams,' she says, looking down at her hands.

We work our way through the crowds, pushing and squeezing into the Christmas frenzy until one of my hands takes hold of Debenhams' door. Inside, two pale men in dark-grey suits stand, legs parted, with puffy faces and gelled hair. The one on the left lifts his chin half an inch then tucks it a little deeper into the armchair of his neck. It's an unpalatable attempt at authority. As we pass, he and his partner raise their hands from their sides and threaten to fire at us with four bottles of perfume. We veer out of their way only to realise that the entire ground floor is steeped in scent they want you to take home.

'I think the café is on the second floor, or maybe the third,' says the woman at my side. I follow her up the escalator through lingerie. We twist around a carousel of children's nightwear, neoteny pink and biddable blue, and pass a shelf of bedroom-door signs announcing 'Daddy's Little Princess' in gold. Beyond this, we find a darkened corner of turquoise walls covered in empty picture frames and a few black-and-white photographs of a bowler-hatted Charlie Chaplin. He died on Christmas Day. The year was 1977. A portable hi-fi is placed on a bare shelf, its plastic speakers buzzing to Tom Jones. Beside this the counter, behind which stands a tall and narrow Englishman with skin like milk of magnesia.

'Teas, ladies? Or will it be coffee?'

We order two coffees and choose a small wooden table pushed snug to the wall. I ask if I can record the conversation. She says she does not mind, 'But I do not want to be named.' So I will call her Ana Nunes.

Our coffees arrive, each with a biscuit wrapped unappealingly in plastic and small enough to perch on the edge of a saucer. Nunes seems uncomfortable. She keeps examining her mobile phone as if expecting a call. I have no idea whether she will be happy to talk for an hour or more, or whether she will have had enough after fifteen minutes. But before I have posed a single question she begins speaking in hurried snatches, flitting in and out of Portuguese.

'Everyone was looking for him. Eventually I managed to speak to this police chief – I wish I could remember his name – anyway, he told me that they had all been sent to Cuba.'

I'm not sure what she means. 'Why Cuba?'

'In those days, it was common slang. We would have lunch and then take a sleep. *Vou cubar*. That's what we'd say: "I'm going for a siesta." But in the political climate that existed, when you heard this expression, *foram mandados para Cuba*, you knew immediately what it meant. "They had been sent to their deaths." Put to sleep, if you like. Of course, Cuba, the country, had political connotations too.'

Nunes' search for her husband continued for weeks, then months. Even though she understood exactly what the police chief had meant, she still held out hope that her husband was alive, somewhere. It was possible that he was being held in one of the concentration camps which had been set up under the Portuguese and maintained by the MPLA at independence. Nunes knew of one camp in the north-east of the country, in the provinces known as the Lundas. She had this feeling that her husband was there.

'I had a friend who had a lover in the Lundas,' explains Nunes. 'She was going to visit him, so I asked her if she would take a letter for me and try to get it to my husband at the camp. She agreed and when she travelled, she put the note in her knickers. *Estúpida!* We knew it might be intercepted and that they might think it was anti-revolutionary, but we did not expect her to be searched like that. So intimately. *Nas cuecas*. In her panties.'

'What did the letter say?'

'Not much. "Have courage... One day we will be together again... In the end, they who have done these bad things will be punished for what they have done." Things like that.'

'What happened to your friend?'

'They arrested her. Then they arrested me. I think it was the last phrase that was the most problematic. But even so, it wasn't much of a letter. I wasn't exactly doing anything.'

It was only after Nunes was arrested, in 1978, that she began to understand what had been happening since the end of May the previous year. 'In fact, they had been following me for months. DISA. *A segurança*. One day they came to my workplace pretending that they wanted something, but they didn't want anything other than the time to check me out. It wasn't until I was arrested that I recognised them.'

DISA searched Nunes' house too, and found several photographs of Nito Alves. He was a friend of the family and it was natural, as far as Nunes was concerned, to have pictures of friends. But DISA was not interested in her explanations. They began seeing her as a dangerous person in her own right.

'It was ridiculous. First, I was imprisoned in Luanda, then I was sent to the re-education camp in Tari, Quibala. They were so afraid, the MPLA!' She laughs. 'They called it re-education but it was brainwashing. They tried to take away all of your bad and anti-revolutionary thoughts. That's what they called them: *pensamentos anti-revolucionários!*' She is smiling at the stupidity of it. 'I don't know what they wanted with me because I was not political at all. I didn't even join OMA,' she says, referring to the MPLA women's wing. 'I went once, but only because my husband pressured me. Afterwards, I told him, "Never again!"'

I'm slightly surprised by this. In those early days, I thought that OMA had done some excellent work, helping the poor and the needy.

Nunes finds my response hilarious and, I fear, rather naive. For the first time, she really laughs from her belly. 'Oh, Lara, *querida*, that is sweet. But there was too much talk! They were all single, these women. I was married. They just talked about their boyfriends. *Tanta fofoca*. So much gossip. I had children. I was busy. It was a waste of my time. I suppose they did provide some political studies but most of the time they just talked about love affairs. They were all desperate to get married.'

Shaking her head, the chuckles continue until other memories get in the way. She rubs a hand over her mouth, smothering more giggles. She looks up at the café ceiling, at its emergency sprinklers, air-conditioners and sets of cameras shielded behind curves of black plastic like large isolated pupils.

'I lived with my conscience, that's all. We had to. We had survived a colonial regime. We had been young then. *Jovens*. We had always believed things would improve at independence. Living under an Angolan regime, we wanted a better life for our kids. The trouble was we could see it wasn't going that way and we all had opinions about that.' With a long sigh, she says, 'It was all of this. It came together as such a dangerous mix.'

Nunes tells me in some detail about her husband's work, but asks me not to mention it in anything I write. Despite living in London, she is very afraid of being identified. All I can say, she says, is that he was completely dedicated to *a causa*, the revolutionary cause. 'Too much for my liking,' she says. 'I was also working and yet I was watching all of our money disappear into *a causa*.' Whimsically, she says, 'I wanted to spend some of it on me, Lara!'

But this is not entirely true. Nunes used her salary to buy books, and set up some of the first public libraries in Angola, *bibliotecas do povo*. 'There was one just a few yards from our house in Luanda,' she recalls. 'It was originally a shop, then I turned it into a *biblioteca*. Now it is a shop again. It shows you the values in Angola, no?' She throws me a wry smile, and we return to her husband.

His work, she says, helped alert people to the revolution, although the MPLA did not see it quite that way. Some time before the Twenty-seventh of May – Nunes cannot remember precisely when – he was dismissed from his job. 'And do you know what? They tried to destroy his legacy as well. It's so complicated. The capacity of the MPLA to destroy things is quite phenomenal.' When she explains what she means by this, she talks about her late husband's name. 'It has become a spectre that haunts our life,' she says. 'People are afraid of being associated with it. It is like it has become a kind of political shaman. People are afraid it will get them into trouble. They are afraid of something that happened thirty years ago. It is stupid. Ignorant!'

'I have never had a death certificate either,' she adds in a low voice.

We are interrupted by her mobile phone. She pulls it from her bag and holds it up, looking at the screen, deciding what to do. Eventually it rings off. 'Maybe another five or ten minutes, Lara. Then I will have to go.'

The urgency prompts me to be more direct. I put it to her that what happened on the Twenty-seventh of May was a coup attempt, that it is wrong to call it a demonstration or even an uprising.

She responds emphatically, utterly seriously, her earlier anxiety sucked clean away. 'I can guarantee to you that it was never a *coup d'état*. Everything that was decided for that day, I witnessed. I was there.' She looks at me sternly. 'It was never never *um golpe de estado*. Do you understand? To have a coup you have to plan properly and they did not. They planned for a protest. My husband and his circle trusted their dreams. They trusted the *mais velhos*, the elders. Primarily, they trusted Neto. However, they also believed that there were some bad potatoes about. People were messing things up, like Iko Carriera and Lúcio Lara. They were leading the MPLA away from the correct line. Many of us knew that this was the problem. So there was tension across the population, a general discontentment, but these young men did not have the capacity to coordinate the entire population to rise up in a coup! This is simply not true.'

I feel I have to persist with the cross-examination. 'But you don't need an entire population to carry out a coup, do you? You need the army. And they had the army. At least, they had the 9th Brigade, according to the MPLA document I have read, anyway.'

'Yes,' she nods, 'yes, I understand what you are saying. But shortly before the Twenty-seventh of May, a man from the 9th Brigade came to talk to this young circle. He told them that the 9th Brigade wanted to help, that they wanted to support pressure for change. So of course the group was really pleased. "Great!" they said. The plan was to open the prison at seven in the morning, not three, as it turned out. It is obvious that someone who was sympathetic to these ideas felt he had a duty to contribute. So this person – whoever he was – led the move to break down the gates. But this was not the plan. It was someone's passion.'

'A very provocative and risky one,' I say. 'I mean, to have a demonstration you do not need to unlock the prisons. Surely it would have been better to demand freedom for political prisoners as part of the deal?'

Nunes looks frustrated. 'I do not think you understand. There were people who had been imprisoned unjustly, who had been arrested and detained simply because of their political views. We knew people in Huambo working in the radio who were put in prison because of their programmes. And after these programmes were taken off air, like *Kudibanguela*, for example, it got even worse.' She pauses. She looks at her telephone. The back of one hand sweeps across her brow. 'So much time has passed. I wish I could remember more. But I knew these people, Lara. I actually knew them.'

She wants to tell me more about the many she knew who disappeared, about where they lived and what they did. 'But it is complicated for you to print this information. I cannot give you names because there are some who helped them who are still alive. It is risky.'

So I try to help her by shifting the direction, and ask her what she was doing on the day itself.

'I was at the radio station,' she says. 'That's where the demonstration was – at the radio and the palace. Then I saw the soldiers coming. Then I realised they weren't Angolans. They were not FAPLA. It was the Cubans, Lara. And then I felt terribly afraid. So I left. I didn't want to stay there and I ran away.'

Many of those who worked at the radio station were killed. Nunes remembers a young man who was in charge of opening the gates every morning. 'He was so young, maybe seventeen years old. He was killed too. And now, I cannot remember his name.'

I mention Michael Wolfers. 'Do you remember a British man, a white journalist, who was training staff at the radio?' She shakes her head. 'No. *Nada*,' she says. So I tell her about his work anyway, about his book and his views on the *vinte e sete*. 'He was there too, and his account is also very convincing.'

Nunes is immediately furious. 'So he guarantees it was a *golpe*, does he?'

'Yes.' I answer. 'As certain as you are that it was not.'

She coughs.

The waiter approaches our table. 'I'm afraid we are closing, ladies.'

But Nunes is oblivious. She touches my hand. 'I want to tell you just one more thing,' she says, staring into my face. 'Real information never gets out of Angola. There are many interests at work that keep all of this stuff secret, simply so that the MPLA can stay in power. This is why we don't have just elections. This is why there has been no justice over the *vinte e sete de maio*. There are many people in the pay of the MPLA. Angolans and foreigners. They tell the lies so they can benefit.'

From the counter, the waiter sounds irritated. 'We are closing now. The café is closing.'

We both stand up and begin gathering our things. Slowly, we start walking back towards the escalators. Nunes keeps talking. She wants me to understand the MPLA.

'Try to think of it this way,' she says. 'Think of it as a big organisation, or a company. There are some people who are there because they believe strongly in the work itself; there are others who are there simply because they want the salary. The MPLA is like that. A great big organisation that everyone belongs to, but for different reasons. It was created by elders who went abroad. The younger ones, like my husband, were militants who were either in urban cells or fighting in the bush. Nito Alves was in the bush, *na mata*. These young ones believed absolutely in the MPLA. They joined the movement because they believed in the cause. They never received anything from the MPLA but they had a strong sense of what it was, its traditions, and its African beliefs. They listened to the *mais velhos*, like Neto, as if he was their father. But apart from him, there was no hierarchy. That's how they saw it. Those in the bush inside Angola had no link with the others living in Congo-Brazzaville and elsewhere. I suppose it is a little bit like al-Qaeda today. No one really knows where they are, but those who sympathise automatically become part of it. They don't have to make contact with the leadership, or sign a contract.'

She pulls me to a halt beside a large double bed, stretching her neck, trying to work out where the descending escalator begins.

'Actually, I really need to go to the loo before we leave,' I say, '*para fazer xixi*.'

She smiles. 'Ha, you know these expressions! OK. Let us find the toilet. It is here somewhere on this floor.' We start walking through the kitchen section. Every few steps, she stops to tell me something.

'When the elders finally returned to Luanda in 1974, the young ones still thought that they – these, who had been outside – knew best. In fact, the leadership that had been in exile was not ready. They were half asleep.'

We potter on, trying to follow the grey rectangles hanging from the ceiling, signposting the ladies' cloakroom.

'The reason we got independence was not because of the MPLA's brave battle, but because of the coup in Portugal, the Carnation Revolution in 1974. This is what is so important to understand: the MPLA did not cause independence. Nor was it ready for it. But I must go now,' she says, breaking into a whisper. 'There are too many Angolans here. Those people over there – you see? – they are listening.'

Two women are standing a few feet away, inspecting some table decorations.

'Those two,' says Nunes, 'with their light skins. Do you see?'

I nod. I do.

'Angolans,' she hisses. 'I cannot be completely sure, but they were also in the café, remember? We cannot stay here and talk.'

We walk to the toilets in silence, and the two women follow us in. Perhaps Nunes is right. It wouldn't be the first time an Angolan had found herself being followed in London.

Back on Oxford Street, she wishes me luck. 'And if there is anything else I can do for you, please get in touch.' She squeezes my hand and looks at me warmly, and then she's gone, swept up into the crowd.

11

◆

CLOSING IN ON THE KILL

At first sight, I dismiss the mousey man standing on the platform with a suntan incongruous for the time of year. I had it in my head he'd be taller. But Ildeberto Teixeira spots me immediately and politely introduces himself. 'You are welcome,' he says. 'Thank you for coming.'

He finally got in touch a couple of months ago from Luanda, where he owns a flat. He invited me to come and stay at his Portuguese home at the foot of the Serra da Estrela mountain range less than fifty kilometres from Spain. So we fixed a date for December: he said he'd pick me up from the station.

We kiss, one cheek then the other, the closeness making me uncomfortably conscious of my larger size. He's unfazed, and leads me to a polished four-by-four already flashing its headlights as we enter the car park. Getting into the thing is a bit like getting onto a horse – it's so high – but once we're seated in the creamy leather, it feels good to be eye to eye. He is impeccably dressed, in greys, browns and beiges, and a stylish cravat adds definition to the point in the beard that smothers his face.

'*Lara gosta de música Angolana?*' he asks. 'Do you like Angolan music?'

'I certainly like some of it,' I say, whereupon a rush of hot air blows into my face and the car fills with some of the cheesiest *kizomba* I've heard in quite a while. Squeezed clutches in Angolan discos flash across my memory: to my great shame I never mastered the art of dancing *kizomba*, a sort of lambada–salsa hybrid, and my initial enthusiasm waned when erections popped up in a string of early partners, an indicator, so I'm told, that I was doing it all wrong. I smile at Senhor Teixeira, who is grinning at me. He releases the handbrake and in one swoop we exit the station, my lifelong tendency to travel sickness lurching into my throat.

'I thought I'd show you a bit of the town on the way back,' he says. 'OK?'

'Lovely,' I say, and for the next twenty minutes or so, he drives me around town, pointing out the local library, the town hall and some of his favourite cafes. It's not an especially attractive place, but the surrounding mountains and large skies are breathtaking after London.

Arriving at his home, his wife greets me in the kitchen. She is a good-looking woman with a neat crown of dark hair. Like her husband, she is smartly dressed, in fitted grey trousers and a light wool sweater. Addressing him, she asks what we'd like to drink. 'Port,' he says abruptly, and leads me into a sitting room where a log fire is burning and a crumpled old lady is seated in a high-backed armchair. Teixeira's mother-in-law smiles when we are introduced, then claws her way to an upright position and shuffles out. Moments later, carrying a silver tray dripping in white lace, Senhora Teixeira enters. '*Com licença, com licença,*' she says, a nervous patter of consonants. She places several white doilies onto a coffee table followed by two glasses of port. For the next few minutes, ever more apologetic about disturbing us, she comes in and out, leaving small bowls of crisps and peanuts on top of more doilies.

But Teixeira barely notices. He's quizzing me about Angola. He wants to know why I went there, which areas of the country I've visited and whether we know anyone in common. As we talk, he encourages me to drink and seems happier when I let him top up my glass. The conversation continues, him still very much the interviewer, me very much the interviewee. When did I learn Portuguese? Have I been surprised by how hospitable the Portuguese are? Do I like Portuguese food? He's about to top up my glass again when his wife appears, hovering at the door. He looks up at her.

'Lunch is ready,' she says.

He turns to me: 'Would you like to see the rest of the house?'

This doesn't sound like a question or even an invitation, but more like a command. I tell him I'd love to, and follow him into the hall and up the stairs to a wide landing with several doors leading off it. He pushes one of them open and encourages me to follow him in. Standing in the corner, between a substantial office chair and a desk, is a young man, I guess in his late teens. He has long, dark, curly hair pulled loosely over his shoulders into a ponytail.

'My son, Michael,' says Teixeira. Michael greets me in English and the two of us look at each other awkwardly across the room, which is spotlessly tidy.

Back on the landing, Teixeira holds up one arm to a collection of rifles chained together inside a glass-fronted cabinet. 'Each one is handmade,' he says, beaming. 'Each one. Such care.' Gazing at the guns lovingly, he talks through the relative strengths of each weapon – its range, what he's shot with it – and goes into some detail about the telescopic sight. 'I rarely need to hit an animal more than once thanks to this. Straight in behind the shoulder. That's the place to get them. The bullet goes into the heart and it's over.'

A call for lunch prompts us back down the stairs. We cross the hallway, decorated in *azulejos*, the traditional Portuguese blue-and-white tiling, and into the dining room, which like the rest of the house and its occupants is the epitome of neatness. A large table is covered in more white lace, pyramids of plates and silver cutlery. What follows is a delicious spread, including a huge dish of *bacalhau* and plenty of wine. During the first course, however, no one breathes a word except Teixeira, who is still asking questions. His wife watches, smiling sympathetically at my answers. Occasionally, her mother looks up from her plate and rocks her head in blank agreement. Michael says nothing, even when his parents start speaking about him.

'All he does is study,' says his mother, apparently disappointed.

'He's not interested in anything else,' adds his father.

'And what are you studying?' I ask, looking at their son, hoping to encourage him to speak. But his mother answers instead. 'Law,' she says, 'like his father.'

A protracted silence is broken again by Teixeira and me, returning to the matter of Angola. This time, it breeds irritation in Michael, who is jolted to speak. He wants to know why I'm so interested in the country. 'It's a dump,' he says, full of adolescent certainty. 'It has nothing to offer anyone. They don't even know how to make the electricity work. Imagine! All that oil and they can't even sort out the energy supplies.' He lets out a rather cruel laugh. 'I have absolutely no interest in visiting any poor countries ever. I want to go to the US and Britain.'

This arrogant little outburst is met with pained glances. I try to engage him but he is more set on promoting his world view than discussing how these ideas came to him.

'I think it's very hard,' offers his mother, her face filling with sadness. 'I couldn't live there now. I was last there in the eighties and I would never go back. It was awful. We were living off rations. I hated it.'

Teixeira looks at his wife, then at me. 'It was much worse in the eighties, but even now she can't take it, can you dear?'

I'm not sure where to look, or whether I should say something to try to ease the tension. Increasingly, it feels like the family row is being played out for my benefit.

'That's why I go on my own,' Teixeira continues. 'I spend six months of the year there and six here.'

'You mean you spend about three here,' says his wife, seeping bitterness. 'You see, Lara, he goes hunting when he's here. The moment he returns from Angola, he's off. Aren't you?' She stares at him.

'Yes,' he says, chirpily. 'We love going hunting. We both go.'

A tired dispute about how much time he spends away is followed by pudding and cheese. To my relief, Teixeira then suggests he and I take coffee alone.

Back in the drawing room, he closes the door and turns his attention, at last, to the whole point of this trip, what he calls 'the darkest page in Angolan history'.

'There may have been terrible killings after the 1992 elections,' he begins quite spontaneously, 'but there was not as much vengeance then as the purge that followed 1977.'

This is quite a contentious statement. In the two-year period following Angola's first and flawed elections at the end of September 1992, about 300,000 people died as a direct result of fighting.[26] I'm not clear whether Teixeira is referring to the numbers killed or the psychology behind those killings. He offers me a half answer.

'During the purge the most violent people were the whites and the *mestiços*, especially those in DISA. Power was in the hands of the whites, you see, and the lighter-skinned people like Iko Carreira and Onambwe, both *mestiços*. There were some blacks in the MPLA, like DISA's Ludy Kissassunda, but the movement didn't have any Ovimbundu in senior posts,' he says, referring to Angola's largest ethnic group, 'just a few Mbundu.'

In other words, the violence that followed the *vinte e sete* was racially motivated. Is that what he means?

'Well, Nito's rhetoric was racist,' he says, coming back from a slightly different angle. 'His speeches were very anti-white and anti-*mestiço*, but this was just rhetoric and he always defended Neto. Always. Even *Kudibanguela*, that very radical radio programme, was never against Neto. That would have been unthinkable. The whole uprising was pro-Neto. It was about radicalising the revolution. Would you like some coffee?' He stands up and steps towards a tray his wife has left for us. He pours me a cup and another for himself.

'I'm not even sure it was really a coup,' he says. 'They only took the radio and the prison. And anyway, the point is it was used as an excuse to kill people who opposed the regime. Once Neto's followers heard his orders on television, they went out and killed. You know about that? "There won't be any pardons. We won't waste time with trials." That's what Neto said. It's all in my book.'

And it is here that my hopes of spending the afternoon discussing the *vinte e sete* are, all of a sudden, disappointed.

'I don't really like talking about it,' Teixeira says, 'and you will get more from my book anyway.'

I watch him disappearing from the room and I'm sure I feel my heart drop an inch. Have I really come all this way for that?

Shortly, he returns, smiling sympathetically. 'These are for you,' he says, handing me two books. 'I've signed them both.' One is his 1993 novel, *As algemas soldadas* (The welded shackles). The other is what he calls his 'testimony', a self-published memoir of the thirty-five years he lived in Angola. Bearing the enigmatic title *E aos costumes disse nada* (literally, To the customary questions, he said none),[27] the front cover is a section of a painting, a fairly haunting image of the Four Horseman of the Apocalypse.

It begins at the start of the 1950s, when baby Ildeberto and his mother travelled by ship from Lisbon to Luanda to join his father. Like many Africa-bound Portuguese families, they were in search of the good life. Arriving in Angola, they lived first in Luanda. In 1953, they moved to Negage, in the northern province of Uíge, which was famous for its coffee, then the country's largest export. In those days, Negage was just a village, with no electricity or running water, but the family enjoyed several good years. Teixeira writes of a childhood full of happiness and simplicity, running barefoot and free. He recalls taking long car journeys with his parents and, every time they saw any black Angolans, watching them wave and doff their caps at these passing whites. But Negage was segregated, with whites living mainly in the centre and blacks on the periphery. The populations socialised separately too. The whites drank and ate in Portuguese-run joints, while the blacks frequented *bares dos pretos* (bars for blacks), where they drank the illegally brewed spirit, *quimbinga*. Any whites who went to these black bars were 'the marginalised', according to Teixeira, and were dubbed the *sanzaleiros* (literally, those frequenting the slave quarters), or simply *bêbados* (drunks). The local coffee industry – controlled largely by white settlers – depended to a large extent on the exploitation of Angolan labour. Blacks were forced into conditions of semi-slavery through contract labour. Among more enlightened members of the white population, paternalism was the order of the day: blacks were treated like children. The only place where there was any semblance of equality was on the football pitch.

Authority, in Negage, was granted to one figure, the *chefe de posto*, the embodiment, says Teixeira, of Portuguese sovereignty. These *chefes* usually gained the respect of the white population by meting out violence on blacks. He recalls one *chefe* in particular who used hot chilli peppers to burn the anuses of Angolans he sought to punish. Nevertheless, Teixeira insists that these men were 'pioneers' in their own right, sent out into a vast, empty and foreign countryside to fly the Portuguese flag. They lived in trying conditions, often alone for months on end. And many, he insists, were decent men, who did their best to ensure that the blacks could also enjoy justice.

Other revealing memories include the fact that many dogs in Negage were named after Patrice Lumumba, the radical Congolese politician, who became that country's first prime minister, only to be executed within months of Congo's independence on 17 January 1961. Less than three weeks after Lumumba's death, Angola's war for liberation began and Negage began to resemble a Western, writes Teixeira: like 'the cinema, in those cities that were waiting for an attack by the Indians'. He writes of an 'incredible wave of violence' sweeping the country, and says that 'racism' and 'tribalism' became suddenly endemic. Remarkably, he never mentions racism in reference to Portuguese practices towards black Angolans. He only uses the term in regard to attacks against the settlers, who, he says, were filled with terror. In 1960, they had met many Belgians fleeing Congo in the run-up to independence and were horrified by tales of whites' heads being chopped off and put on top of sharpened poles. The Portuguese in northern Angola had supported their fellow Europeans, offering them shelter, food, clothes and political solidarity as they fled south. Now, they themselves were running too. Little Ildeberto, by then a growing boy, fled with his mother to Lisbon, where they remained for one year.

On their return to Angola, they found Negage pumped with Portuguese troops and the war for liberation well and truly under way. Yet Teixeira says that the period from 1961 to 1974 saw the 'greatest progress' Angola had ever experienced, at least in terms of material development. In Negage, an asphalt road was laid, street lamps erected, shops built and electricity and water supplied. Across Angola, the economy 'entered into a truly explosive phase', with the construction of new roads, bridges, airports, hospitals and schools. This massive investment from Lisbon, he thinks, 'demotivated' the guerrilla activities of many Angolans. Perhaps it did assuage a few, but the idea that the demand for national liberation could be bought off with improvements to the infrastructure is to fail to understand the fundamental purpose of the struggle – to be independent, free of racism, state brutality, torture, daily humiliation and imprisonment. Moreover, the 'benefits' of increased public transport and schooling were accompanied by an escalation of military violence. Portuguese planes began dropping napalm across the country, and the authorities arrested an unprecedented number of Angolans, torturing and killing many of them. It is therefore a little galling to read, towards the end of Teixeira's account of this period, that the main problem with the arrival of the military was the boom in prostitution. He even states that despite the war, whites and blacks got on 'absolutely peacefully even to the point of being friendly' and that, 'compared to the rest of black Africa, Angolans were relatively advantaged', because the Portuguese 'radicalised themselves and put down roots'.

It was only after independence, in Teixeira's view, that material conditions of life collapsed and, for the first time, Angola experienced 'the plague of hunger'. Charting what he clearly saw as the steady disintegration of the country, at times the book reads like a lament for colonialism. He mourns the collapsing infrastructure, the scarcity of goods, the growth in diamond-trafficking and the ever-declining white population. He refers to Neto's alleged alcohol problem and the growing tendency of the MPLA to refer to the president as 'the guide of the revolution'. He notes, solemnly, that one of the first laws to be published in the MPLA gazette, *Diário da República*, was that which created DISA, a 'sinister organism' staffed by racists and people motivated by tribalism. He says DISA took over the best buildings in cities and towns across the country, and opened up several concentration camps, which filled rapidly.

In June 1976, Teixeira began working in the southern town of Lubango, in Huíla province, as the local representative for the Attorney General. He'd not been in the job long when, with dozens of others, 'both black and white', he was arrested and detained by local police. They were all accused of conspiring against the MPLA and of having links with the defunct MPLA faction, the Active Revolt, and the communist grouping OCA. Coinciding with this development was the arrival in town of the minister of interior administration, Nito Alves. During a speech, he made reference to the arrests, describing the prisoners as 'reactionaries', and held up a gun, which he claimed belonged to one of them. '[I]t seemed to me,' writes Teixeira, 'that [Alves] was going to take advantage of [our arrests] by making one of his demagogic and incendiary speeches.'

Nevertheless, Teixeira was relatively lucky. After three days, he was released on the orders, he thinks, of the prime minister, Lopo do Nascimento. He had escaped the torture and beatings suffered by many of the other prisoners, particularly the whites, he says, who were beaten with the butts of guns until they bled. One man, nicknamed Igrejas (Churches), was beaten so badly he died. His body was thrown off the Tundavala, a vast and beautiful volcanic fissure, over 2,500 kilometres above sea level and offering outstanding views of Huíla province.

Determined to get justice, the day after his release Senhor Teixeira travelled to Luanda to inform the Attorney General and the justice minister of what had happened. As a result, disciplinary procedures were taken. In an extraordinary reversal, Teixeira, now in charge of the inquiry, set about trying to recover Igrejas' body and ordered the arrest of those he believed were corrupted senior police officers in Lubango. However, on the day he ordered the imprisonment of these officials, he received instructions to suspend the punishment immediately. The order had come from none other than Lúcio Lara, 'one of the most hardcore and inflexible militants' in the MPLA. Teixeira tried to reason with him, insisting that political power and judicial authority should remain separate. But Lara dismissed his ideas as 'bourgeois theories' and said there was only one power in Angola, 'the revolutionary power of the MPLA'.

The disagreement did not end here. The Attorney General weighed in, defending his representative's actions. This did not go down well with

Lara, who was becoming sick and tired of the whole process and viewed our author as 'a Machiavellian individual "possibly in the service of the *nitistas*"'. But Lara, alleges Teixeira, had 'an extreme complex about the paleness of his skin', which is why he was so keen to promote 'tremendous populism' and make 'demagogic attacks, constantly, against colonialism and the Portuguese'.

Eventually, things reached a head. A high-level meeting was held, including the Attorney General. Also present was Lara, who compared Angola with the Soviet Union 'in the time of Stalin', insisting that the MPLA had no choice but to take certain actions given the extreme circumstances. He announced that the final decision about the Lubango police officers would be taken by the Politburo. A few days later, Teixeira received instructions – he was told they came from Agostinho Neto himself – to free the prisoners immediately. They were all released that day.

According to Teixeira, these were all signs of an increasingly corrupt and authoritarian state. Other examples could be found in the nature of the media, whose sole objective was 'to eulogise the regime' and reinforce the idea that Neto was the 'uncontested leader'. Indeed, not only was Neto the head of state, he was the head of the party, the head of the Council of the Revolution, the head of the army and even the head of the country's only university. Portraits of the president were made more visible, as were pictures of Marx, Engels and Lenin. Teixeira felt that the MPLA's claims to Marxism were hypocritical, however. He remembers the prime minister speaking about the need 'to get in step with the working class' but to 'crack the teeth of the petite bourgeoisie', while 'the teeth of the leadership were becoming every bit sharper and they were learning quickly how to chew on the privileges of the bourgeoisie'. Neto, he says, was also learning how to play the international community. While he may have been happy to see his supporters escape from justice, others were banged up for no reason, and he made sure that a group of European mercenaries, who had been captured fighting on behalf of the FNLA in 1976, were given fair trials in Luanda. In other words, says Teixeira, they received more justice than the vast majority of Angolans could expect.

Against this increasingly ugly background, the crisis of the Twenty-seventh of May unfurled. There was, states Teixeira unequivocally, no factionalist action in Lubango at all. However, when Neto spoke on television that evening, insisting there was no time for pardons or trials, it was the '*sinal de arranque*' (the starting gun) to go out and kill. DISA immediately swung into action, arresting many people, sending spies into every corner of the country, beating on people's doors and breaking into their homes. If you were found with a copy of Alves' document, 'Treze teses em minha defesa' ('Thirteen theses in my defence'), you were killed. In Lubango, access to the Tundavala was suspended, rousing suspicion that it was being used to carry out more assassinations. Teixeira writes of a frenzied contest among friends, neighbours and colleagues to outdo each other's hatred for the nitistas. He describes a growing competitiveness in the hunt to track down and kill factionalists. Everyone was desperate to prove their loyalty to the state, to the MPLA and to the president. Meanwhile, Cuban 'specialists' were brought in to kill people, and Nito Alves – widely believed to have been executed – was, claims Teixeira, tortured to death.

Although he was appalled by the factionalists' murder of the six MPLA leaders in Sambizanga, Teixeira writes critically of the way the party commemorated their deaths. 'They were all given state funerals, including all the pomp,' he writes. 'However, before and after these funerals, hundreds of other corpses were thrown into mass graves or hurled off the top of precipices.' He stops short of estimating the numbers, but he is certain that there were many unlawful killings in Lubango, Huambo, Benguela, Luena and Malanje, where the number of women wearing black was 'astounding'. Some had lost all their sons. He is certain that 'nothing justified the bloody repression.' However, he admits that 'it might have been a lot worse' if the *nitistas* had taken power.

Once the uprising was over, the political situation deteriorated further. There was 'a complete remodelling of the structures of the party and the state'. The MPLA youth wing, the women's branch and the army were all stripped clean of opposition. Teixeira was sickened when the MPLA added to its name the letters PT, meaning 'Workers' Party', given that Angola's working class was, in his strict view, such a tiny minority.[28] It was nothing more than 'a construction of Neto's', Teixeira felt, rather like the state-run shops, which, he says, were usually empty of supplies. The only people who could shop at leisure were those in power, and most of them went to Angodiplo, which was exclusive to diplomats, VIPs and wealthy people with strong European currency. For the majority of the population, life grew unbearable. No one was allowed to go out at night without a pass. Police and military patrols sprang up everywhere, and the sound of gunshots became more and more common. Rubbish mountains piled up, potholes multiplied, street lamps were stolen and trees torn down. Schools no longer had seats or benches, and escalators in office blocks, high-rise flats and hotels stopped working. The number of people with mental-health problems multiplied, and men, often 'completely nude', could be seen scouting for food in rubbish bins. It seemed now that the only people who had any fun were the MPLA leaders and the businessmen: every weekend, they partied hard on imported whisky.

Horrified by these developments, Teixeira left Lubango and went to work in Namibe province, in the south-west corner of Angola. Here, he visited the famous prison Campo de São Nicolau, which, he says, had never held more than 500 people under Portuguese rule. By contrast, in 1977, 'there were more than a thousand living in the most degrading conditions.' And dying, too. On the day he visited, a funeral was taking place and he noticed a number of fresh graves.

In the middle of all this misery, Neto abandoned the presidential palace and moved south to Futungo de Belas, a modern Luanda neighbourhood that had been built by the Portuguese shortly before their departure. The presidency took over the whole *bairro*. Here, right on the coastline, Neto had access to his very own nautical club. Apparently he also began accumulating foreign cars, including a Mercedes 600, similar to the one President Mobutu Sese Seko owned. With the creation of a special presidential military guard, Futungo de Belas became 'an authentic fortress'.

Senhor Teixeira believes that 'Neto's presidency had been a total disaster for the country, leaving it in ruin and chaos'. By the time the president died in Moscow, on 17 September 1979, Angola was 'locked into an internal civil war', he writes, its economy 'completely destroyed' by 'an incompetent elite'. A 'huge popular discontent' remained hidden because of 'strong repression', and the only reason the regime still existed was because of 'a contingent of foreign forces numbering about 40,000'. Teixeira was even more appalled when a mausoleum was built, to the south of the presidential palace, in commemoration of Neto. This giant concrete shard, shooting from the ground like a massive stalagmite, was, he insists, nothing more than 'a megalomaniac work'. Nevertheless, he believes that Neto came to regret the purge that followed the Twenty-seventh of May and suggests this is why DISA was dismantled shortly before his death.

◆

Here, now, in Portugal, Teixeira doesn't want to discuss any of this. He wants to show me his dog. I follow him out of the back door and into the garden. He lets me take a peek inside a beautiful old brick shed, with a wood-burning stove and lines of red apples collected from an orchard. When we climb some steps to the garden's upper terrace, half lawn, half cage, we are met with a mangey, chocolate animal, pacing among piles of faeces, looking through the wire wall, hopeful that the two humans gazing back might be about to touch or feed him. It is freezing out here. A cold wind slices the air and the short-haired dog looks miserable. Noticing my pity, Teixeira insists, 'He's a hunting dog, he's very tough.' Frankly, he looks too old to be chasing after much more than a biscuit. I'd like to take him inside and put him by the fire, but Teixeira has other plans. He and his wife are taking me to see their *quinta*, their country cottage, on the edge of a forest. We shall all spend the night there.

Three fallow deer are grazing on the clipped lawn beside the cottage. Normally such jumpy creatures, I'm amazed they don't run away when Teixeira swerves into the driveway. Unfrightened, they remain perfectly still, their spotted coats a beautiful bright orange against the green grass. Perfectly still and – I now realise – perfectly plastic.

We park up and jump out. Teixeira wants to show me around. He leads me across the garden, a large patch of green with a swimming pool dug into one side. At the far end, a small slope leads to bushes and trees, thickening into a dense forest that covers the hills beyond.

'There are lots of wild boar around here. I've shot several in a little clearing just about there,' he says, pointing into the trees. 'What I do is put food out so that they learn it's a good spot to eat. Soon enough, a few will start coming regularly and on about the third day, I'll shoot one of them.'

How disappointing. I'd been under the impression, what with all his equipment, that Teixeira was a real hunter. 'That's not exactly giving the animal a fair chance, is it?' I say.

'Oh, it is. Yes,' he says. 'It means I can shoot them faster and quicker because I'm so close. It means I'm very accurate.'

Any notion I might still have that the fun of hunting is in the chase is dispelled inside the *quinta*, which is really a converted barn. The walls are covered from top to bottom with the heads, hooves and paws of wild boar, wild bear, rabbits and different deer, antelope and buck from Europe and Africa.

'There's a zebra coming soon too,' Teixeira tells me. 'We're just waiting for the taxidermist to finish stuffing it. We'll have the head on the wall and the rest of the body will be a rug for the floor.'

At night, the three of us eat out. The Costas order big chunks of meat and red wine and watch as I wade my way, alone, through pudding. For reasons I find hard to follow, when we leave the restaurant, we drive back to their town house to collect a second car. We dip briefly inside to check on Michael. His mother wants to make sure he's eaten. Stilted moments in the kitchen follow. Michael catches my eye while his parents bicker about some trivial matter of housekeeping. As we leave, Teixeira turns to his wife and pleads with her not to drive too fast.

'You will keep checking in your mirror, won't you, to make sure I'm there? Don't just drive off without me, will you?'

'Probably,' she says, soberly.

I walk back to the four-by-four. Senhora Teixeira takes the driver's seat. We roll backwards down the steep drive and, through the windscreen, I watch her husband, now clumsy and vulnerable at the side of the low-slung saloon car. Beside me, Senhora Teixeira pushes us out of reverse and presses her foot hard on the accelerator. We shoot off down the road, back to the *quinta* at top speed. Teixeira arrives about fifteen minutes after us. He looks drunk and afraid. She switches on the television and sits down; he opens a bottle of wine and offers me a drink. But I don't think I can bear being between these two much longer. I bid them both goodnight.

The following morning, Senhora Teixeira is nowhere to be seen. She left at dawn, having prepared our breakfast of coffee and toast, now cold on the table. My visit has come to an end. I am to return to Lisbon with two of Teixeira's old friends, a father and son, who also lived in Angola.

The journey takes a little over two hours. The old man spends much of the time complaining about the MPLA. 'They destroyed Angola,' he says, over and over, 'they completely destroyed Angola.' I'm not sure what to say in response, but in my head I keep thinking about the threads of continuity from colonial rule to self-rule, and the possibility that the *vinte e sete* was, in many ways, a clear expression of that.

◆

Back in Lisbon, I have the afternoon to fill before flying home, so I walk up the cobbled streets to Castelo de São Jorge, the Moorish castle at the top of the city's highest hill, to a favourite café. From here, you can look out across the oldest part of town and rest your gaze on the tiled orange roofs and the pastel-pink, yellow and white walls. The view fills me with a nostalgia I don't fully understand. Someone is playing the piano and I can hear a woman calling instructions over the top. The music and her orders keep breaking and starting again, and I imagine little girls in pink, leaping like frightened frogs around the room, and an old woman stamping her cane into the floorboards.

I order a glass of red wine and ask an elderly waiter for a single cigarette. I gave up several years ago, but I'm desperate to shed the tension from the weekend. I've convinced myself I need a smoke.

'So where did you learn Portuguese?' he asks, lighting the Camel in my mouth.

'Angola,' I say.

'Angola?'

'Yes. Angola.'

'I was there,' he says. 'In the 1960s. What about you?'

'Much more recently,' I reply. 'I first went in 1998.'

'I was in the Air Force,' he says, pouring the wine. 'I bombed them.'

'You?'

'Yes,' he says with a sort of smile, but there's nothing very happy in his face. 'We used napalm. You know about that?'

'So I've heard.'

'We used a lot,' he says. 'We killed a lot.'

I'm not sure what to say in this strangely cathartic conversation. I look up to him, but he's looking over the view.

'I still dream about it. We had to do it, you know, it was our job.'

'It's the same everywhere, isn't it? Soldiers have to do as they're told.'

His eyebrows flicker in what I think is agreement and he pulls another cigarette from the pack in his shirt pocket and places it on the table. 'Take as long as you like,' he says. 'You enjoy yourself.'

I wish he hadn't said that. I can feel tears welling. I've been feeling so angry with the Portuguese – the endless denials of the damage wrought by colonialism, the foolish insistence that it only went wrong at independence – and now, just like that, my fury evaporates. All I have left is pity.

PART II

'Is there any difference – and, if so, of what sort – between what happened during the colony and "what comes after"? Is everything really called into question, is everything suspended, does everything truly begin all over again, to the point where it can be said that the formerly colonized recovers existence, distances himself or herself from his/her previous state?'

Achille Mbembe[29]

12

♦

SO MANY DRAGONFLIES

'*Alô?*' A deep voice, gloopy as honey.

'João?'

'*Sim?*'

'*É a Lara que fala.* I'm here! In Luanda!'

'Lara! You're back! When will I see you?'

'In an hour or so, if you like.'

'Make it two.'

It's past midday by the time I climb the eighteen flights of stairs to João's flat and rattle the bars of the large metal cage that surrounds his front door like a passageway to a prison. When, eventually, he appears, he's naked, save a narrow towel the colour of mustard wrapped round his hips. He looks at me with a full smile of stained teeth and a cigarette.

'You're looking older,' he says, unlocking the gate, 'definitely older.' He releases a rumble of laughter and we kiss cheeks.

His ninth-floor flat is unchanged since my last visit over five years ago. The black-and-white portrait of Karl Marx is still hanging high on the wall, its paper corners peeling up from the chipboard beneath. A small television sits on a low table that is covered in pink cloth, and a white shelving unit holds battered books on economics and politics and a selection of Angolan poetry and fiction. Piles of newspapers are stacked along one wall, mostly the weeklies, *Agora* (Now), where João works, and *Folha 8* (Page 8). He has written for both for years.

He offers me a cigarette, ignoring me when I say I've given up. 'Have one anyway,' he says. 'Smoking suits you.' So I pull one from the red and white pack. They're AC, an Angolan brand that plunges new depths in nicotine's destruction of your health: you can actually feel them killing you with each puff.

Encouraging me to sit down, João smacks at a cushion moulded concave in the seat of an armchair, springing dust and crumbs into the air. Beside the armrest, in the perfect position for a smoker's fingers, a free-standing ashtray rises from a steel column overflowing with butt ends and ash. 'Hold on, I'll empty that,' he says, disappearing from the room. He returns with an old margarine tub full of water.

'Because I have a guest, I'm watering the plants,' he quips. 'They will love you for this.' He walks the length of the windowsill, which is as long as the room is wide, tipping the tub over the cracked soil of a row of cacti cloaked in dust.

I first met João Faria in the offices of a US aid organisation in Luanda in 1998. I remember being impressed when he told me that he'd read all of Sigmund Freud's work in French and English, and then showed genuine surprise at my psychoanalytical ignorance. I felt more inadequate when he ran through a list of political literature that he thought any self-respecting foreign correspondent should have read. What warmed me to him most, however, was his keenness to challenge my political ideas and to question my preconceptions about Angola and the wider region. 'What you need to understand,' he explained early on, 'is that Angola was colonised by Portugal's underbelly. My family were crooks, Lara, prisoners, and they were sent here to develop Angola. Can you imagine?'

As we became friends, his loyalty and sense of humour became clear. It was João who rescued me and my car after I insulted one of my neighbours – I didn't realise he was a police chief – who had the vehicle removed in the middle of the night. And it was João who told me, through tears of laughter, that the pale-skinned man whose Angolan nationality I had been questioning over the dinner table was none other than General Hélder Manuel Vieira Dias Júnior, head of the Military Bureau in the presidency and, after the president himself, the most powerful man in the country. Of course I knew him by name – everyone's heard of Kopelipa, as he's known – but I had never actually seen him in the flesh. So when he and his four mobile phones sat down next to me and chose an old piece of Edam cheese and biscuits over the Angolan staple of *funje* and stew, I assumed he was a stuck-up Portuguese businessman. If only I hadn't made my views quite so public. But João thought it was hilarious. He and Kopelipa grew up in the same neighbourhood and knew each other as children. But whereas Kopé has devoted himself to the pursuit of power and wealth, João has put his political ideals first. In so doing, like many other Angolan journalists, he has spent much of his life fighting off depression and disillusionment through a determined combination of the written word, women, political action and alcohol.

It was only when I started researching the Twenty-seventh of May in London that I began to get a sense of João's past. While reading through some old files from Amnesty International's archives, I discovered that he had been arrested in 1976 for being a member of the Grupo Joséf Stálin. This was one of several left-wing associations that were banned shortly after the MPLA came to power under the watch of the then minister of interior administration, Nito Alves. In July 1980, twenty-seven-year-old João became seriously ill when he and nine others went on hunger strike for over a month to protest against their detentions and the fact that they had received no trial. They were released in August.

Then someone gave me the memoirs of a Portuguese author, Américo Cardoso Botelho, who was held in Luanda's São Paulo prison in the late 1970s. During his detention, he smuggled out pages of notes detailing life on the inside. His recollections about the man in the cell opposite his – João Faria – is not an easy read. We learn how João was physically and psychologically tortured during regular interrogations.[30] They 'broke his nose then made him suck up his own blood from the floor'. On one occasion, 'Faria was forced to remove staples from the elbow of another prisoner who had been tortured with a stapler.' He was also subjected to the *n'guelelo*, or 'eastern torture'. Amnesty describes this as a common form of MPLA torture that involved

> tying the victims' arms and legs together behind their backs, usually with wet rope that contracts; these cords being sometimes also tied to the victims' testicles, then attached to two curved sticks around the victims' heads, the two sticks perhaps being tightened by a tourniquet putting tremendous pressure on the victims' temples.[31]

Botelho says it 'was applied to the head of the victim to drive him completely crazy'. While João was restrained like this, burning matches were run over his body and lit cigarettes were used to scorch his mouth and tongue. On other occasions, recalls Botelho,

> two of his fingers were tied together with copper wire and, with his hands in front of his body, his elbows were tied behind him with rope; salty water was then poured over the rope, which made it dilate, increasing the pressure on his elbows and his fingers, causing excruciating pain. After an hour, the rope would be cutting into his flesh, causing deep wounds and leaving serious scars.

Sometimes João was subjected to the '*chinkwalia*' torture: his wrists, his ankles and head were tied together with rope, which was tightened until his body had been pulled back into 'a true human arc'. He would then be lifted into the air and dropped 'helplessly' to the floor. One night, Botelho recalls, João's nose was producing so much blood that it was spurting everywhere, even staining the clothes of the torturer. Despite this cruelty, João's courage did not falter. On 10 June 1978, he was interrogated by Onambwe, second in command at DISA and a member of the MPLA Politburo. Asked whether he had grounds for complaint against the MPLA, João responded, 'I do, sir, yes.' He later told his father that he would sooner die for his political ideals than be allowed to return home for giving the authorities what they wanted.

Beneath a pile of papers under the windowsill, I notice a copy of the book. João catches me staring at it and grins. 'I'm in there,' he says, 'but he's got some of his facts wrong. I was inside for four years, not a year and a half. Never mind. I knew he was writing a lot, every day, scribbling it all down.' He lights a cigarette. 'I need to wash. Then I'll get us some coffee.'

I tell him I've read the book. 'It was pretty bad, João. I didn't realise just what you'd been through. I wish you'd told me before. When I read it, I felt terrible.'

'Well, it's the past now. A long time ago. Do you want a coffee?'

He leaves the room and I listen to him in the kitchen.

Shortly, he returns with two cups of strong coffee sweetened with a sickly amount of sugar.

'I know it was the past, João,' I say, 'but the present is made from the past, isn't it?'

'Of course it is, but revisiting it doesn't help. We live in the present now. We have different problems. Those were different times. We were very young.' He lights another cigarette. 'I ought to go and wash.'

He stands up and pulls his towel away from his body, then wraps it tightly back round his waist and sits down again. For several minutes, we are silent, staring at the grey television and the wall behind it where two wooden carvings hang, the profiles of a man and a woman.

'I want to try to understand why the MPLA was so brutal,' I say. 'Why were you treated so badly? What had you done?'

He lets out a heavy sigh. 'Oh, Lara! Do you want another coffee?' He stubs his cigarette out, and stands up again. 'I was going to wash, but this is a conversation. We will have to drink more coffee.'

He returns to the kitchen and calls out answers.

'Long before I went to prison, there were lots of purges in the MPLA! Can you hear me? They were killing people all the time!'

I shout back: 'Why?'

'Nobody knows!' He breaks into loud laughter. 'They were already killing each other before independence. You should know all this already.'

He returns with a dented metal jug in his hand and pours more coffee. Then he pushes another cigarette into my mouth. 'If we're going to talk,' he says, 'we need to smoke.' So I oblige, and light up.

He tells me about Matias Miguéis, a veteran nationalist who was executed with another senior comrade, José Miguel, in an MPLA guerrilla camp in Congo-Brazzaville in November 1965. Some reports allege that, prior to the executions, Neto's most loyal ally Lúcio Lara conducted a trial that lasted ten minutes. Both Miguéis and Miguel were key figures in the MPLA, but they were part of a different faction to Neto's. They were allies of Viriato da Cruz, one of the MPLA's founders and its first Secretary General, from 1956 to 1962. 'Da Cruz was our only decent poet and our best writer,' says João. 'He was the biggest thinker in Africa. It's no wonder he fell out with Neto.'

'When?' I ask.

'Early 1960s. Da Cruz followed the Chinese school of communism. He was a Maoist. Neto was a Soviet communist, although he wasn't really quite that.'

In 1964, da Cruz and his supporters joined forces with the rival liberation movement, the FNLA. The year before, the FNLA's Revolutionary

Government in Exile had been recognised by the Organisation of African Unity. Da Cruz believed it was crucial, for the sake of the liberation struggle, to join forces with the FNLA. Neto disagreed, and the executions of Miguéis and Miguel were widely interpreted as his revenge. The men's deaths left da Cruz completely demoralised. This intellectual, whose radical vision and energy had helped create the MPLA, never regained his political strength. In 1969 he went to China, where he became the secretary for the Organisation of Asian and African Writers. In 1973, at the age of forty-five, he died in Beijing in relative obscurity.

'We like to destroy our best, you see,' says João. 'Here, have another.' He chucks the pack of AC onto my lap. 'The trouble was,' he continues, 'everyone wanted to be leader. All of them. Even me.' He starts chuckling. 'I was the leader of the Josef Stalin Group.' He laughs a little harder and repeats the name of his old party. 'The Josef Stalin Group! I was a Maoist, Lara.'

'Surely you were a Stalinist?'

'Yes,' he says, through more laughter, 'but Mao supported Stalin.'

'So why not the Chairman Mao Group?' I ask.

'The point is, I was not a Leninist. My communism was about being led by the peasants, not a vanguard group.' He's laughing even harder now and it's infectious. I'm not quite sure why, but every time he says 'Josef Stalin Group' I laugh even more. It seems so incongruous, so old-fashioned and, somehow, so naive.

'Of course the MPLA had to have a leader,' he says, relenting a little. 'Because Neto was in Lisbon's Aljube prison, it meant he was well known. It helped, so he became the figurehead.'

'Isn't that why Amnesty International was created?' I ask. 'Because of Neto's imprisonment?'

'Of course! Neto was their *raison d'être* – and just look at what Amnesty's hero did in 1977! Killed all those people!' He shakes his head, suddenly sinking with the tragedy of it all. 'The amazing thing is how Neto escaped from that prison. He made an extraordinary escape. I don't know how he did it but he just did. It was incredible. Anyway, I need to wash.'

When João comes back, his hair is wet and combed, and he's dressed in a sun-bleached shirt and a pair of old chinos. A bottle of wine is tucked under his arm and he's holding two glasses. He pours the wine and strides to the bookshelf.

'These are my principles today,' he says, placing a dictionary of economics open on my lap, a thumbnail digging into the word 'efficiency'. 'This is what I'm interested in now.'

'What?'

He grins at me: 'Getting the maximum returns for the minimum effort. I have no values any more, Lara. I am a positivist. All true knowledge is scientific. We must eradicate emotion from our discussions. It is completely unhelpful.'

'I'm not sure I follow,' I say.

'I've moved on. When I was young, I didn't know what I was on about. In those days, we all talked about communism and Leninism and Maoism but none of us knew what it really meant.' His mouth twitches as he tries to suppress another urge to laugh. 'We thought the dictatorship of the proletariat, or in my case the peasantry, was the best way forward. Then we thought democracy was the best way forward, but that isn't bringing us any benefits either because it is not properly democratic. Any fool can see that. And globalisation is also a disaster. Too many people remain too poor.' He pauses and tosses his head back to the wine. 'Let's stop this now. I want to eat.'

I follow him into the kitchen, where a single window opens onto another tower of flats, blocking the sunlight and darkening the room. A slab of thawing meat is lying in a pool of blood in a glass bowl. João wipes away the remains of some chopped onions and slaps the meat onto the wooden sideboard, whereupon he produces a hammer and begins smashing it into shape. Blood spurts from the flattening beef, splattering the walls and João's pink shirt. I watch a drop slide down the side of the cupboard, forming a long red line to the floor. I think about his nose being smashed in São Paulo prison and the torturer whose clothes were stained with João's blood. He takes a lemon and squeezes it into a small pan. He adds the onions and places it over the gas. He dips the meat in flour and chucks it into the pan with the onions. Then he opens his large rusting freezer, the sort you could hide a body in, and pulls out a bag of frozen tomatoes. He saws through them and throws them into the pan with the meat. 'Don't worry,' he says cheerily, 'we're having potatoes too.' The pan has no handle. Each time João shakes the food, he takes a cloth and holds the side of the pan high up and for a brief second only. 'There's no water today,' he says, 'so I'll have to cook with wine.' A bottle of white is pulled from the freezer and glugged over the meat. 'Give it ten minutes,' he says, placing a small plate over the top of the pan, 'and we'll eat.' He ushers me back into the main room.

We stand at the window, leaning over the cacti, admiring the Luanda skyline and the faded horizon of the ocean in the distance. We count the cranes across the city but can't agree on the final number. I've heard there are more in Luanda than anywhere else in the world, but João is sceptical. 'They can build as many skyscrapers as they wish, but we've still got all these millions of poor,' he says, letting out another line of laughter. In fact, after decades of being written off as a failed, war-torn but resource-rich state, Angola's reputation has started to change since the end of the war in 2002. In the past ten years, it has had one of the fastest-growing economies in the world. At points, growth has peaked at an incredible 20 per cent, and between 2003 and 2011 it averaged 11 per cent. This has largely been due to the oil sector – Angola is Africa's second-largest producer after Nigeria, with oil constituting three-quarters of government income and 97 per cent of export revenues – although manufacturing, agriculture and construction have also contributed a bit. But for all the shiny new hotels and office blocks there is little sign that the average Angolan is benefitting. Sixty per cent of Angolans still don't have electricity, even those who do have to put up with repeated power cuts, and around 65 per cent don't have access to piped drinking water and proper sanitation. Meanwhile, many of the labourers on the construction sites are Chinese men, who are bussed in to building sites first thing in the morning and bussed out last thing at night. The construction companies are also Chinese or Brazilian or Portuguese. Only a minority of educated and often politically privileged Angolans could be said to be doing well. Even the massive oil industry employs just 1 per cent, and many people here believe that it is the foreigners who are gaining the most. In a historical U-turn, whereas half a million whites fled to Portugal as independence loomed in 1975, tens of thousands are now turning to the former colony for economic and employment opportunities they cannot get back home. Recent estimates suggest that as many as 200,000 Portuguese are now living in Angola.

The gloom of our conversation is lifted when a dragonfly appears, darting back and forth a few feet in front of us. It is joined by another, and then another and another, until I lose count of the large brown *libelinhas* zigzagging before us.

'Where do they all come from?' I ask. 'I've never seen so many before – certainly not this high up.'

'It's Sinfo,' says João, referencing the intelligence services, Angola's main internal security organ – the secret police, modern-day DISA if you like.

I start laughing. 'You mean the *bufos*?' I ask.

'Sinfo, yes,' he says, seriously. 'Why are you laughing?'

'Come on João, it's funny.' I'm still giggling, but he, most definitely, is not.

'That one there is from Sinfo,' he says, his finger moving in sudden jerks backwards and forwards. 'It's a tiny camera and a tiny microphone. They are here listening to us and watching us.'

'Is that really what you think?'

He shakes his head and looks at me in a sideward glance. 'Lara, you are so naive. The trouble is you come from a country where this sort of thing doesn't happen. In Britain, you don't need to watch your back and worry about the phone being bugged. You don't know the meaning of fear. You simply don't know what it is.' He pauses and draws on a cigarette, heaving on the nicotine and blowing smoke at the insects busying before us. 'Big Brother...' he says in a voice so deep I can almost feel it vibrating, 'always there, always listening, always watching. The phone, the computer, the lot. It's all bugged.'

'I thought you said you didn't have internet up here.'

'You think they need internet to know what's in that!' he says, pointing at his laptop on the table.

I feel stupid, even though I'm pretty sure they do. 'OK, OK!' I say. 'But the dragonflies? Seriously?'

'Why not?' he barks. 'The KGB can make those tiny things, so why not here? We were raised on the KGB. That's where our training comes from. We might not be good at many things, but we're good at that.'

'You mean like that fat brown one there?' A large dragonfly is hovering above one of the succulents.

'I don't know which one, but I'm sure that if they want to they can do it. And it would explain why we've had so many this year.'

He stubs his cigarette into one of the small mosaic blue tiles that cover the outer sill and flicks the butt high into the air. 'Come on,' he says, 'let's eat.'

The meal is surprisingly tasty. João follows it with the offer of whisky for pudding. I'm already feeling mildly drunk from the wine and all the cigarettes.

'Have you not got anything soft at all?' I ask.

He shakes his head. 'I only drink water once a year,' he says, his lips twitching to laugh. 'Have a whisky and stop worrying so much.'

I relent, again, and wonder why I seem to apply such different rules to life in Luanda compared with London. Is this hypocrisy? Am I not taking the place seriously? João slams down two glasses of whisky. We clink and drink. I'm starting to feel sleepy, but João is starting to wake up. He wants me to read his recent work, the articles he's been writing for *Agora*. He passes me the current edition and urges me on. The first paragraph is a wash of words without any commas or full stops. I'm not sure I can fully comprehend what it's about, but I press on, trying to make head or tail of his argument. I think of my passion for Samuel Beckett – line after line, page after page, empty of punctuation – and wonder if I am looking at the work of a genius here, or a madman? João pours me more whisky and I persist with his piece, certain I can detect a lurid anger in the never-ending sentences even though I can't fathom his argument. We sit in silence for perhaps half an hour. I can feel him watching me as I read. When I've finished the second piece, confused by his structure and roaming language, he starts speaking in a stern voice.

'We cannot be afraid,' he says. 'We must write what we see and what we feel.' He touches my arm and looks at me affectionately. 'Lara, don't worry about what people will say. You must write what you see.'

'And if I write about you? If I write about this?'

'Write what you want to write. Don't think about the subject. Just get it down. Say what you believe and what you see and hear. Say what matters.' He smiles at me, and I feel dreadful because I'm remembering that another friend told me that recently João had come close to ending his life. I wonder if it is true. I wonder whether I should ask him. I wish I could do something to make him more happy.

'Let's have one more cigarette,' he says, 'I really like watching you smoke.'

He pushes another on me and strikes a match. I've had so many now, I'm starting to feel sick. But I smoke it anyway, for old times' sake, in the heat, with the wine, and the whisky, and my friend.

◆

The sun is setting when I begin my walk home. It must have gone six. My head feels fuzzy as I cross the sandy car park that stretches out behind João's block of flats towards a large yellowing secondary school. At night, this space fills with men and women laughing and loving in cars and open-air bars that serve cold beer and spirits and occasionally skewers of peppered goat cooked over coals. The first time João and I spent an evening drinking beer here, he told me about *as sereias* (the mermaids). This is where they gather at night, he said, when they come ashore, drifting over the land to mingle among the muddy bars beneath the moon. I laughed, of course, but he wasn't having any of it. He encouraged me to look for their tails, magically transformed into legs until sunrise.

This evening there are no *sereias*. It's too early. Instead, I spot a ginger cat lying in the shade of a rotting tree trunk, her stomach convulsing like bellows, in and out and in and out, while a tiny pair of kittens knead on her empty belly, sucking hard on dry teats, desperate to feed their tiny frames. Still, she licks their little heads over and over until, eventually, they give up on their mother. Step by wobbly step, they walk towards a puddle of glistening black water, where they crouch down beside a pigeon and drink.

It's midnight now, and I'm lying beneath a single sheet in a white room with a high ceiling. Above me a large fan is spinning, its plastic parts rattling with each rotation. From a nearby flat, I can hear the melancholy voice of Paulo Flores, one of Angola's most popular contemporary singers. I close my eyes and my head fills with couples swinging, hip to hip, happy and hot in the heart of the city. But soon, this colonial bungalow where I now lie will be no more. These old pink houses, built during the first half of the twentieth century, are disappearing. One by one, their owners are selling off their tiny plots of land for $3 million and rising; in their place, towering blocks of concrete and glass are climbing out of the ground. The next-door neighbours recently sold up to a hotel group. So the gossip goes, the neighbours on the right-hand side are considering following suit. Rumour has it that a footbridge will be built on the twelfth floor between the two buildings, and a tunnel will be dug underneath. Sandwiched in the middle, this little house will stand like a relic from another world. Already, the demolition has begun. As well as Flores and the fan, lying here now I can hear a JCB digger slamming into the walls of the house next door, the thud of machinery sending tremors down the street. The project is behind schedule, so the workers must labour through the night. I know I have no right to mourn the passing of Portugal's architectural legacy, but I'm sad that whole swathes of this city will soon be unrecognisable to visitors like me. I've heard predictions of 'an African Manhattan', but *Jornal de Angola* says the stated goal is Dubai.

13

◆

SAVED BY A POET

Budgerigars wake me. Squawking and talking. Four of them, fluorescent blue, green and yellow. Colours of candy living in a cage outside my window. I check my watch. It's ten past six. Already streams of traffic are rushing past the house, reminding me how early people here start work.

I get up and open the windows. I push back the shutters until they slam against the walls, and immediately I feel the brewing heat slip into the room, to warm the throbbing hangover in my head.

Armed with black coffee, a glass of water and some ibuprofen, I drop back onto the bed, slumping into a pyramid of pillows I've just built. I'm feeling mildly panicked. After eleven months of waiting, I was suddenly given a one-month visa to return to Angola. In principle it can be renewed twice, but it might not be renewed at all. So I need to come up with a plan, and I need to be quick.

I take a shower and get dressed. Then I make some more coffee and bang off a few emails to old friends, letting them know I'm back in town. Next, I run through my list of senior figures who were involved in the *vinte e sete*, pondering which ones might speak. Afraid of tempting fate or being stopped at the airport, I decided not to do any of this before arriving in the country, just in case it all went wrong. Now that I'm in, I'll need to lean on intermediaries, people who can put in a good word on my behalf. Without elite lubricant, you are nothing here. Even with it, there are no guarantees. Those at the top of the MPLA are notoriously tight-lipped, and critical journalists rarely get near them. My chances, let me be frank, are slim. On a brighter note, the other part of my plan, although more random, should be more successful. I will simply approach members of the public and try to persuade them to talk. In my experience, the less power a person has, the more open he or she tends to be. Some say they have less to lose: I believe they have more courage. But right now, what I really need to do is immerse myself back into the beat of this city. I need to get out and walk.

At the bottom of Rua Dr Américo Boavida, where the traffic is wrestling itself to a standstill, a young man in a red wheelchair is coming at me at speed, leaning into cars, pulling and pushing off burning bonnets and chrome bumpers. I try to manoeuvre myself out of his way but I'm caught between the crush of a gold Pajero and a black Cherokee and my hand signals through their darkened windows seem to be going unnoticed. The man in the wheelchair thrusts down on the wheels, as if he's about to mow me down, but then he's twisting suddenly, pushing towards the pavement, faster and faster, until the simple metal chair smacks into the kerb. Hands, hips and locks of hair slam to the ground. Shooting out of this mess, something tiny catches my sight. It flaps and flutters, chased by the young man, whose feeble legs and stunted, rubbery feet are bouncing behind his pelvis like intestines unravelling. Hurling himself forward, he vanishes in a tussle of limbs and feathers. Seconds later, he's swinging himself back into the wheelchair in an arc so graceful it defies gravity. Upright again, he beams with delight. I'm dying to know who he is, this character begging at the busy junction, and I'm tempted to stay and talk. But what is there to say after such a spectacle? '*Obrigada*'? So I drop some money in his lap and he opens his fingers to reveal the scratch of life pulsing in his palm. A tiny pet sparrow.

I cross the junction and head up Nossa Senhora da Muxima, a steep hill that leads past the Catholic university and, at the top, to the museum where the *nitistas* are alleged to have focused their first, failed, coup attempt. Soon I can see the crescent of the bay swooping into the Atlantic and a queue of cargo ships stacked up along the horizon, where they will be waiting for weeks to enter the port. I detour down a stump of road that pushes up the spine of a line of dull apartment blocks. Here, the road reduces to a gnarled dogleg that passes through the belly of Hotel Trópico before emerging back onto Rua da Missão. Cars are hooting and I can hear polyphonic ringtones bursting from people's pockets. I turn left, climbing another short hill beside four lanes of traffic, passing a man in a pressed suit. He's holding a briefcase in one hand and, with the other, wiping his waxed hair back over his head. I catch him looking at his fingers, stretched wide in front of his face, as though searching the lines in his skin for an answer to a question he's been asking all his life. Beside him, a woman dabs a tissue at her blouse while gesturing impatiently at the plump drops of water falling from above. I follow her gaze, up the sides of the high-rise hotel and I notice, for the first time, the colonies of air-conditioners nesting across the concrete. So this is what is producing this glittering curtain of excretion. I look down at my feet, to where I am standing on a lime-green spread of syrupy leaves. A shining stream is rushing in broken currents around my heels to where a large slab of concrete has sunk, producing a rock pool of clear water at the side of the pavement. I look back to the woman, still blotting her blouse, and we share a smile.

I continue up the incline towards Kinaxixi, a public square made famous in a poem by Agostinho Neto. It used to be home to a large market, built in the 1950s but recently closed down. Today, like so much of Luanda, Kinaxixi is a building site soon to be transformed into a shopping mall. They have even removed the vast statue of Rainha Nzinga, the seventeenth-century queen under whose reign the kingdoms of Matamba and Ndongo became the most powerful in the region.

From here, I fiddle my way along more streets, remembering times past, and searching, I'm ashamed to admit, for a way back there. I head for a small café, a place I used to like, tucked into the shadows of a heavy block of flats, all its faded shutters pulled down tight. I choose a table on the pavement outside, in an enclosure of miniature hedges grown inside wooden boxes. I've barely sat down when the waiter appears. He looks to be in his fifties. He looks exhausted. He pulls out the other chair at my table and half sits on it, holding my gaze, eyeing me firmly.

'*Finalmente, a senhora da BBC voltou*,' he says in a steady voice, as if I'd only been gone a couple of months. 'So finally, the BBC lady has returned.'

'I arrived yesterday,' I say, trying to hide my amazement. 'It's the first time in five years. I'm honoured you remember me.'

He doesn't smile. 'Of course I do. We used to talk. It's Laura, isn't it?'

'Nearly,' I say. 'No U. It's Lara, like Lúcio Lara.' But I'm ashamed because I've completely forgotten his name. I only remember his face. 'Didn't you used to work somewhere else?' I ask.

'I was a security guard behind Hotel Continental, at Prédio Limpo. Do you not remember?'

Vaguely, I do. It's coming back.

'We went to the plane crash together,' he continues, 'when that Antonov came down near the UN headquarters. You were in a terrible state. All those bodies, but you seemed to be so busy on the telephone to London that I wondered if you'd even noticed them. Do you remember?'

'If it wasn't for you, I'd never have found the crash site.'

He smiles. 'That's right.' He offers me a drink.

'I'd love a Coke,' I say. I'm gasping.

'I'm coming right now,' he says, striding away. 'Don't go anywhere.'

In a flash, he's back, with the Coke and a glassful of ice. He sits down again, a little more relaxed this time. He wants to know where I've been and what I've been doing. He wants to know about the BBC and London and my family. My parents, are they well? And my husband? Why didn't I marry an Angolan? And why haven't I got children? 'A life is not complete without children,' he warns.

'And you?' I ask.

'I've been here,' he sighs. 'Always the same. Nothing changing.' He sounds resigned to his life.

'And your family?' I ask.

There's a pause before he replies: 'I lost my only son in the war.'

'I'm sorry,' I say, pathetically. 'I'm very sorry to hear that.'

He bows his head a little, acknowledging my sympathy. 'But you English are strange,' he continues with a sudden surge of energy. 'You let your sons go to fight a war in another country and you don't even protest!'

'But we do,' I reply, slightly taken aback by how defensive I sound. 'It's just that our government doesn't listen.'

'What about the big war in Iraq?' he argues. 'Your country still went to war. You didn't stop it.'

'We tried,' I say. 'More than a million protested, possibly 2 million. Hundreds of thousands of us protested more than once.'

'You British are very fortunate,' he says. 'We don't protest here. We can't. If we did, they'd kill us.'

'Still?' I ask. 'You really think they'd kill you now?'

'Of course!' he snaps. 'But you won't get killed, and still you don't protest.'

'But we did!' I insist. 'We do! It's just that no one with any power seems to listen.'

'Well,' his voice full of disbelief, 'I saw nothing about this on the television.'

He looks up. A woman from inside the restaurant is tapping at the window. He tells me to wait while he goes inside to talk to her. I watch him through the window, folding his hands over one another, listening to her patiently, not saying a word until she gives him a piece of paper from her pocket. Then he returns to my table.

'You have to trust me,' I say. 'We really did demonstrate against the war. Many of us. Truly. But our leaders don't care. And if you didn't see it on television, that probably says more about the way the Angolan media cover foreign affairs than the British propensity to protest.'

'OK,' he concedes, 'but I also watch Portuguese television, and I didn't see anything there either.'

'Well, all I can say is that we did demonstrate. I give you my word.'

His tone softens. 'Well, we didn't,' he says, 'but at least it was our war. What I don't understand about the British is that you are losing sons and they aren't even fighting in your country. They're fighting in someone else's.'

I'm not sure I understand either. I used to think I did until I came and lived here. Then I started to realise how nebulous everything is. Especially war.

'I don't think I fully comprehend the English democracy,' he says. 'I've thought about it a lot. We were told it was the best in the world, the very finest.'

His comment makes me laugh, albeit drily. 'Many people have been told that,' I reply, 'and a lot still seem to believe it. But I don't.'

'Well, this Iraq war shows that it is not the finest at all,' he says.

I agree. 'What I've learned,' I say, 'is that successful democracies allow the public to demonstrate, but the rulers don't respond. That's the beauty of it. They let the public protest while completely ignoring them.'

'You think that's how it works?' he asks.

'Well, that's my interpretation of how it works,' I say.

'I see,' he says, now sounding disappointed. 'But I suppose that's still better than what we've got here.'

A part of me wants to disagree with him. I certainly don't think the West is best. But it would be churlish to refuse to appreciate the many freedoms we do have. 'I suppose it is a bit better,' I say, reluctantly.

The conversation fades. I finish my Coke. He asks me how long I will be staying for. I tell him I don't know. 'At least a month,' I say. Then he asks me what I'm doing here. So I tell him, ignoring my own advice to keep that to myself.

He looks surprised. 'Nito Alves?'

I nod. 'Yes. Nito Alves.'

'Well, you be careful,' he says, his voice reducing. 'You be very careful.'

He tells me he'd like to pay for my Coke. 'And make sure you drop in again while you're here. We can talk more about your country.'

An hour later, I'm exiting the press centre in the Baixa (downtown), where I've just registered as a foreign journalist. As I'm crossing Rua Amílcar Cabral, a teenager in flip-flops calls out to me. '*Branca! Vem!*' he shouts. 'White lady! Come here!'

I walk over to where he's standing on the edge of a small crowd held back behind a strip of orange-and-white tape that spans the width of the road. Pulling me in with a hand on my shoulder, he points down the street to where a fresh layer of asphalt is being raked out and rolled over by a team of workmen. They are all either white or *mestiço*. I wonder if they're Angolan.

'Do you see?' the boy whispers. 'The tiny hole, just there!'

In the centre of the road, a small dribble of water is bubbling up from underground. 'See!' he says, nudging me. 'They come from Brazil to mend our roads but the water outwits them!' He breaks into a giggle which ripples out among the other onlookers. I laugh too, but I get told off.

'It's not funny,' an old man growls. 'You foreigners get paid to work on our roads and we get left with the consequences.' He stares furiously at the leak. In the short period of time I've been standing here – two or three minutes – it has developed into a rush of water, as if a tap has been turned on. Fifteen minutes later, when I manage to extricate myself from the conversation and the crowd, it's starting to look like the beginning of a flood.

I wander off, down a little backstreet which leads across a small square into Rua dos Mercadores (Grocers' Road). From here I enter a network of narrow lanes, barely the width of a car, where low-slung colonial buildings are thick with dirt and greenery growing from the cracks in the old brick walls. It feels like an archaeological site down here, but inside, young families are squatting. I can see washing hanging on lines, I can hear people talking and I can smell food cooking. I round another corner and find the old restaurant with tiny windows that used to be decorated with white crocheted curtains tied back in little bunches, like an Alpine hideaway. Inside, there used to be a black bull's head fixed to one of the walls and the tables were always covered in red and white chequered cloths, and tiny vases holding plastic roses. Most of all, I remember the waiter, immaculate in a bow tie and a maroon waistcoat over a long-sleeved shirt. Today, the place is abandoned. There is no sign of a bull's head or a gentle waiter and where the tables once were, plants are pushing up through the concrete floor.

I plod on, heavy-hearted. My desire to verify the past by revisiting the places I've held in my head all these years isn't coping well with its dismantling. Wherever I walk, bulldozers seem to be burrowing into the broken land, turning ancient sites into crumbling craters emptied of history. I ponder the connection between memory and landscape. Once the Baixa has been remodelled, will I discover that my memories have been remodelled too? Perhaps this is precisely that: an attempt by the elite to persuade people to forget the past. Or am I guilty of romanticising the architecture of a European power because of my own cultural upbringing? Why should Angolans maintain the bricks and mortar of colonialism? Maybe it's more appropriate to demolish every last particle of that brutal past.

I drop in on Lello's bookshop, fingering the books of poetry I think I like. But they all seem to disappoint, and the Angolan authors who most interest me don't appear to be here. That's MPLA politics for you: if you don't toe the party line, you're excluded. I exit, and follow the road east, up towards the roundabout where I once saw a woman sliced in half by an articulated lorry carrying United Nations emergency food supplies. I remember staring at this extraordinary sight from my car window, half expecting the magician Paul Daniels to appear and tell us all, in his squeaky voice, that it was just a trick. But he never came, and we were left with a long skirt filled with stomach and hips, stout legs and feet complete with little shoes. A few metres away, a T-shirt puffed proud with a pair of breasts and the woman's head still sticking out of the top, her hair tied up in a colourful cotton wrap.

Crossing Mutamba, I pass the bus station, busy with vehicles squeezing for space at the foot of the Finance Ministry. On my right, I notice the headquarters of Angola's union for musicians and artists. How odd that in all the time I lived here, I have never noticed it before. I stride up the hill to the neat grassy square with the pink Carmelite church on its south side. Strange to think that this is where my research began, with those demonstrations, years ago. Today, there are no protesters, just a handful of gardeners spraying the lawns and clipping the hedges. Crossing the pavement before me, a young man is wrapped in white bandages. Around his feet, layers of plastic bags, frayed like filo pastry. A length of heavy chain is wound round his ankles and up his calves, then to his wrists and his arms and his neck, where a thick collar is bolted with a padlock. He is dragging his feet through the dust of the street, clinking and shuffling and shifting his arms. As he steps onto the road, some of the cars let him push through the traffic, his entire body in white, his face covered in chalk. He looks like a performance artist, or a spectre from the slave trade. It may be that he has escaped the confines of Papa Kitoko, another performer of a sort, the stereotype of the African witch doctor, a magnet for foreign journalists, who locks up Luanda's insane on the outskirts of town.

It's past midday when I arrive back in my room, shining in sweat. In my absence, I've received some invitations. One is from a Brazilian man, a friend of a friend I've never met. He's having a barbecue on a balcony when the sun goes down. He'd like me to be there.

At eight, a South African photographer picks me up. I don't know him either, but we chatter away in the car about our different experiences here. He says he's only got a few days in Luanda, then he needs to get back home. Next week, he's going straight to Congo, he tells me, 'to capture Kinshasa'. He says he finds the rush conducive to taking decent pictures, but by the time we arrive at the party he's convinced me he's probably wrong. Several beers later, I'm in conversation with a large man who introduces himself as a poet. When I tell him my full name he says he knows who I am. He remembers my reporting from Malanje, he says, in 1999, when the town was being bombed for weeks and weeks by UNITA rebels. He tells me I was brave and embraces me and even now, all these years on, I'm overwhelmed to learn that someone somewhere noticed the work. At the time, I was certain no one had heard. 'And now?' asks the poet. 'What's brought you back?' I tell him about my current research into the *vinte e sete* and his response is stunning. 'I have a car,' he says, 'and a few good contacts. If you will allow it, I'd like to help.' His name is Aloisio Serrano.

14

TO SAMBIZANGA

From the other side of the garden wall, Aloisio signals his arrival with a loud honk. He's bang on time. As I pull myself up into the battered old four-by-four rumbling at the side of the road, he releases the brakes and we roll into the waiting traffic.

Sambizanga is less than four kilometres away, but it takes us nearly forty-five minutes to reach its borders at São Paulo market. I suggest we'd have been better off walking but Aloisio is certain I wouldn't be able to cope. 'It would be too hot for Lara,' he says, fixing his eyes firmly on the landscape of cars, trucks and *candongueiros* stretching ahead of us. When we eventually reach Avenida Ngola Kiluanje, the main route north out of Luanda, he changes into third gear for the first time in the journey and a welcome breeze whirls into the cabin. It doesn't last long.

Suddenly he is pulling us sharply off the main road and we are bouncing towards a large pond. My Pavlovian right foot reaches for a brake pedal that does not exist; Aloisio's presses down on an accelerator that does. I push myself back into the seat, my right hand snatching for a handle that probably fell off several years ago. With a splash, we roll and rock deeper and deeper into the water, Aloisio shaking his head in frustration and muttering under his breath, '*Esses buracos, pá!*' These bloody potholes! But with a diameter at least the length of an articulated lorry, this one stretches the limits of even the broadest definition of a pothole.

Muddy waves fan out behind us, a motorised tidal surge that chases up the ankles of a woman stepping carefully around the edge, a washing bowl of bread balanced on the crown of her head. As we trundle forward like passengers on a bad fairground ride, returning tides slap against the panels of the four-by-four, catapulting bubbles of brown spray over the bonnet.

'You'd never believe the president of this country was born here, would you?'

I want to say I wouldn't – I know exactly what he's getting at – but the story of the president's birthplace is another disputed point of Angolan history. Many of dos Santos' detractors insist he is not even Angolan, but a foreigner who came to Sambizanga as a child, having been born in São Tomé and Príncipe, the small archipelago in the Gulf of Guinea that was also colonised by the Portuguese.

'You'd think they'd want to make it look nice, wouldn't you? Smarten it up a bit.' Aloisio's voice, though gentle for such a large man, is heavy with despair. He points a finger to our right, to an elderly man in a red baseball cap collapsed into a deckchair that just about fits on a sliver of dry land. One hand is curled around a can of beer, the other about the toddler balancing on his knee. As we roll by, a crest of brown water unravels from our tyres to his toes. The old man drops his head, no matter the wet, and Aloisio raises a hand, a sign of respect and mutual exasperation.

The road–river narrows now. We pass between the wall of some kind of warehouse on one side and a row of low buildings on the other, an unofficial gateway into this vast network of family homes, drinking dens and the occasional shop, all disguised behind a collage of rusting iron and breeze blocks held together with mud, string, plastic bags, barbed wire and decades of resolve. Whether or not the president was born here, there is another, far more important reason why one might expect Sambizanga to be more than an overcrowded slum oozing neglect. For it was an underground MPLA cell from here that is credited with having started the fight for liberation in 1961, an event bursting with so much significance that one of the first feature films to be made about Angola, Sarah Maldoror's *Sambizanga*, tells this very story.

We weave further and further into the waterlogged maze, Aloisio turning to look at me every so often, tipping his head as if to say, 'Shall we pull over here?' I shrug. I have no clue where we are or where we are most likely to find someone willing to talk about the Twenty-seventh of May. It all seems a bit of a gamble to me. And then we spy what is signposted in chalk as '*a cantina*' tucked in among the inspirations of shelters and tin roofs. Aloisio reverses the Toyota hard up against a whitewashed wall from which a small boy wriggles and offers to keep guard. 'Fine,' says Aloisio, 'but if I catch you playing about, there won't be any payment!' The boy leaps into position.

We settle ourselves at a table covered by a thick square of floral plastic, with a pot of toothpicks and paper napkins placed at the centre. Bare concrete surrounds us, a clean soft grey that merges the walls and floor into one. From behind a fridge-freezer that doubles as the counter, a man in spectacles held together with tape shuffles towards us, an ice-cold *gasosa* in each of his heavily veined hands. 'Any *jinguba*?' asks Aloisio. The barman leaves the fizzy drinks on the table and shuffles away. I watch him disappear through a curtain of multicoloured ribbons on the far side of the room. When he returns he has our bowl of peanuts. Aloisio takes the opportunity to ask him for help. Waltzing carefully around the matter, never once using the words *vinte e sete de maio*, he tells him why we have come to Sambizanga. The barman listens carefully, but when it comes to his time to respond he says he does not like to discuss these things. 'But he will,' he says, looking over his shoulder and pointing with his nose to the table behind ours.

José Domingos Francisco Gonçalves is not the most reassuring of sources. His eyes are so bloodshot and his breath so heavy with alcohol, I'm sure I'm inhaling ethanol when he stands in front of me introducing himself.

'It's da UNITA,' he explains. 'You must remember the bit at the end: José Domingos Francisco Gonçalves *da UNITA*.'

I say I will try, and with that he agrees to lead us to the '*área sinistra*'.

As it turns out, the sinister area is just around the corner, less than a minute's walk. But Gonçalves da UNITA is certain we need the car. So Aloisio steers us along more flooded pathways to a large opening, completely underwater, with several different paths and muddy roads leading into it. In effect, it is a large, flooded junction shaped by a hotchpotch of buildings at its edges. We sit at the top end, the four-by-four rumbling in neutral, trying to decide where to park. There is so much water that wherever we end up, we will inevitably soak our feet and legs when we try to get out.

'Where is best?' Aloisio turns to our guide, who bats him away with an impatient hand. '*Espera, espera!* Wait!' he says, putting a mobile phone to his ear with the other. There begins a long conversation in which Gonçalves da UNITA barks down the phone, ordering someone to go and find his father. 'Tell him there are journalists who want to speak to him about Kiferro. It's very important.'

Aloisio switches off the engine and we sit in the heat, waiting for Gonçalves' father to arrive. I am struck by the balance displayed by people as they cross the junction during the following half-hour or so. Bits of concrete and large stones form dry pathways that cut diagonals through the floods. Women with containers of water on their heads, some with babies wrapped on their backs, step with remarkable skill from one awkward object to the next, their feet feeling and gripping and working hard beneath them. Not a single one displays even the slightest wobble, like gymnasts on the bar. Meanwhile, one tiny entrepreneur in oversized gumboots is making the most of the rainy season. He's selling piggybacks to the elderly, the lame and the lazy. His tiny frame folds down to allow each passenger to clamber on, then, legs spread, he rises slowly upwards, finds his balance and marches smartly through the lake. We watch him passing back and forth with all shapes and sizes clinging to his skinny body, gleefully rolling his kwanzas into the pocket of his shirt. I think back to primary school, to the story I learned of St Christopher, and wonder how on earth it is that so many Angolans believe in God.

A tap on the back window signals the arrival of Gonçalves' father. Taller and thinner than his son, he holds his upper body in a stoop, his neck angled forward, vulture-like, to a long chin. Half of his face is a mix of blues, greens and dark purples, heavy bruising from a fall or a fight, and he's wobbly when he walks. He clambers into the front of the car, puffing and coughing, his rich breath confirming what he later admits – that like his son, he lives for alcohol.

'*Careca*,' he croaks through a smile when we ask his name. 'Baldy. But my real name is Lino Gracia Mateus.' He points to my sound recorder and asks whether I am going to turn it on or not.

'If you don't mind,' I say as politely as possible, but managing to irritate him profoundly.

'Why would I mind?' he asks angrily. 'What do we have to lose talking to you? I have nothing. Of course you can record it. Of course you can use my name. Say what you like! It's time they were told the truth.'

Humiliated or humbled, I'm not sure which, I turn it on.

Senhor Mateus begins slowly. 'It's like this,' he says, instantly gaining the full fix of our attention. 'Factionalism began as a sort of joke.' I think of what Victoria Brittain told me – that some of the people she knew made the odd joke about the *vinte e sete* – but Mateus is saying something quite different. 'It began as a game of football,' he explains. The youth wing of the MPLA, the JMPLA, formed a football team for a tournament in Sambizanga. 'It was on the Bukavu football field, which we used to call the field of independence.'

The words echo. 'The field of independence.' It's his son, who develops this rather theatrical repetition quite intensively over the course of the next hour. Mateus flicks his wrist at the back seat, a casual shut up, then continues resolutely with his story.

'Progresso was the name of our team. It wasn't a big team back then – there were nine players – but it won the tournament. After this came the championship, the first nationwide championship since the nation became independent. For this we had the Jubas, the Gingumas and the other big guys like Augusto Pedro, who brought the team to eleven players. It also got its first president, this man who had various fishing boats and who had grown up here in Sambizanga. The trouble with him was, he never turned up, partly because he had gone to live in another neighbourhood, in Bairro Operário. But the team was doing better and better.'

'So what happened?' I ask.

'*Calma!* I'm getting there!'

Aloisio agrees: 'He's telling the story very well. Let him take his time.'

I mouth a silent apology.

'What happened was that Nito Alves was elected as the new president, and the football meetings grew larger. They stopped taking place at Kiferro's house...' Mateus points through the windscreen at a pale-blue bungalow to our right, 'and they started taking place at Salão Faria. We used to go and listen, and soon... *eh pá!* It became something that happened every day at six o'clock in the evening. And by this time, they weren't talking about football: these were party political meetings with Nito Alves. They were preparing for mass participation and were recruiting followers for the factionalists and for the *vinte e sete de maio*.'

A loud tapping noise distracts us. Three children are trying to climb onto the back of the vehicle. Aloisio leaps out of the car, cursing the water as he lands in it, and shoos the children away. '*Sai! Sai!*' he shouts, clapping his hands, and they run off laughing to the other side of the water, where they sit down on a long concrete step to watch us from a safer distance. Aloisio gets back into the car, tutting and apologising.

Mateus carries on as if he'd never been interrupted. 'On 24 May, the meeting was much, much bigger than anything we'd seen before. There were people turning up from Cazenga,' he says, swinging his voice around the words, almost in song, 'and other *bairros* too. In fact, there were so many that Salão Faria did not have enough space to fit us all in. The whole world was there. So us kids, *os kandengues*, we were sent outside.'

At the time, Mateus was just fourteen years old, which surprises me because I had assumed from his face and body that he was well into his sixties. He's not even hit fifty.

'Then on the night of 26 May, we were all here, sitting around talking in a nice crowd, when at midnight a whole lot of arms were distributed by followers of Nito, like Kiferro and the late Ginguma. Everyone was given a gun. All the young ones were obliged to take one. No one was left out.'

Mateus and his friends were terrified. 'We were shouted at,' he recalls, '"*Kandengues!* Nobody is going anywhere. These arms are for the morning. Stay alert for when we come and knock on your doors!"' he says, looking at me hard in the eyes. 'The aim, you must understand, was not to kill Agostinho Neto.' He is speaking in long, slow syllables now. 'All of us were conscious that this was a revolt to change the system.'

After independence, the people of Sambizanga had become increasingly frustrated. Their living standards had remained very low. Mateus recalls Nito's speeches with real enthusiasm, his wet eyes opening up with excitement, his voice getting louder and louder. I notice the red light on my sound recorder flickering, a warning of distortion.

'He used to explain how, in the bush, when they had been fighting for our freedom, they had dreamed of an equal society in which blacks would enjoy the same rights and opportunities as others. Nito used to tell us that everything and everyone had to be equal. He used to say that there shouldn't be any more problems of colour or race. But we could all see that the whites were still running things, and he told us that we should be running things. He told us that we shouldn't be ordered about any more. He said that if you have an illiterate white, he too should be a road sweeper. And if there was a *mulato* who hadn't studied properly, he too should be sweeping the streets.'

A loud echo, 'Sweeping the streets!' punctuates the pause. Mateus is catching his breath. He wants to show us exactly where these conversations happened. He points to the children sitting on the step opposite us: 'I used to sit with Nito Alves just about there. He was a man who was much better accepted and much more popular than Neto, especially in the traditional *bairros* like this one. He didn't have any bodyguards. He just hung around with us on his own. He'd sit with me on the floor, just hanging out on the floor.'

'Do you mean, then, that you did not like Neto?' I ask.

Mateus releases a frustrated sigh. '*Eh páaa...*' He shakes his head at me, and I feel another telling-off coming on. 'We were not angry with the president. It was the men around him we disliked. Lúcio Lara and Iko... Iko...'

'Carreira?' I offer.

'Eish! Let me tell the story, will you? All right. Yes. It was Iko Carreira, this lot, this ring of *mestiços* surrounding Neto, who were filling his head with this stuff. This is why, on the Twenty-seventh of May, we left here and went unarmed to the palace to talk to Neto, to be heard by Neto.' He pauses. He seems to be running over the events in his mind, his eyes cast down, wrinkled concentration gathering on his forehead. When he starts speaking again it is to himself, under his breath, very softly. 'We went to the palace and we were met with Cuban bombs.'

'Cuban bombs,' comes the echo.

'How many of you went to the palace?' asks Aloisio.

'All the people from Sambizanga. We went without arms. Some went to the radio station, but the rest of us went to the palace.' Shouting, he says again, 'We did not have arms. We went on this demonstration peacefully! *Pacífica!*'

'*Pacífica!*' his son shouts to the window.

'But because it was the time of the one-party system,' Mateus comes back, 'the people who were in charge were them.'

'Them,' says his son with a thud.

Mateus continues: 'The chief of the army sent tanks, Cuban tanks, to fire at us, to make us go back home. We each tried to protect ourselves. Some of us managed to get away, some did not. And it was this that provoked some of those in Nito Alves' support base to come up with some other ideas.'

I am not sure what he means by 'other ideas'.

'It was not Nito Alves who sent anyone out to kill,' explains Mateus. 'Do you see? I hope you are listening carefully.'

'I am, I am.'

'These ideas about those bodies. It was the group, the crew who supported Nito Alves, who brought them here. There were some very big names among them. *Grandes cabeças!* Helder Neto,[32] Bula, Gato, Saydi Mingas... They were all brought here. Then Kiferro took them to his mother's house. That house there.' He points at the same blue house he mentioned earlier and begins to shout. 'When they realised – Kiferro and his friends – that there was no way out, that the whole of Sambizanga was surrounded by tanks, this is when the panic set in. The entire neighbourhood was being held. You could not breathe for tanks, nor even take a step without bumping into a Cuban soldier or a DISA.'

The mention of DISA sets father and son into rivers of laughter, and soon we are all laughing. 'DISA!' shouts Gonçalves da UNITA. 'DISA was a nightmare, wasn't it?'

His father is nodding. 'Even if you took one tiny step backwards they would arrest you on the spot. Like this, everyone was taken prisoner. Every man, every youth. All of us, herded up and taken to the Campo Académico up the street, where we were made to lie on the floor, tanks all around us, for hours. I was fourteen at the time. Fourteen! And I was sure it would be my last day on this earth,' says Mateus, his voice dropping to a low rumble.

Word had spread that Iko Carreira had given the order to reduce Sambizanga to rubble. 'He wanted to finish us off completely. Our only hope was that Neto would intervene.' But while they were all lying on the ground, certain of their pending deaths, Kiferro and his crew were wondering what to do with the people they had captured, these leaders of the MPLA. 'They killed the lot of them just here.' Mateus points to an alleyway straight ahead of us. 'Just down there at the black hole, we called it the *carro de Ngunga* [Ngunga's car]. That was the place where we used to dump our rubbish.'

When news got out about the murders, the situation became considerably more dangerous. Cuban and Angolan soldiers went on the rampage, looking for Kiferro and his followers.

'They should only have gone after the people who were involved in the conspiracy of the Twenty-seventh of May,' says Mateus. 'The innocent should have been left alone. But it was too late. Many innocent people died. Many, many.'

His son leans forward, his hand on his father's shoulder. 'Many innocents died.'

'How many do you think died in Sambizanga alone?' asks Aloisio.

Mateus becomes quite distressed by this question. '*Eh pá! Woah!* I don't know the numbers.' He shakes his head and flaps at the air in front of his face. 'I didn't count. But among my group of friends there was a lad called Chikokai and another called Moises. But every family in Sambizanga lost one or two of its own. Many were killed by soldiers while they were searching for Kiferro.'

'So where was Kiferro?' I ask. 'Had he run away?'

He drops his chin to his chest, almost smiling, but his head is still shaking from side to side. 'Kiferro,' he says eventually, 'had been touched by witchcraft. He became a stick.' Mateus raises his left hand in the air. 'So he could be here with us one moment' – he shakes his hand about – 'but as soon as the soldiers arrived, he'd disappear.' The hand comes down sharp and vanishes between his legs. He bursts into laughter again, and we all start giggling at the image of Kiferro the magic stick. 'The troops looked everywhere but they could not find him. Wherever they went, Kiferro would disappear. And so they began taking other people who looked like Kiferro and killing them instead.' Our laughter fizzles out. 'The longer it went on, the longer they could see that Kiferro wasn't going to come forward, the more they killed. Once they had caught everyone from that group who supported Nito Alves they began taking members of Kiferro's family instead. His brothers.'

'They killed them too?' I ask.

A long hiss whistles from Mateus' mouth, like air being forced from a tyre. 'Ayyyyyyy!' He winces, twitching his head, as if an invisible hand is hitting him about the face. '*Eh Papa! Papaaaaa!* They put a noose around anyone. Fina lost a son who looked like Kiferro. He was called Idílio. Idyll.' He smashes a fist onto the dashboard, making us all jump. 'They made a mistake. They got it wrong.' He groans, painfully. 'Eyyyyyyyy! They took nephews too, and when they had killed his nephews they came and got their mothers as well.' Mateus looks even older. Recalling these times seems to be ageing him, a year for every sentence, greying his skin, exhausting him. 'Eventually it became clear that Kiferro would have to come forward. And he did.' He slaps a hand over his head. 'We never saw him again. *Nunca mais*.'

His son offers a final word, '*Nunca*', which seems to bring the conversation to its natural end, but Mateus has other ideas. He suggests we go for a bit of a stroll. There is something he wants to show us. We all clamber out of the four-by-four, leaping for the shallows, and he beckons us around the edges towards a larger building that might be a school.

'On 28 May, this is where the tanks came. They swept through the entire area and came down here.' Mateus chucks an arm forward, signalling to a long line of shacks stretching away from us. 'They destroyed more than 100 houses right here. It was the Cubans. They used so much force.'

We follow him down the pathway, walking beside the line of corrugated-iron homes, listening to his mutterings. 'All along here. All these homes crushed.' The building I thought was a school is, he says, an indoor basketball court. 'It used to be homes as well, but they crushed them too.' He begins to moan about basketball. 'We had some of the best football players in Angola, here in Sambizanga, and they were all killed. It's a pure lie to say that the footballers were behind the deaths of the commanders. It wasn't them.'

From one of the shacks, bent over in black, a figure appears, smoke blowing over its back. This very small, very old woman wears no shoes and walks with a stick. Her body is so worn down that the length of her back is curled over, her head at the same height as her hips. As she passes, all I can see of her face is the long wooden pipe tucked into one side of her mouth.

'Good day, mama,' says Mateus. She mumbles something back about a funeral. We stand in a row watching her as she steps slowly into the water, prodding her stick ahead of her, the hem of her dress floating on the surface.

'Today,' says Mateus, 'the Angolan people are completely tranquil and quiet. We watch, we see and we say nothing. This is purely because of what happened in 1977. People remember this. They cannot forget. That is why so many of us drink. We need to forget what is in our head.'

I think about the response one friend had when I told him I was going to Sambizanga to try to find out what happened here: 'I don't know why you bother. All you will find is drunks.'

I don't know what to say to Mateus, nor to his son. I could offer them some money, pay them for their time and their courage, but I fear this might offend them. We turn and start walking back towards the car. The old lady has only just reached the other side of the water. Mateus is watching her. He grips my arm, tightly, desperately, and looking to his son, he says, 'We held a funeral for him in 1994. We thought he was dead.'

Gonçalves da UNITA butts in. 'I was captured by UNITA in 1990. I was made to go and fight for Savimbi. I stayed with them for over ten years.'

'He didn't come back till 2002,' says his father, blinking back his grief. 'People didn't believe he was still alive. It has been hard for me because he is UNITA and I am MPLA. He speaks Umbundu and Kikongo. I speak Kimbundu. UNITA have forgotten him now, just like the MPLA have forgotten me.'

His son explains, 'He also spent so much time away fighting that when he came back, his daughter, my sister, didn't know who he was.'

'She calls me uncle,' says Mateus, 'because she doesn't believe I'm her father.'

With that, he seems to have said all he wants to say. Now it's time to walk back to wherever he came from, his son following a few steps behind. Aloisio and I offer our thanks, but it is only the son, Gonçalves da UNITA, who turns and waves.

Back at the house, I put a chair on the porch outside my room, and sit in the shade for the afternoon, transcribing the morning's recording onto my laptop. I'm almost at the end of the interview when I'm joined by the two dogs of the house. One is a little white thing with smudged, pink eyes, a miniature poodle of sorts whose name I can never remember. Her son is Alfredo, a long, low blonde, the spitting image of a Dandie Dinmont. I'd find him hard to resist were it not for one particularly unpleasant habit he has, a daily indulgence often performed in front of me. Here he comes, sidling up to his mother, now cowering by the wall. He edges closer and closer then throws himself on top of her, proceeding to hump his hips against her head for several long and painful minutes, pausing briefly to catch his breath, then to alter slightly the angle of assault by shuffling his hind legs in a frantic pirouette. Finished, he trots off to the flower bed and flops onto his ribs, panting and contented beneath the shade of a bush. His mother, now pitifully sad, is pawing at the dollop of semen between her ears and repeatedly sneezing. What I find most disturbing about this performance is that she never attempts to defend herself from her son, not even to run away. She simply crouches down, her stained tail tucked hard as a bullet between her hind legs, and waits miserably for the business to begin.

15

◆

THE LITTLE RED BOOK

'Are you sure he's not dead?' I ask.

'He's sleeping,' says Aloisio, for the second time, 'but don't worry. Someone will know who he is.'

In the wing mirror, I keep watching the body – more like a pile of clothes – and it stays perfectly still until the road twists, snatching it out of sight.

'The last time I came along here, it was tarmacked.' Aloisio's memory makes him laugh; his cheeks bulge, all taut and shiny. 'The president was making a visit so they smartened it up – it was the Chinese – and after a few months the rain washed it all away. You can't see any tarmac now, can you?'

I cannot. 'Are you sure it was this road?'

My question makes Aloisio snigger, but the cynicism remains etched into his voice. 'Why would they do it properly? It's not as though he is going to come back any time soon, is it?'

We round another bend and the subject switches again. Now, I can see flat banks and roll-ins, launches and pyramids, and even a section that could pass for a wall ride. What could be the perfect skatepark is the perfect nightmare for drivers of cars and trucks, and men thrusting their bodies behind big-wheeled wooden barrows loaded down with carburettors, raw meat, sacks of charcoal and God knows what else. Aloisio urges his lumbering four-by-four towards the first steep hump pushing up from the red earth. The vehicle pitches into a steep angle and I calm myself with the myth that even London's double-decker buses can tilt to forty-five degrees without falling over. 'He's just around the corner,' says Aloisio without the remotest hint of distress, 'on the other side of this.'

We park up outside a row of detached, two-storey houses, their faded shades of pink paint a marker to the metropole. These neat brick buildings, each with a small courtyard encased in fronds of iron fencing, stand out in the sand slum, not far from where we were yesterday in Sambizanga. They are colonial housing, abandoned by Portuguese traders and downwardly mobile whites when they realised that the privileges of colonial dictatorship were coming to an end.

A svelte man is standing in loose nylon trousers and pointed leather shoes in the shade of a corrugated roof. Aloisio leads me towards him and introduces us.

'So you've come to talk to me about the *vinte e sete de maio*?' The man's voice is filled with suspicion.

'Yes,' I reply, a sense of dread scampering up my throat.

But he's not interested in my anxieties. He takes me by the hand and leads me across the concrete patio to a pair of rickety wooden doors with dirty mosquito netting nailed into the panels. We enter what appears to be a classroom, the dusty air thickening in the heat of the afternoon. A whiteboard stands at one end, and plastic tables and chairs are positioned in clusters, as if some sort of strategy meeting has been taking place. I wonder what the Portuguese is for blue-sky thinking and brainstorming – has management-speak reached the depths of Luanda's *musseques* too? – but my musing is interrupted. The man I am here to interview is keen to get started. He gestures to a chair.

'The *vinte e sete de maio* marks one of the most significant stages in Angola's development. It tells you something about our true history, so you are quite right,' he says, breaking into a smile, 'to want to know.'

His voice is polished and smooth. The sentences roll out, oiled and fluent, each word pinned to the next with a tidy consonant or a carefully rounded set of vowels.

'I will begin,' he says, 'with Nito Alves.' But before he does, he explains the conditions of the conversation. I can quote him as much as I want but I must not identify him. 'And it would be better if you refrained from asking questions about my work. I have a family and children. I know you understand.'

This is fine with me. From now on, he will be Senhor Carmoto.

'Good. And so to Nito!'

He crosses his legs and lengthens his back and begins talking in methodical sentences, as if he is giving an important lecture – which I suppose he is. 'He was a wonderfully expressive man who spoke excellent Portuguese. He had a very good grounding in political theory, mostly in Marxism–Leninism. He was also influenced by Maoism. In those days, we all had little pocket books produced in China by Mao Zedong. A lot of Nito's speeches were scattered with his words. These were the speeches he gave at the CPBs [Comissões Populares de Bairro], the neighbourhood commissions, when huge crowds gathered to listen to the leaders. Dr Neto also gave tremendous speeches but the trouble was' – Carmoto's right index finger suddenly springs up, erect, between us – 'the people liked Nito more than Neto.'

'Why?' I ask.

'Because Nito was more eloquent. His speeches were *terra a terra*,' down to earth, he explains, 'but most of all, he focused on the fundamental problems of poverty and inequality and, critically, of racism.' He gives a little wink as he says the word 'racism' and I'm not sure if this is to tease or comfort me and my whiteness. 'Nito would ask questions like, "Why, after defeating the Portuguese, are whites and *mulatos* still dominating blacks?" and he told us that there would be peace only when whites and *mulatos* were also cleaning the streets, not just us, the blacks.'

I tell him I've heard this before. 'But do you think he really meant it, or was it simply a populist rhetorical device?'

His eyes sprout surprise. 'Certainly not,' he says. 'What is more, only the whites and the *mulatos* received fellowships to study abroad.'

That can't be true. I know black Angolans who studied in Russia and Cuba. 'I've met them.'

'Maybe a few,' he says, 'but most were whites and *mulatos*. And when it came to manual labour, the only people who did it were blacks. Even the whites and *mulatos* who had not studied did not do manual labour.'

This is no moot point. During the final decade of colonial rule, more than half of the Portuguese immigrants to Angola had received no formal education. Between 1965 and 1972, fewer than 17 per cent had been educated beyond primary school; and in May 1975, six months before the MPLA took power, a Portuguese newspaper reported that only 15 per cent of whites in Angola were skilled.[33] The bulk of Portuguese immigrants were illiterate farm labourers with ambitions to become small businessmen earning much more money for far less work than was possible back home.[34]

In Carmoto's view, the trouble for Nito was that although he was a minister and also a member of the Central Committee, he was not at the top of the elite's social hierarchy. With unmistakeable bitterness in his voice, he explains, 'Above him came men like Iko Carreira, Lúcio Lara and Henrique Onambwe. They tried to silence him, but the thing about Nito was that he could not be silenced.'

'So did you ever hear him speak?' I ask.

'Oh yes. I was a member of the MPLA youth wing.'

'The JMPLA?'

He claps enthusiastically, '*Sim, sim!* What we wanted was independence based on equality, and we could see it wasn't happening. The Central Committee never spoke about this, so we began listening to Nito instead.'

'So he was the de facto youth leader?'

'Not quite. But he began to emerge as the leader in the shadows,' he explains. 'We had the formal leader, Neto, and the informal leader, Nito. And you know what an informal leader does, don't you?' He gives me another little wink.

Alas, I do not.

'Power is usurped!' he says, releasing a strange hissing sound, then drawing a sharp breath and raising a finger to his lips, running it around them, his eyes narrowing. 'You see, Nito began scooping sympathy away from Neto. But Neto was intelligent and very temperate. He was someone who would insist on the importance of waiting. Unfortunately, while he was happy to wait and to observe, he got exploited.'

Presumably, by Nito.

'No!' he says, shaking his head impatiently. 'Like I said, it was Lara, Iko and Onambwe. They're the ones who fed Neto ideas. But while they were doing that, students, artists and musicians had all become part of FAPLA and this helped to increase support for Nito within the army.' He names David Zé and Urbano de Castro, two of Angola's most popular musicians during the late 1960s and early 1970s. 'They all supported Nito.'

'Wasn't Artur Nunes another?' I ask.

The reference sparks delight. 'So you know!'

I know a few, but regrettably cannot understand all of the songs because many are sung in Kimbundu, a language I've yet to learn. 'I prefer to listen alone,' I admit. 'That older music floods me with memories of the time I lived here. It makes me feel so sad.'

He nods generously. 'The tragedy is that they were banned. Their music was prohibited and, later, they were killed.'

In fact, there never was an official ban, but it is true that after 1977 their songs were not broadcast for many years.[35] In itself, this silence was quite a feat: de Castro alone produced more records than any other Angolan artist from 1969 to 1978. Yet such was the self-censorship that followed the Twenty-seventh of May that, even in 2001, only one of his records could be found in Angola's national radio collection. In many ways, the killing of de Castro, Nunes and Zé mirrored the jailing, by the colonial authorities in 1959 and 1960, of members of the iconic band Ngola Ritmos, who defied colonialism by singing in autochthonous languages and using local instruments.[36] In both cases, the musicians were so popular, particularly in the *musseques*, that the governing elite viewed them as a threat.

Notwithstanding, Carmoto believes that the real trouble began when an elite group from the army, the 9th Brigade, came out in support of Nito. 'It is crucial,' he says, pointing at my hands, 'that you remember, when we talk about factionalism, that the 9th Brigade was fundamental. It was they who broke down the doors of São Paulo prison, what I call "the coup in the prisons".'

So it *was* a coup!

'Oh yes,' he says, confidently, 'it was definitely a *coup d'état* – the central idea was to take power – but it was a crashing failure. Thousands protested, but there would have been even more if they hadn't been so afraid. I, for one, did not go because I was too scared. We knew that the country had to change and that this would only happen with a *coup d'état*, but we never thought it would be violent.'

I'm astounded by this admission of naivety. Surely they must have known that violence was inevitable in a coup?

But Carmoto blames the involvement of the 9th Brigade, the distribution of arms across the *musseques*, and also the release from São Paulo prison, not only of political prisoners, but of hundreds of thieves, no-gooders and what he calls 'dangerous delinquents'. Another factor, he says, was that many people were afraid of how the defence minister would react. 'We didn't know what Iko Carreira would do when he realised that the uprising was racially motivated. He was white.'

As it turned out, he believes they were right to have been afraid, 'Because then the Cubans were sent in and, oh my goodness, the moment they got involved, the most awful things began to happen. People started fleeing for their lives.'

Carmoto hesitates.

'Tell her what happened,' Aloisio encourages him, 'you need to tell her.'

'Yes, yes, I know,' he says, smiling at me. 'Well, that's when the real retaliation began. Persecution. Man against man. And because most of the meetings with Nito had taken place in Sambizanga, that's where the repression started. It was just like Soweto.'

This is an astonishing comment. He's referring to the Soweto uprising, which took place on 16 June 1976. Thousands of pupils in the Johannesburg township took to the streets to protest against the apartheid Bantu education policy, which forced all schools to teach in Afrikaans as well as English. By the time the protests ended, hundreds had been killed, the overwhelming majority of them black Africans shot by the state security forces. Ironically, the Soweto uprising had been inspired, in part, by Angola's independence: that a socialist liberation movement could defeat a US-backed South African invasion gave great hope to the African National Congress and the broader anti-apartheid movement. Is Carmoto really putting the MPLA government on a par with South Africa's National Party, and the Cuban army with the SADF?

'The people of Soweto and the people of Sambizanga shared a characteristic of great courage,' he says, diplomatically.

This may be true, but the Soweto students weren't attempting a coup and they didn't kill any members of the regime.

'But Nito Alves did not order it,' he counters. 'It was a moment of anarchy, an appalling error. Even Comandante Bula was killed and he was one of our own, from Sambizanga, very dear to us all, a man who did a lot for this country. He was normal. Like us. He was black.'

'So why was he killed?'

Carmoto looks a little upset. 'Like I said,' he says gently, 'there was confusion.' He is certain that the footballers from Progresso carried out the killings, but he is quick to remind me that, in turn, they were also killed for their actions. 'You must understand,' he says, almost pleading with me, 'that the people of Sambizanga are still reluctant to build anything on the land where those killings happened, on the *área sinistra*.

They think that if they do, they will be accused, even today, of being factionalists.'

It is this enduring fear that fascinates me, and the fact that so many people still carry with them this deep anxiety of guilt. Even Carmoto, an educated man with a relatively well-paid job, seems to be afraid.

'You're right,' he says. 'My memories of that day remain very clear. The first thing I did was dig a hole and bury all my stuff in the ground. Everything I had that related to Mao Zedong I buried. Even my copy of *The Little Red Book*. It must still be there in Sambizanga.' The thought brings a smile to his face. 'But I had to evacuate. We all did. We knew we couldn't stay because factionalism was associated with the young. They had seen us listening to Nito. There is no question about it. They would have killed us.'

Having hidden his belongings, Carmoto disguised himself as a woman and fled to the home of a relative. 'Not even the children in the house recognised me,' he says with a bit of a chuckle. I'm tempted to ask him what he wore: did he don any lipstick, or was it just a headscarf and skirt? But as gentle as he is, I'm not sure he'd appreciate my more banal enquiries. 'I was lucky to have survived,' he says. 'Many thousands were killed. Many friends too. Most of them were buried in a mass grave in the cemetery of Mulemba with just a bit of dust thrown over them. There wasn't even time to make coffins.'

Like Maria Reis, he believes that many of the deaths resulted from people taking revenge for petty matters: 'It became an excuse to kill those you didn't like.'

So does he blame Neto for the statement he made, insisting there was no time for pardons or trials?

'No, no. Neto wanted to give them clemency,' he says. 'He said he wanted to resolve it nicely. It was the men around him who were so awful. Lara, Onambwe, Iko.'

These three again. Surely Neto had some independence of mind. He was president, after all. Isn't Carmoto simply blaming these three because of their skin colour?

'I don't know about that,' he says. 'But the trouble we have now is that many of us are completely depressed because of the *vinte e sete*. There are people with psychoses, people who are completely unhinged. It's just like the war. Families who lost three, four or five children. Totally dejected. They have nothing. They think their lives ended that day.'

This comment rouses Aloisio, who's been sitting quietly in the heat, listening to us talking while crunching his way through two packets of Jacob's Cream Crackers. '*Coitado, coitado.* The poor wretches,' he says, swaying back and forth. 'Our dreams used to be for revolution. We had social activists and singers who insisted on independence, who insisted that we could not have whites and *mulatos* running the place. We had ideology back then, something to believe in. Now, the only dream you can have is to be a member of the MPLA. That's the only way to get rich. Everyone else has been reduced to beggars, paupers and tramps.' He punctuates the end of the sentence by pushing two more crackers into his mouth, my own drying up just watching him.

I look to Carmoto.

'He's right,' he says. 'The MPLA is too strong. It's a party–state and a state–party. Angolan people, even MPLA people, always hoped for a strong UNITA in opposition. But we don't have this. All we have is MPLA.' He pauses to swallow the last drop of a pineapple fizzy drink that's going flat at his feet. He holds the bottle upside-down, high in the air, catching the last of the viscous yellow liquid with his tongue.

'But this isn't all,' he says, placing the bottle carefully back on the floor. 'Public transport here is so unsatisfactory that people have to walk kilometre after kilometre on foot every day. They are totally exhausted. So we have this situation where everyone is against the government, but they are too tired or too afraid to do anything.'

Aloisio holds up half a cracker, signalling an intervention. 'Even the few we have, who are good and brave... they will all end up like Mfulumpinga.'

Mfulumpinga Nlandu Victor was an outspoken political leader, a man never afraid to criticise anyone, not even the president. His voluptuous character was captured in his face, a sculptor's dream, so thick with flesh that at times he looked like a bloodhound of a man. Then, one day, on 2 July 2004, he was shot outside the Luanda offices of the mainly Bakongo political party he had led since 1991. The authorities insisted he was killed by gangsters. Few believe that story.

I turn to Carmoto again. 'Does this mean there can never be change?'

'It is still very dangerous,' he says. 'The MPLA has such force and, with our history, you cannot joke.'

He stretches his arms above him and starts to laugh. Aloisio is muttering agreements and I feel persuaded by the general pessimism of their analysis. However, there are some changes afoot already. At least, today, Angolans can go to the ballot box and vote. 'Doesn't that show that society is beginning to open up?' I ask.

Carmoto is still a bit giggly. 'Oh, yes,' he says, enthusiastically, 'the door is definitely opening.'

'Yah,' picks up Aloisio, like a low rumble of thunder, 'but on the other side someone is standing with a machete.'

Disturbing for its seriousness, this image seems suddenly hilarious. In our plastic chairs, we find refuge in laughter. When we finally calm down, Aloisio suggests we call it a day. He's concerned about spending so much time in one place, talking so critically. You never know who might be listening. You never know who might be watching. Also, Carmoto has another appointment in a *bairro* on the other side of town. Since rush-hour traffic can easily turn a five-kilometre hop into three hours of fume-filled misery, he needs to get moving. He bids us both farewell, apologising for having to leave and offering to meet me again if there is anything I don't understand or any questions requiring 'better answers', as he puts it. I feel vastly undeserving of such generosity.

Later, when Aloisio drops me back at the house, he offers to take me to Mulemba cemetery, the place Carmoto spoke of, where so many of his friends are buried. 'It's critical you see it,' says Aloisio thoughtfully. 'I could pick you up tomorrow, towards the end of the day, when I've finished work.'

16

◆

KILOMETRE FOURTEEN

I must be hearing things. Someone has just walked down our street whistling 'O come all ye faithful, joyful and triumphant'. For a few peculiar seconds, I'm a child in a church half listening to a sermon while pondering the vicar's bald patch and the fringe of brown hair that circles his head. I'm trying to remember whether he really did look like Friar Tuck, or whether that's my imagination at work, when the phone rings.

'*Alô*,' I say.

'Lara Pawson?' a male voice responds.

'*Sim. Eu sou a Lara.*'

'This is Justino,' says the voice, sounding awfully official, 'from the press centre.'

'Justino?' I don't know anyone by that name.

'Justino,' the voice insists.

I'm racking my brains for a face. 'But I've never met anyone at the press centre called Justino.'

'I'm calling to check this is your number,' he says.

'Well now you know it is,' I reply. 'Is that it?'

'We want to know what you are doing here,' he says.

'Reporting. You know that. I wrote that in the form.'

'We know what you say you are doing,' says Justino, 'but we also know what you don't say you are doing.'

'You've lost me there,' I say, trying not to display any anxiety.

'We know why you are really here,' he says, cross.

I lie: 'I don't know what you mean.'

'I'm sure you do,' says Justino. 'And I will be calling you again.'

He hangs up, and for a moment I feel very bothered. Then I engage my brain and telephone the press centre.

'Please can I speak to Justino?'

'Who?' says the woman at the end of the line.

'Justino,' I say.

'Hold on.' There's a click. I'm not sure if she's hung up or put me on hold. So I wait. A few seconds later, she picks up. 'Justino is not here,' she says.

'Do you know when he will be?' I ask.

'Hold on.' Another click. She's gone a bit longer this time. When she finally comes back she apologises. 'I'm sorry, madam, but we don't have a Justino here.'

I thank her and hang up. Now I'm starting to feel uncomfortably conspicuous. Was the call simply to let me know that the *bufos* know what I'm up to? Or was it a one-off, some joker who has nothing to do with the secret police at all? Flashes of paranoia start to rattle me. Perhaps I shouldn't be doing this research? Perhaps I should be more careful about whom I interview? Perhaps Senhor Carmoto was a set-up? Maybe he threw in that line about cross-dressing for a bit of a laugh. Was it the brainwave of some bod from the Ministry of the Interior, paid to cook up stories to feed foolish foreign journalists like me? I wish I'd never given him my mobile number.

When Aloisio turns up, I'm hugely relieved, even if going to the cemetery does mean enduring more traffic. I say traffic, but as we head north, beyond the port of Luanda, swathes of people are marching beside us. They walk so close, I can hear them panting as they pace along, fully focused on the business of getting home. The odd pedestrian flashes a smile our way, but at no point does Aloisio consider giving anyone a lift. 'Take him,' he warns, 'and the whole lot will be climbing on board.' So on we go, cool and comfortable, while the lithe stride forward, loaded down with buckets and briefcases, and basins of belongings. Occasionally we are overtaken, even by a young woman with a baby bouncing on her back, a toddler curled around her hip and a bowl on her head.

Eventually the jam loosens and we progress at jogging speed. Still some of the people keep pace, mainly young men with nothing to carry, trotting along, marvels of energy, keen to get home.

Still on the coastal road, to our left is the Atlantic and to our right, Boa Vista, a tidal wave of rubbish and red earth rising high above the road. Its panorama of the ocean is what gave the neighbourhood its name – Good View – but given that it is a slum it seems like a sick joke. I let out a sigh of what is probably pity, appalled by the poverty, but Aloisio encourages me to look closer at the complexity of this community. A small building at the foot of the clay cliff is an evangelical church that doubles as a medical centre. Higher up, a boy is herding a group of goats, chivvying them along the steep slopes of pulped plastic bags that suck the animals' legs down into the soil. Along the ridge there are hundreds of shacks, the minority built from breeze blocks, the majority sculpted out of supermarket trolleys and wheelbarrows, abandoned chassis and old car bumpers, clay piping, corrugated iron, bent bike frames, chicken wire, bottles, rubber gloves, fishing nets, tree branches, flags, and even the odd shoe. Lower down, some of these homes have rigged-up electricity, a cat's cradle of wires syphoned from somewhere else. Above all of this, a flock of cattle egrets are flapping and scrounging, their snow-white bodies bright against the mounds of litter into which they needle their beaks.

Aloisio points to a young girl upon the brow of the hill. I spy on her through my camera's zoom, admiring her twists of hair decorated with beads that swing and rattle around her shoulders. She's playing with someone I can't see from down here. On the next ridge, a man in a baseball cap sits back to front on a chair, his jeans rolled up and a shirt flung around his neck like a scarf. He seems to be looking far beyond the horizon, as if commanding this entire space. Further along, a group of men are hunched in a circle, playing cards. Beneath them, groups of children lug containers of water up the huge treadmill of rubbish, heaving and hauling one after the other all the way to the top of the hill.

Long after we've left Boa Vista behind, we are still stuck in the tightness of traffic. I cannot imagine what it must be like to endure this commute every evening, at the end of a day's work. Aloisio says many don't bother. During the week they sleep in Luanda's city centre – on office floors, down darkened side streets, in the compounds of friends and family or the bed of a girlfriend – only returning home at weekends. I ponder the complaints we make in London about a forty-minute bus journey in a comfy seat with a newspaper and feel a sudden rage at Britain, where despite our own flaccid flesh we continue to regurgitate the idea of the lazy African.

My temper abates when, after an hour and a half, we finally turn off the main road and head inland towards the cemetery. Leaving the tarmac creates its own set of problems. Now we are faced with several kilometres of flooded, muddied tracks. Ahead of us, a single *candongueiro* is empty of passengers but still so low-slung it looks close to sinking. In front of that, an articulated lorry loaded down with sacks of cement is rocking from side to side, its metal joints creaking so loudly they sound as if they might snap. As usual, the problem is the potholes. Chasms of sludge. In places, we slalom through the mud, skidding into pits of water where the track drops so deep our wing mirrors level with the doorsteps of the shops and bars on either side. If that were not enough to worry about, we are also losing the light. Alarmed, I look to Aloisio. 'This is nothing,' he says, as calm as ever, 'and anyway, we're almost there.'

The sky is wrapped in ribbons of pink by the time we park up in front of the long white wall. From a darkened gateway steps a man in a burgundy body suit and a brown beret. Aloisio jumps out to greet him. They shake hands and huddle in whispers for several moments before I notice Aloisio's right hand rise up, signalling me to join them. We follow the guard back through the gate into the cemetery. On the other side, fresh mounds of clay bulge out of the soil, but further off we can see hundreds of gravestones poking up from an expanse of green stretching into the distance. The guard leads us along a wide path beside the cemetery wall. Aloisio walks next to him and I walk behind, trying to pick out words from their hushed conversation. Shortly, we reach a corner, where we are met by a large hole in the wall. 'It's here,' says the guard, hopping straight through.

On the other side, an old man is leaning against some bricks, puffing on tobacco. Beside him, a much younger man leaps like a cat to the top of the wall, snatching a glance at us before hurrying away, his tall slim figure balancing easily at least a metre above our heads. The guard whispers something to Aloisio. Aloisio turns to me. 'This is it,' he says.

I don't want to admit my first thought. Not even to myself.

Straight ahead of us is a single grave, a long rectangular block of concrete decorated with the sort of glossy brown tiles that were popular in middle-class kitchens across the UK in the 1970s. Apart from that, the rest of this section of the cemetery seems to be abandoned, overgrown by grasses and weeds. In one corner, close to where we are standing, traces of smoke are snaking into the wind, rising from a charred pile of litter so big that it levels with the top of the wall. But where is the mass grave? I was expecting something more obvious, perhaps some sort of dome rising up from the earth. I look to Aloisio. I'm a bit confused.

'Where, exactly?' I ask.

He shrugs his shoulders and twists round to the guard, who looks at Aloisio and then at me before saying something in a small voice. For a moment, I'm distracted by the man on the wall. He's still up there, striding around the edge of the cemetery as if it were a stage, his figure darkening to a silhouette as the sunset fades to grey. I take a few steps forward, towards the thickening undergrowth, wondering whether I am walking on the dead right here, right now. I turn around to Aloisio, who comes to join me. Together, we walk forward, half looking at our feet, half further afield.

'I think the bodies are buried throughout this bit,' he whispers.

'I see,' I say, still scanning the grasses for some sort of clue. I feel like I should be having a more immediate response to the presence of death, or at least be thinking something profound. But my mind seems to be empty and I'm starting to wonder why we have come here. What was I hoping to see? Skulls and bones? Have I been propelled forward by some frenzy of desire to witness more dead bodies in Angola? Am I stuck in my own othering of the African continent as a site of catastrophe? It all feels so anecdotal, so vague and voyeuristic – and none of it proves anything. Surely what is actually needed here is a team of forensic scientists armed with pickaxes, shovels, paintbrushes and transparent bags, experts who can exhume whatever is down there and start to tell us all the truth. Anything less, I'm starting to think, amounts to little more than some sort of weird necro-tourism.

I hear someone whistling. It's the guard. He's getting twitchy. He encourages us to follow him back through the hole in the wall. The old man, who hasn't moved an inch, stays put.

On the other side, the guard leads us further along the inner wall, perhaps another fifty metres or so, towards a tombstone fit for a giant. Behind it, on the wall, printed in blue paint, are the words: '*Aqui jazem vítimas de 27 de Maio 77. Honra e glória.*' (Here lie buried victims of 27 May '77. Honour and glory.) On either side of this are four columns of seventeen names each, all painted in black capitals. I recognise some of them – Nito

Alves, Urbano de Castro, Monstro Imortal, Rui Coelho – but I'm not sure how to interpret them. Does this mean that only these people are buried here, or are there others, lesser-known men and women, who have fallen into obscurity?

Aloisio and I are standing side by side in front of the wall, studying the names and the large grey gravestone. I don't know what he's thinking and I'm not sure I know what I'm thinking either. I seem only to have questions about death. I want to know how these people died. Were they shot? Were they hacked to pieces? Perhaps they bled to death after days of torture, cruel techniques passed down by the Portuguese. Maybe some of them died from shock. Heart attacks. Perhaps they were buried alive. Did they even know why they were dying? Did their killers know why they were killing?

Aloisio interrupts my thoughts. 'Would you like me to take a photograph?' he asks.

'Yes,' I say. And I confess that I take my position, smiling, in front of the names of the dead, as if I were standing in front of a palace or a statue or some other symbol of the state.

Aloisio hands me back my camera. 'Have you had enough?'

'Sure,' I say. 'Let's go.'

He walks ahead with the guard, the two of them talking softly to each other. My mind, meanwhile, is filling with ideas that shame me. I'm surprised that it is so peaceful here. I feel entirely relaxed inside these walls. It's not what I was expecting, this site of death. I had this idea of what I thought would confront us and what I thought I would write, but now I've actually come to the place, the physical space feels like an anticlimax. Does this mean that all the horror was in my head?

17

COLD WAR PARADOX

It's the sombrero that's thrown me. Although the two men I'm here to meet are from political parties I've never heard of, I was still expecting something more austere than the jaunty pair before me.

José Júlio, the one in the hat, and Mário Tito have the manner of a practised double act. Júlio is the larger of the two. Wearing shorts to his knees and open-toed sandals, he walks with a slightly clownish gait. When he speaks, the words seem to lollop from his lips in a low boom of vocal expression that's so slothful, you wonder if he'll reach the end of the sentence. Tito, a slighter, slimmer figure, is tighter in comparison, shooting strings of words as we introduce ourselves in an empty *candongueiro* station in Bairro Rangel.

It's still early for a Saturday morning. Not many people are out and about. So Júlio's concern for our safety is surprising. 'There are a lot of pickpockets and bandits here,' he says, looking around uneasily, 'let's get moving.'

He ushers me along the pavement, past a small government building wrapped in razor wire to some steps leading down to an underground bar. Inside, a young man is standing behind a wooden table examining the head and looped horns of what must have been a large black and white goat. Blood leaks from the stump of the animal's neck, but its bulbous eyes are glistening with so much life I almost expect it to blink.

Apart from us, this small eating and drinking den is empty. Júlio chooses one of the plastic tables on the far side of the room and we all sit down. Immediately, the meat man produces a large cleaver and starts chopping his way through a slab of goat meat. Raising the rectangular blade to his shoulder, he swings it down in a perfect arc, slicing through the splay of flesh, spinning a fly into the air. Bit by bit, the goat is divided and subdivided – Bang! Bang! Bang! Bang! – hammering our conversation into bite-size pieces.

'So that you know I'm real,' shouts Júlio, slapping something small down in the middle of the table, 'I've brought this.' It's a metal badge in the shape of an inverted arrowhead, in red, black and gold. At the bottom of the badge is a small gold tank; above that, a slightly larger gold star; and above that, across the top in black, it reads '9th B.R.I.M.', which stands for the 9th Brigade Motorised Infantry. This is why I am here: José was in the 9th Brigade.

'There's this as well,' he says, pushing a FAPLA identity card across the table. A small black-and-white photograph shows a fresh-faced boy in a beret looking confidently into the camera. 'In those days,' he says proudly, 'I was called Relâmpago.' Lightning. 'I chose the name myself.'

I'm impressed – how many people can boast a *nom de guerre* at fifteen years old? – but I find it hard to believe that the 9th Brigade could have been so sophisticated if it was made up of teenagers. My doubt provokes a burst of laughter. 'You need to understand,' says Júlio, pulling his hat from his head, 'that we all became military at a very early age.'

But let's get this straight: the 9th Brigade was in a league of its own. Such was the skill and bravery of this elite military division, it won the respect of senior Cuban soldiers, leaders of the troops sent by Fidel Castro on the eve of independence to fight the US-backed invasions from South Africa and Zaire. The first Cubans arrived just in time to support the 9th Brigade, which was single-handedly defending the capital from advancing FNLA soldiers and their foreign allies, including the SADF, the Zairean army and the CIA. The Battle of Quifangondo, as it is known, was the first major victory for the MPLA and Cuba. In the following weeks, the 9th Brigade continued working with a handful of Cubans to take control of most of northern Angola by the end of February 1976.[37]

Eighteen months later, however, these national heroes swung their support behind Nito Alves. On the Twenty-seventh of May, not only did the 9th Brigade conduct what Senhor Carmoto called 'the coup in the prisons', they also captured the six MPLA figures who were later killed in Sambizanga. This is why most of the brigade were wiped out in the days, weeks and months that followed the uprising. Or so I've been told.

'It was us, the young ones, who really wanted to move,' explains Tito, who was sixteen years old in 1977 and also a soldier, though not in the 9th Brigade. 'The elders were permanently delaying everything, and we were fed up of waiting for change.'

Júlio recalls acute discontent at the heart of the armed forces. In 1975, he was sent for training at one of the centres for revolutionary instruction. 'Even then, there was no food,' he says. 'We were eating *mukwa* [the fruit of the baobab tree] for months on end.' Over thirty years later, he is still incensed that they had to drink water from a ditch. 'We even had to fetch it ourselves,' his voice suddenly rising above the blast of a sound system from a passing car. The vibrations rumble into the room, climbing the legs of the chairs, shaking our buttocks and thighs, and Júlio has to bellow above the bass beat and meat man's hammer: 'Our uniforms were in very poor condition! Our boots were splitting at the seams! Many of us didn't even have laces! It was calamitous!'

When the situation deteriorated even further in 1976, Júlio was among a group of soldiers who became so hungry that they hijacked some trucks transporting food. I'm sure I detect a quiver of shame in his voice when he admits this, but I'm surprised that he seems to have no clue as to why they were without food.

'All we ever knew was that there wasn't any,' he says.

Tito tips forward, stretching his arm across the table, tapping his forefinger: 'You have to remember that we were hoping for a better life, but when independence came things stayed the same and then started getting worse. You'd be standing in a queue for bread and you could see that everyone around you was suffering.' Furrowing his forehead, he adds, 'It was the reality of the life we were living, and it is the life we are still living. Things have never changed.'

I'm not going to dispute this, but I'm puzzled that they still believe, all these years on, that an immediate improvement in their living standards was possible at the moment of independence.

'Look, it was like this,' says Júlio. 'The MPLA had fed us a doctrine of hatred and militarisation. They told us that the FNLA and UNITA were our enemies, just like the Portuguese had been. To make us pick up arms against our brothers, they even told us that the FNLA ate human flesh slapped on top of potatoes. We believed it all until the fiasco of the Twenty-seventh of May, when we realised that everything was a lie and a farce.'

I can't believe he really means 'everything'. Surely this is nostalgia speaking?

'Well, we'd already heard about the corruption,' he replies. 'We knew about these men like Iko Carreira.'

'The minister of defence?'

Júlio's eyes widen. 'Indeed.' He smiles. 'We wanted to know why we had no food while he was making money trafficking diamonds.'

'But did you have any proof?' I ask.

'Everyone was talking about it!' comes his slightly startled reply. 'And we all agreed that we would have to substitute this group of men for some others.'

'Which group of men?'

'Carreira and Onambwe, but also Lúcio Lara – they were not genuine Angolans, you know.'

'Genuine?'

'They were not Angolans of origin,' he says.

'But they were born in Angola, right?'

Júlio looks to Tito, who looks agitated. 'Listen!' says Tito. 'There were cultural differences, cultural problems. They came from Portuguese families.'

But I've read that Lara's father was a *mestiço*, so possibly the son of a black Angolan mother or father.

'Those three were all born in Angola, it's true,' says Tito, 'but their parents were not of Angolan origin so *they* were not Angolans by origin. They were like the Rhodesians! They wanted to turn Angola into a Rhodesia.'

'You mean *former* Rhodesia,' says Júlio.

'Former, yes, former,' says Tito, annoyed at the interruption. 'They wanted to have a regime like Ian Smith's, which is why there was this secret accord within the MPLA which explains why there is still a certain number of *mestiços* and whites in the party.'

I've never heard of this accord, but it is not difficult to understand why many black Angolans resented the whites, and to a lesser extent *mestiços*, who enjoyed power after the Portuguese left. For decades, they had learned that the lighter your skin, the more you benefited from the racist policies of colonial rule. Moreover, Angolans had witnessed something of a surge in white domination during the decade preceding independence: Lisbon was so desperate to cling on to the colony, it had tempted more and more Portuguese to Angola. Come the early 1970s, the white population doubled to around 400,000, making it the second largest in Africa after South Africa's.

Júlio is nodding vigorously: 'Neto was a figurehead, but the person who led the movement was Lara. We had to get him and the others out of the heart of the MPLA. They were clinging to Neto. Everything he did, he had to get their approval first.'

'He's right,' says Tito. 'Neto had his back against the wall with that lot. We had to save him.'

A man bursts into song beneath the table, making me jump. It's Júlio's mobile phone. He raises his hand at me while fending off the caller – 'I'm coming, I'm coming!' – then hangs up. His hand drops, and he picks up the thread from Tito so smoothly that I wonder if they've done this before. 'He was always drunk,' he says, referring to Neto. 'They would get him completely intoxicated so that he would sign anything they wanted.'

I'm not sure how this could be more than rumour. When I ask for another example, Júlio's response is immediate.

'The petroleum contract!' he says, his lips thickening into a pout. 'Not even the Central Committee knew about it. It was a secret accord organised by Lara and Iko in 1976, and Neto signed it. It was with the Americans. With Cabinda Gulf.'

'We were Marxists!' Tito interrupts, furiously. 'Socialists! How can you speak against the United States every day while, behind everyone's backs, signing deals with them?'

This question cuts to the core of the conundrum facing the MPLA as it sought to become a credible contender for government. Oil extraction in Angola began in the mid 1950s, off the coast of the enclave of Cabinda. By 1973, it had overtaken coffee to become the country's biggest export, with 150,000 barrels per day being extracted. In November 1974, the MPLA boldly declared that were it to gain power it would rid the country of all foreign oil companies and seize their assets.[38] But halfway through 1975, it reconsidered and established a special national commission to take charge of the petroleum sector.[39] Placed at the helm was Percy Freudenthal, a white Angolan businessman whose family had long been close to Neto's.[40] In order for the oil sector to avoid a decline like that experienced by the coffee industry, Freudenthal was certain that most of its existing employees would have to be kept on. So even though the Portuguese oil company, ANGOL, was nationalised at independence, a prior agreement with Lisbon ensured that nearly all of its white Portuguese staff retained their jobs and pensions. Freudenthal also knew that if the MPLA was to gain the income it would desperately need as a government, the US-owned Cabinda Gulf Oil Company (Cabgoc) would have to remain. Despite its distrust of the US administration, the MPLA leadership was happy to go along with this. Unfortunately, not everyone in Washington felt the same.

In December 1975, three days before Christmas, Cabgoc shut down its operations – partly because of the war, but mainly because of political pressure in the US. Henry Kissinger, then secretary of state, was determined to destroy the MPLA government and was livid that US dollars were filling the coffers of a socialist state. For the next four months, Angola did not receive a single cent. Neto was so incensed that he pondered kicking Cabgoc out for good. He even made contact with Romania to find out if they would be willing to take over operations instead.[41] Ironically, strong opposition to this move came from Havana. Jorge Risquet, one of Cuba's most senior officials in Angola, wrote to Castro telling him that the socialist states were not a suitable option since they had little or no experience of oil production.[42] In the end, Kissinger backed down. On 9 March 1976, $200 million of royalties and taxes owed by Cabgoc were finally paid to the MPLA and, a few weeks later, the operator resumed work in Cabinda. Not long afterwards, another US oil company, Texaco, signed its own contract to operate in Angola.

A further twist in the contradictory oil sector was the founding, in 1976, of the national oil company, Sonangol. Right from the start, it held a curiously autonomous position within the otherwise socialist state.[43] Just as the MPLA was officially adopting the ideology of Marxism–Leninism, Sonangol's leadership were developing key partnerships with Western companies. In fact, it was precisely because the MPLA's allies were the Soviet Union and Cuba that Sonangol's top team were so motivated to prove to the West that they were trustworthy and competent. Every time they encountered a new problem, they would hire US consultants to help overcome it. A favoured firm was Arthur D. Little, a company that had previously worked with the Portuguese administration.

Another poignant example of the topsy-turvy Cold War world was that early on in Angola's civil war, Cuban soldiers using Soviet weapons were deployed to protect Cabgoc's Cabinda base from US-backed UNITA rebels. I mention this to Júlio and Tito, who look at me as if I'm deluded.

'No, no,' says Tito with a rather patronising grin. 'The Cubans came to protect Angola from the South Africans.'

That may have been their main aim, but they also protected the oil installations. I've been told this by a senior Chevron staffer and I've read it in several books. 'It's a known fact,' I insist.

'I guess it's possible,' Júlio says, more charitably, but clearly he doesn't believe a word either.

Tito rolls his lips in on each other, nodding at me and stretching his facial muscles into an awkward smile. 'The fact is that Nito was the one who brought everyone's attention to the oil contract,' he says. 'He was a proper Marxist, which is how he managed to mobilise so many people for the coup. Except,' he adds, hastily, 'it wasn't a coup, because in Marxist theory, coups do not exist!'

This isn't the first time I've heard this argument, and I don't find it convincing. Plenty of Marxists have conducted coups, Portugal's Carnation Revolution being one of the most obvious examples. It was a military coup that not only brought down the government and sent the president and prime minister fleeing to Brazil, but also ended colonial rule in Portugal's colonies. Surely Tito wouldn't dispute that?

Júlio intervenes: 'We wanted to protect Neto. In a *coup d'état*, you do not protect the president.'

'But you did want to get rid of very senior members of government, no?' I look at them both, unsure of which one I'm speaking to. 'What about the men killed in Sambizanga? The *nitistas* did that, didn't they?'

Júlio laughs at my question. 'It was not the factionalists who killed the *comandantes*,' he says, 'it was a *mestiço* by the name of Tony Latão.'

'Tony who?' I ask.

'Latão,' Tito replies. 'It's slang for *mulato*. *Mulatão* shortened to *latão*. See?'

Sort of, yes, but I've never heard the man's name before.

'He worked directly for DISA,' Júlio explains. 'His role was to eliminate the *comandantes* in order to place blame on the factionalists.'

'You mean a conspiracy?' I say.

'We saw it with our own eyes!' he replies.

On the Twenty-seventh of May, Júlio was with the 9th Brigade breaking into São Paulo prison on the edge of Sambizanga. 'When the MPLA *comandantes* arrived in Sambizanga – Bula, Dangereux, all of that lot – they were taken to Kiferro's house. Have you heard of Kiferro?'

I nod, 'The footballer.'

'Well, at this very point, the Cuban tanks arrived in Sambizanga. And when the people saw those tanks, they all started running and then the soldiers started shooting, and...' Júlio pauses and turns to look over his shoulder.

A group of men have just come down the steps into the bar. Meat man stops hammering. Now Tito turns round too. There are four of them and they are staring at us. They walk straight towards our table and for a moment I feel like I'm in an old-fashioned cowboy film, about to be caught in the crossfire. But all they do is sit down at the table next to ours. Meat man starts chopping again. Slowly, Júlio turns back to face me, offering Tito a sideways glance and squaring his body up against the table in what looks like a display of male assertiveness. I don't know about them but I'm feeling distinctly uneasy.

Continuing in a low voice, Júlio finishes his sentence: '...and it was then, during this confusion, that the *comandantes* were killed.'

The first part of this story chimes with what both Carmoto and, before him, old man Mateus told me: that the killings took place after Cuban tanks surrounded Sambizanga, causing panic. But neither of them talked of a conspiracy. Moreover, I don't understand how this Latão character could have killed them all, especially if they were in Kiferro's house. I want to put the question to Júlio, but his attention is fixed on the four men, now talking quietly among themselves. Are they *bufos*?

When Júlio eventually returns his focus to our conversation, he's forgotten Kiferro and moves to another point in the day. 'As I was saying,' he says, confusing me, 'when I went to the palace to demonstrate, Cubans and Angolans opened fire on us. We had to run and spread out as fast as we could.'

I turn to Tito, hoping for clarification. 'I was elsewhere,' he says, beginning to laugh. 'I had gone to the radio station and when I left there, it was to go to the hospital. I was sixteen and I'd been shot...' He breaks off into loud cackles.

'Show her the bullet wound!' says Júlio, pointing to his friend's leg.

Tito duly pulls up one of his trouser legs to reveal the hole in his flesh. The sight of it sets them both off giggling. But what happened to both these men following the uprising is not funny. Júlio's story is even worse.

On 30 May, he was picked up at a warehouse, here in Rangel, thrown into the back of a truck, and taken to the same prison he'd helped break into three days earlier. 'I was absolutely terrified,' he admits. Shortly afterwards, he was ordered to strip to his underpants, and was tied up. 'We were no longer being treated like human beings,' he says. 'To them, we were simply creatures who happened to be alive.'

Later, all the men who had been captured were rounded up into sets of sixteen. Júlio's group were put back on the truck and driven up to the Fortaleza de São Miguel, the fortress where Zé Van Dúnem would later be tortured.

'They were taking people up there to kill them,' says Júlio, who was certain he too would be killed. But instead, he was put back on the truck and taken to another neighbourhood, Morro da Luz (Mount of Light). 'There, they had a mass grave,' he says, 'and again, I expected that this would be my death.' But once again, he was not killed. On 1 December, he was taken to the military prison in Luanda where he remained until 7 January 1978, when, finally, he was transferred to the São Nicolau prison in the southern province of Namibe, the one that Ildeberto Teixeira describes in his book. He remained there until 1981.

'I was lucky,' he says. 'I'm here with my life, but many soldiers simply disappeared.'

'Some units were decimated,' adds Tito.

'Yes, the 9th Brigade was ended for good,' says Júlio.

They run through a list of all the groups of people who were killed: most of the political commissariat of the army, one of the best women's military units, and entire provincial military units around the country.

'They all vanished,' says Tito.

'Eyy!' Júlio slaps the table. 'And Moxico was unspeakable.'

Tito is shaking his head. 'Entire families wiped out,' he says, his voice softening. 'It makes it very difficult to calculate, but at least 80,000.'

That's a big figure. In 1977, that would have been more than 1 per cent of the population. 'How did you reach that?' I ask.

'Well,' he replies, 'you need to count all the 9th Brigade, the women's brigade, the youth movement and a whole lot more. It would take ages.'

Maybe it would, but I can't help thinking that three decades is an awful lot of time.

'We've wanted to gather signatures of enough people to send to The Hague,' says Júlio, raising a slightly different point. But again, given how much time has passed, I wonder why they haven't done it. Is this a symptom of what psychologists call learned helplessness, when someone becomes so accustomed to having no control over his or her circumstances that even when there is a way out, he or she does not take it? Or could it be that they've not been able to get enough people to sign a letter to the International Criminal Court because their claims regarding the number of dead are exaggerated? Perhaps it's simply that people are still too afraid. I want to have this debate with them, but in the moment of our discussion I chicken out. I'm afraid of offending people who've suffered so much, especially after Júlio has told me how some of the accused were killed.

'They poured gasoline into people's mouths,' he says, 'and made them run and run until it would start to leak out, and then they would strike a match and throw it, and then' – he takes a large breath, his cheeks ballooning with air – 'BOOOOM!' His fingers stretch out over the table, expressing an explosion. 'Another way they killed people was with a bayonet,' he says. 'They'd bayonet them in the stomach, pour over gasoline, strike a match and' – his hands leap into the air – 'there you go.'

We're interrupted by another burst of song from his phone. He apologises and takes the call, listening with intense concentration to the caller and, every now and then, turning to look at the four men sitting nearby. His eyes flicker briefly between me and Tito, then he hangs up.

'This happened in prison a lot,' he continues. 'Angolan agents from DISA did most of the torture and the killings, but sometimes they were helped by Cape Verdeans, São Tomeans and Portuguese. You see, we knew many of these people who did this. We still know them.'

'To this day?'

'Oh yes,' he says, 'and they turn away in shame.'

'You don't say anything?'

'What is there to say?' Júlio's voice scales up in despair. 'We know they know and they know we all know.' He jerks his head to the left, signalling something about our four neighbours. 'Time to go,' he says.

If the four men really are here to spy on us, they are remarkably unsubtle. We get up to leave and they all stare, their eyes following us as we move towards the doorway. Júlio throws them a last sideways glance before we take the steps up to the pavement.

Outside, he releases his frustrations: 'Just look at this country today, will you? Nothing changes! The government receives all this money to invest in the country, but spends it on itself. That's why you still hear the expression "the people continue in captivity" – because it continues to be true.' He places his hat back on his head and hastily grips my hand, giving my arm a good shake. Tito also takes my hand and offers me a friendly smile. Then they stroll off, shoulder to shoulder, down the centre of the street, Júlio joshing and joking, the two of them talking and laughing.

Watching them now, it's hard to believe what they went through as teenagers. At times, our conversation seemed so removed from reality that it was like listening to fiction. Bayonets in bellies? Of course it happens, I know that, but there was something about the way they spoke that seemed to deny any emotion. Yes, they sounded angry, but they were also curiously upbeat. Was that all a front, I wonder? Will they go home and weep?

18

◆

APPEARANCES

Beauty parlours link women the world over. Never more so than in Luanda, where it helps to be well turned out, especially if you are female. On one occasion, I was actually sent home from a press conference with orders to find a dress and put on some make-up.

So here I am, surrounded by mirrors on the first-floor balcony of an international hotel with Gina at my feet. She's hacking off dead skin from my toes and heels and from beneath the balls of my feet. She is snipping at my cuticles and rubbing down the ridges that run along the tops of my nails.

'Would you like a massage?' she asks, pushing her thumbs hard into my soles, squeezing tickles up my spine. Now she's pulling at my toes, kneading my ankles and running her fingers down my calves and shins. It's bliss.

Until a few moments ago, the woman next to me was having an all-over transformation. Feet, hands and hair. But the process came to a temporary halt when we noticed that her head, encased in a heated helmet, was producing smoke.

'*Fogo!*' she shouted. 'Fire!'

Gina didn't bat an eyelid. She says she's seen many emergencies. She used to be a teacher, but when she didn't get paid for two years she swapped educating children for buffing nails.

'What colour do you want?' she asks.

'Isn't gold all the rage?'

'It's popular,' she says, squeezing my big toe, 'but you'd be better off with a deeper colour to hide this fungal toenail.'

I leave the salon painted plum-red.

For the next hour, I am in the home of a French woman. She's a hairdresser '*pour les femmes européennes*', as she puts it. Her husband works for an oil company. They've been living here for years, but she speaks barely a word of Portuguese. So while I'm being washed, cut and blow-dried, I do my best in French.

'*Vous aimez Angola?*' I ask.

'*Ah oui!*' she replies. 'Much better than France.'

I'm intrigued to understand how she's managed to be here so long without learning even the colonial language, let alone any indigenous ones. She insists it's not hard. Most of her friends are French. 'But you don't need to speak a language to understand a people,' she assures me. 'I can tell that the Angolans are fed up of being poor while everyone else is getting richer. They're angry. And they're going to get more angry.'

Tonight, I've been invited out for dinner again. The man who's offering to cook for me heard about my research through a mutual friend. He phoned me up and said he'd like to talk. Apparently his father knew Nito Alves and, like Nito, was executed. He encourages me to come early so we can discuss the matter at length. I say I'll be there at around six.

When he opens the door to his flat, his lips spread into a huge smile that seems to hold the rest of his face, and his eyes suggest a man with a big heart. He welcomes me in, enthusing in Portuguese, but quickly switches to fluent English. I ask him if we can stick to Portuguese: I don't want to get lazy. 'When you come to London, we can speak English,' I say, and he roars with laughter.

We spend the next hour in the kitchen, me on a stool watching him work his knives on fish and vegetables. We talk across topics. Kafka, peak oil, Tony Blair, French nationalism, contemporary art and slavery. He tells me that Angola has so much oil because of Atlantic slave trading. 'Over the centuries,' he says, 'the remains of these men and women, the ones whose bodies were thrown into the sea, is what formed the oil. And because we've had so many wars, yet more and more flesh and bones have been lost to the sea. That is why the oil keeps coming – because we keep killing. When the oil dries up, it'll be a good sign.'

His flat is huge and well furnished. We eat dinner in the dining room, seated across a large table. Afterwards, we have French cheeses on the balcony with wine. Finally, over coffee, we move on to the matter of the *vinte e sete*. He shows me a photograph of his father, a good-looking young man.

'I barely knew him,' he says, tears appearing on his cheeks. 'He was killed when I was a kid.'

He says he doesn't know much more about what happened, or what his father did. He thinks he was a *nitista* but he isn't sure: none of his relatives will discuss the matter. His hope, he tells me, is that I will be able to find more out for him.

But I've never heard of his father. 'How can I know more than you?' I ask.

He agrees that it might be difficult, then asks me what I do know about the *vinte e sete*. So I explain everything I have learned so far, including the contradictions, potential distortions and all the uncertainties. We talk and talk late into the night and I get the sense that, in truth, he knows quite a lot about his father's role but is too nervous to tell me. He admits that he's afraid of losing his job.

'If they find out I'm talking to you, my career will be finished.'

'What do you do?' I ask.

'Just a bit of business.'

I try to persuade him to open up, but he insists it's too risky: 'You shouldn't even be here.'

'Why not?' I ask, but he comes back with a question.

'Why don't you stay here tonight?'

That's a neat U-turn.

'It'll be easier to talk in the morning.'

Oh, will it just! Over the years, my relationships with men in Luanda have proved tricky. In my experience, if you turn them down they can get quite nasty, spreading rumours that you've slept with half the men in town. I've had lengthy discussions about this with a number of female friends. They normally advise me not to take it too seriously. But once, a female minister in government became quite animated in her insistence that I must never be tempted to marry an Angolan. 'You will have to share him with six other women,' she warned, blaming forty years of war for a gender imbalance, with women outweighing men seven to one. Not that this has got much to do with the dilemma facing me right now.

'No,' I say firmly. 'It might make it easier for you to talk, but it will make it much harder for me to ask questions. And anyway, I love my husband.'

My rebuttal makes no difference. He continues trying to persuade me that a night with him will be a night to remember forever, until I can't stand it any more.

'I want to go home,' I say, stiffly, 'right now.'

My certainty seems to have tipped him into a mood. He leaps out of his chair and leads me to the front door. But when we get there, he can't open it.

'I must have lost the keys,' he says. 'We're locked in.'

Goodness me. What to do now?

'Well you'll have to find them,' I say, hopelessly.

For the next few minutes, he rushes in and out of different rooms, apparently hunting for the keys, which are nowhere to be found. He offers me another glass of wine. 'We haven't finished the cheese,' he says. But I stand firm. He's beginning to really wind me up.

'You've got to find the keys!' I demand.

He pours himself more wine and sulks into the glass.

'You come here all dressed up,' he says, 'and then pretend you aren't interested in me.'

I tell him that I am interested in him, but not in his body. This goes down badly. He starts telling me how much he loathes women like me – 'Hypocrites!' – and pulls a key from his pocket.

'You can go!' he shouts.

We walk to the front door again. This time he unlocks it and lets me out. An earlier offer of a lift home has been retracted.

'You can walk,' he says, slamming then double-locking the door behind me.

19

♦

A DEATH CAMP

Less than a kilometre south of the goat-head bar where I sat with José Júlio and Mário Tito lies the abandoned underbelly of an alien spacecraft. Rising from the sand of Bairro Indígena, this monolithic structure is known as the Cidadela. It is Luanda's largest stadium, a legacy less to science fiction than to the brutalist tendencies of modern European architecture. Constructed during the final years of colonialism, this 50,000-seater was initially intended for major football matches that could showcase Portuguese power. However, at independence, it became the stage for massive MPLA rallies, such as that which took place on 21 May 1977.

That day, a Saturday, thousands of party militants streamed into the Cidadela, squeezing onto every available bench. They were there, reported *Jornal de Angola*, to witness 'a historical moment rarely experienced by a revolutionary People'.[44] President Neto was to make the speech of his life.

He arrived at five o'clock in the afternoon alongside his scrupulously neat Portuguese wife, Maria Eugénia. First, he apologised for his late arrival. He explained that he had come from a two-day meeting with the Central Committee in which the decision had been taken to expel Nito Alves and José Van Dúnem. His announcement, according to the newspaper, was met with applause. However, when the clapping and the cheering had died down, Neto warned the people that if any of them opposed his leadership, they too would be presumed to be factionalists and would be thrown out of the MPLA.

'There cannot be any factions inside the MPLA! Either you are of the MPLA or you are not! Whoever is not in agreement with us, get out!'

He further threatened, 'This is a dictatorship and if it is necessary to take more severe measures, we will take more severe measures. It is the MPLA who is in charge here.'

Refusing to acknowledge the internal divisions within Angola – remember, there was a civil war going on – he spoke of the need 'to conserve' what he called 'national unity'. He claimed that the country was being divided by external forces, 'forces that are not rooted in Angola'. However, he proceeded to point the finger at a number of groups inside the country, including the working class, who, he said – somewhat curiously for a self-professed socialist – should not be 'fighting the other classes' nor 'isolat[ing] itself from the rest of the population'. He poured scorn, too, on Jehovah's Witnesses and Tocoists, a minority group that followed the twentieth-century Angolan visionary Simão Toco. The only religions that could 'belong to the MPLA', said Neto, were Protestants and Catholics. He further advised all comrades to be on their guard for those he dubbed 'false militants' – people who were really members of the FNLA or UNITA – and for any 'elements that think they have a historic vocation to make a complete Revolution in Angola'.

His thumping rhetoric extended to an impassioned defence of DISA, which he described as 'a fundamental aspect' of national defence. He railed against those who compared it with the Portuguese secret police and insisted that any misdemeanours by DISA agents resulted from 'a lack of experience'. 'We must forgive them,' said Neto.

He also defended several of his closest allies, including Iko Carreira, 'one of our best commanders', and Lúcio Lara, whom he described as one of the MPLA's founders and who had played a crucial role in its survival and been active in several regions of the country during the national-liberation war.

Towards the end of speech he spoke passionately about race and class. 'There is no immediate or logical relation between skin colour and class condition,' Neto insisted. 'It's not like this at all.' He described those who 'divide the People up on the basis of their skin colour' as 'counter-revolutionaries' and 'ultra-revolutionaries', who should be known as 'counter-ultra-revolutionaries'. Defending his own position, he added, 'they think that this comrade who is speaking to you cannot defend the Angolan working class because his wife is white, because his children are *mestiços*.' For Neto, it was precisely the opposite: 'Nobody is in a better position than I am to defend everyone.'

From here, he nudged the audience towards his final, incendiary message: 'I ask all comrades, all activists of the movement, members of the committees and action groups, in accord with the decisions taken today by the Central Committee, that they carry out a true and serious fight against all factionalists they meet in their path. Thank you very much.'

While Neto was rousing the crowds in the Cidadela, a twenty-one-year-old gunner from the reconnaissance corps of the 9th Brigade was in agony in the nearby army barracks. Miguel Francisco felt as though his stomach was being tied in knots. Eventually, the pain became so intolerable that he signed off and walked slowly back to his flat near the Primeiro de Maio, a major road junction in Luanda. The following morning – the day *Jornal de Angola* published Neto's speech beneath the headline 'Liquidate factionalism!'[45] – the pain in Francisco's gut got worse. On the Monday, his condition deteriorated even further; and on Tuesday, instead of returning to duty as he was scheduled to do, he went to hospital to get help. He was seen by a Cuban doctor, who prodded and peered at his abdomen before instructing him to stay at home without working for eight days.

'This is why I am alive!' Francisco tells me when we meet over thirty years later. 'If I had been in barracks on the Twenty-seventh of May, I would definitely be dead.'

Our conversation takes place on Rua António Saldanha da Gama, a short residential road named after the Portuguese aristocrat who governed Angola from 1807 to 1810. Today, a stagger of four-by-fours straddle the street, making it more like a Toyota showroom than a thoroughfare. When I arrive on foot, sweaty after a nostalgic stroll up Avenida Lenine and Avenida Che Guevara, a young man in a strip of filthy jeans is on his knees polishing the rubber tyres of one of the cars. As I pass him on the pavement he calls out, 'Madam! I will do yours next!' and looks incredulous when I tell him I have no car, as though it is not possible for a foreigner, a white European one at that, to be without wheels.

'I have legs instead,' I say, 'and I walk.'

He bursts out laughing and shoots back another idea. 'So I'll wash your legs, *senhora*, your legs and your feet.'

He's still cackling into the hubcap when I press on the bell at the side of a two-metre-high wood-panelled gate. Disconcerted by its lack of noise, I cannot tell if anyone has heard the bell or whether it is broken – and then the gate opens. A tall man beckons me with a smile. He wears a pressed-cotton security-guard uniform, a boxy baseball cap and heavy black boots that lace around his calves like corsets. Behind him, a large metal container housing a generator swallows much of the outdoor space, and yet another shiny four-by-four clogs up the rest. He shows me to a heavy front door, and pushes it open.

Inside, the house is as cold as a butcher's fridge. It's also very white. The walls are white and the floors are covered in glossy white tiles that seem to go on forever, like Arctic ice. The large front room doubles as the entrance hall, furnished with a pair of desks, some swivel chairs and a long sofa behind a coffee table that's covered in copies of *Jornal de Angola* and a selection from the private press.

These are the rooms of the BBC. Although the corporation no longer has a dedicated correspondent in Angola – it seemed to lose interest after the civil war ended in 2002 – it does have the World Service Trust, which describes itself as 'an international charity' that uses media technology 'to help reduce poverty and promote human rights'. Make of that what you will. The point is that the man currently heading the trust's Angola arm is João Van Dúnem. After I interviewed him in London, he managed to escape the constraints of Bush House and return home, to live in Luanda for the first time in nearly three decades. It is thanks to him that this meeting is taking place.

He'd told me about a man writing a book on his experiences of the Twenty-seventh of May. 'He was held in a concentration camp,' João had said. 'You do know about the camps, don't you Lara?'

I did not, but João offered to help me anyway. And it is he who greets me now, and introduces me to the author.

'Meet one of our freedom fighters,' he says.

Leaping to his feet, Francisco explodes from the leather sofa with overwhelming energy. He curls his fingers around my hand, squeezing bones into tendons and sending a shot of charisma up my arm. Apart from his silver hair, which is clipped to a military-style flattop with short back and sides, he doesn't look like a man in his fifties. Tall and slim, he cuts a fine figure in a bright-orange T-shirt and bomber jacket over slimline blue jeans and a pair of brown moccasins. He has thick black eyebrows and a thicker, blacker moustache, a broad face and large, kind eyes, one with a slight squint. Releasing my hand, he smiles and I notice a strangely reassuring gap between his front teeth.

'Why do you say you'd be dead?' I ask, responding to his opening statement.

A finger darts towards me, making me flinch. 'Why?' he shouts. 'Why?' There's a slight pause while he investigates my face. 'Because I was young and active. Because I participated and discussed. Because we could all see that Nito Alves was right! *Sim, senhora!* A crack of laughter cuts the air between us and he punctuates the sentence with a bark. 'Yah! This is why if I'd been in barracks on Friday, the Twenty-seventh of May, I would have been killed.'

I'm keen to hear more of his memories of the day, but before proceeding any further, he insists on setting me straight on what he calls 'the fundamentals'. First, that the Twenty-seventh of May was a problem internal to the MPLA. 'It's absolutely critical that you get that right,' he says, every bit the schoolmaster. 'It was, in essence, a problem about who should have been leading the MPLA from 25 April.'

'You mean, after the Carnation Revolution?' I ask.

'Very good,' he says approvingly. 'It was about whether the revolution should have been led by the majority or the minority.'

'Meaning?'

'We! Us! The blacks. We were the majority!' he says, already sounding exasperated. 'The *mestiços* and a very few whites were the minority, yet they were the ones who'd formed the leadership of the MPLA. It is, you understand, a very delicate subject.'

'The subject of race, you mean, and class?'

'*Pronto!*' He pats me on the knee. 'You have spoken very well indeed.' He turns and smiles at João, who is watching us from the other side of the coffee table. 'You see, Senhora Lara, the problem of Angola is that we were colonised 500 years ago. The coloniser was white, yah? Yet during these 500 years, the true owners of this land – that is us, the blacks – were held beneath Portuguese supremacy. Now there are some who say the coloniser has no colour and that blacks can have a coloniser's mentality too, but the fact is that the coloniser was white!'

When I tell him I agree, he looks mildly surprised, even unbelieving, and emphasises his argument with another one. He explains that the main reason he joined FAPLA in November 1974, a few weeks after his nineteenth birthday, was because of what he had learned about colonialism as a teenager. Working in a factory in the late 1960s and early 1970s, he was paid less than all the whites and *mestiços* working alongside him. 'Even the ones doing the same job as me!' he exclaims. It was because of the way this made him feel, as an intelligent young black man, that he was prepared to risk his life for liberation.

'So the question is,' he continues, 'why did some of these whites and *mestiços* embrace the rebellion to end colonial rule? Did they do so in order to devolve power among the majority, or was it in order to take power for themselves and continue running the country their way? *Senhora*, the problem of the Twenty-seventh of May resides precisely at the heart of this question.'

This provocative point about the persistence of racial hierarchy seems to have brought his introduction to an end. I suggest that we return to these questions regarding race at the end, after he has taken me through the day itself.

'Shall we go back to the moment when you were lying in bed?' I say.

'Hold on!' he shouts. 'You still need to understand the truth.'

'Truth?' I say, questioning such boldness, but really loving the spirit and candour of this man.

'Yes,' he says, once again looking rather frustrated by my questioning, 'that Nito Alves' cause was that of the majority. You see, the trouble with those *mestiços* in power was that they confused the question of legitimacy with racism. Was it not Jean-Jacques Rousseau and Kant who talked about the theory of legitimacy and democracy? Eh?' He looks at me expectantly and I find myself nodding even though my knowledge of both thinkers is poor. What I remember most about Kant is that he held 'the Negro' in very low esteem.

'Yet despite all these theories,' Francisco continues, 'we had a minority ruling over a majority.'

Except it wasn't quite that simple. 'What about Neto?' I ask. 'And Ludy Kissassunda, the head of DISA? They were black. They were the majority. And there were other blacks too.'

'Neto was black, *sim senhora*, but he was only the face of power. He did not have real power. And it is also true about Ludy – yes, black – but he did not make the decisions. He was a figurehead like Neto. It was Onambwe, the deputy of DISA, who made all the decisions. So when the Twenty-seventh of May broke out, those who decided the fate of thousands of our young people were our compatriots of *mestiço* race. It is unfortunate and it will cause me problems to say this so frankly, but it is my contribution to history and I have said it now. Moreover, as a cultured person, I am sure you will understand.'

I certainly think I understand, but I'm still keen to steer him back to his personal story, to the facts of the Twenty-seventh of May as he experienced it.

That day, Francisco woke at three o'clock to the sound of shooting, but he brushed it off as the usual antics of deserters – those he calls 'turncoats' – returning from the front drunk and with guns. It was gone six when he woke again and reached for the radio. When he switched it on, he could hardly believe his ears: it was the *nitistas*' programme, *Kudibanguela*, and they were playing the music of Urbano de Castro and David Zé. Sitting bolt upright on the edge of the sofa, looking straight at me with rigid concentration, he says, 'I remember thinking, "*Eh pá*! Something's not right here, something's definitely not right."'

He got out of bed and walked to the window of his tenth-floor flat, scanning the city for signs of trouble. His eyes whiten and he lets out a sort of squeal, 'Wow wee! There were loads of cars and masses of people. Hundreds. No, thousands, *pá*! All out in the road, moving towards Rádio Nacional. The whole world was running that way, *pá*!'

Watching Francisco, I feel a wave of empathetic exhaustion for him. He seems to turn the task of talking into high-speed gymnastics: not only does he speak incredibly quickly, but he also manages to enunciate each syllable perfectly, appearing to wrap his lips and cheeks and all the muscles in his face around them.

He wanted to join the crowds, he tells me. He wanted to find out what was happening. So he dressed and left his flat. He took the lift to the bottom of the building and when the doors opened he found the hallway crammed with people. '*Muita gente, pá!*' As he squeezed through the crush, he noticed several soldiers standing guard and felt someone tapping him on the shoulder. It was Guerra (War), a colleague from the 9th Brigade. Dramatically recalling their conversation, Francisco adopts Guerra's whisper and mimics the movement of his head and arms: 'What are you doing? Why are you in civilian clothes?'

'I've been ill and off duty,' replied Francisco. 'I've just come to see what's going on.'

'At the barracks, things are really hot,' said Guerra, who explained that during the night, the most senior members of the 9th Brigade had appeared and given orders to all units to organise into groups, go out at dawn and support the demonstrations. 'So that's what we did,' he told Francisco. 'We went out in tanks. Some went to São Paulo prison, others like myself came here, and there are more who have gone to Rádio Nacional.'

Guerra also knew that some senior MPLA members had been taken prisoner. 'The biggest commanders from the ministry are being held,' he said. 'Mingas, Bula, Petroff – the whole lot.'

Francisco was alarmed by what he heard, but he wanted to know what was happening on the streets so he decided to follow the crowds to the radio station. 'Everyone was going there,' he says. 'Everyone.'

Outside the radio, people were chanting *'Viva Nito Alves! Viva!'* and singing to the music of Artur Nunes, Urbano de Castro, David Zé and the group Kissanguela. Francisco recalls a feeling of revolution in the air and a sense of achievement. He remembers the man beside him suggesting that President Neto should reverse the Central Committee decision to expel Alves and Zé Van Dúnem. In that moment, Francisco thought the man was probably right. There were tanks everywhere, as well as police and armed soldiers, all in favour of Nito Alves. Francisco stood among the crowds, delighted that everyone seemed to want the same thing. Then, at about eleven o'clock, a rumour began spreading that 'the coup', as he calls it, was taking hold and that Nito was about to make a speech. But no sooner had the news spread than the atmosphere began to change. Francisco's voice flattens and he leans back in the sofa, exhaling in a heavy, slightly forced manner: 'President Neto gave orders for the Cuban forces to intervene. This was his greatest mistake. They wiped out all these young people who had done so much for the country.'

Francisco panicked and raced home. Back inside the safety of his flat, he turned on the radio to find out what was happening. Instead of Nito's speech, an official was talking. 'It was a Portuguese journalist of Goan or Indian origins,' he says. '"We're going to find out where those lizards are hiding." That's what he said, and I knew then that something had gone badly wrong.'

From his flat window, Francisco watched as more and more tanks began to appear. At first he thought they were the 9th Brigade's T34s, but as the numbers grew he realised he was wrong. 'Only the Cubans had that many,' he says. 'They had legions of tanks that had come off the ships.' He's rubbing his hands up and down over his knees. 'I saw so much repression. Bullets. Gunshots. Endless firing.'

Were it not for the Cubans, Francisco believes 'the coup' would have succeeded. 'There was not a single soldier in the 9th Brigade who was not in favour of it,' he says. 'They all backed Nito.'

As the violence unfolded, Francisco knew, he says with chronic understatement, that 'things were going to get tricky'. He spent the rest of the day indoors and come night-time he tried to get some sleep. He stands up in front of me to pull down imaginary blinds and switch off the lights. The flat was pitch-black. He lay on his mattress staring into the darkness, trying to relax. Eventually he nodded off. But not for long. At half past one, he woke to the sound of loud banging on his front door.

Francisco's voice is gravelly now, and the semantic speed has dropped off. '*Eh, pá!*' he says. '"What could they want?" That's what I was thinking.' He hunches up, rounding his shoulders so his leather jacket climbs up his back. '"I bet they've come to kill me." That's what I was saying to myself. "They've come to kill me."'

He got out of bed and walked, barefoot, across the bedroom, slowly tiptoeing down the short corridor that passed through the kitchen into the sitting room. It was completely dark, apart from a line of light that shone beneath his front door from the landing outside. Francisco stepped slowly towards it, feeling his way carefully across the room. He stopped a few steps short of the door, his eyes fixed to the funnel of light. He leaned forwards and peeped through the small security lens in the middle of the door. Cupping his hands to his eyes, he turns them on me like a pair of binoculars. In a soft whisper, he describes what he can see. 'Five men. All of them *mestiços* with beards, though I cannot tell if the beards are real. Through these peepholes, it's hard to tell what people really look like.' He leans towards me, the binoculars within inches of my face. 'One of the men is standing right outside the door, another is in the doorway of the elevator, keeping it open with his shoulders and his feet, which are spread a foot or so apart; and two others are standing at the doorway that leads onto the roof of the building.' He drops the binoculars and looks at me normally now. 'I was terrified, absolutely terrified. I could hear them all talking. And they were armed to the teeth.'

Francisco tiptoed back to his bedroom and looked through the slats of the blind to the road below. He could see two armoured vehicles and two four-by-fours parked up. His heart began beating harder than ever. He was certain it was only a matter of time before the men on the landing knocked down the door. So he took a piece of paper and wrote a note explaining that he had been taken by five men and if he could not be found in hospital or prison, it was because he was dead. He placed the note under his mattress. Then he crept back to the front door and looked through the peephole once more. The men were talking. One of them was telling the others to go downstairs to see if the room was lit up from the outside. Francisco heard them get in the lift. 'Tock! Tock! Tock! Tock!' he says, spitting the sound from his lips. 'Bang! It arrived.' He hurried back to his bedroom and looked through the gap in the blind again. They were staring up at his room. He watched, terrified, until they walked back towards the flats and out of his sight of vision. Moments later, he heard the lift again. 'Tung! Tung! Tung! Tung! All the way back up!' Francisco crept back to the front door.

'The guy's not in there,' he heard one of them say. 'Let's go!'

And with that, to his sick relief, they went.

Abruptly, Francisco stops acting out parts and looks at me earnestly, as if he's about to say something embarrassing. 'I am naturally, I swear, a very courageous person,' he says, 'but that night I was full of fear.' Even though they had left, he was certain they would be back. He was sure this would be the last day of his life. He lay on the mattress, waiting for the hours to pass. 'Two o'clock,' he says, raising a wrist to one ear. 'Three o'clock. Four o'clock. Five o'clock. *Eh, pá!* At half past six, the sun was rising. Francisco got up and crept back to the front door. Still, there was no one there. Beside himself with fear and confusion, he decided to visit a friend in the adjacent block of flats. But when he got there, his friend had a visitor, a cousin from the general command of the army. Francisco crouches over his knees, huddling me into a secret. His voice drops deep.

'Listen,' said the officer. 'Every single unit of the 9th Brigade is being taken away by Cuban troops. You guys are being polished off. Don't go to the barracks.'

'Ahhaaaaa!' shouted Francisco. 'So it *is* the Cubans!'

'Sssssh!' said the officer, flapping his hand at Francisco's mouth. 'You must not go to the barracks.'

So Francisco returned to his flat and glued himself to the radio for the rest of the day. He was horrified when he heard the news that the MPLA leaders – those Guerra had mentioned the day before – had been found dead. But he was even more disturbed to hear President Neto's speech. '"There will be no pardons." That's what he said, Lara. "We will not waste time holding trials." This was a death sentence for many people,' says Francisco.

Hour after hour, information began coming through about the persecutions of anyone thought to have been involved in the uprising. There were also endless appeals for the whereabouts of 'the ringleaders' – Nito Alves, Zé Van Dúnem, Monstro Imortal, and others – and an order was broadcast to all military officers to return to barracks immediately. Francisco was in despair. Terrified of what might happen, he began sleeping over with friends. 'I slept here, I slept there, and here, and there and...' His voice peters out, a rare lapse of concentration and energy.

Come the Tuesday, he plucked up the courage to go out. 'And that was when I was amazed. Absolutely amazed and shocked.' He pauses, a conscious attempt at dramatic effect. 'The city was crammed full of *mestiços* and whites. Packed with them! They were all in uniform. New uniform! They were armed. They were everywhere! Especially in the Baixa, *pá*! Downtown. It was the *mestiços* who led all the investigations, who conducted the searches, the witch-hunts.' His hands and legs are twitching, itching to express each point physically.

On the afternoon of Friday, 3 June, Francisco was in his flat with his fiancée. A curfew was now in place every day, starting at sunset. So at five o'clock, they left to go to her parents' home. As they were leaving the building, they saw one of Francisco's neighbours being escorted out by two soldiers. He was a young man, a member of the MPLA youth league. 'We didn't know each other well,' Francisco admits, 'but well enough to exchange greetings. "Good day", "Good evening", things like that. My God, Lara, I felt dreadful.'

Francisco and his fiancée hurried out. He escorted her to her parents' house, and afterwards returned home to find out what had happened. While he had been out, the doorman explained that another one of his neighbours had also been arrested, and that they had also been looking for him. Francisco took the lift back up to his flat. His front door had been smashed in, but nothing had been taken. It was now way past the curfew, so he decided to spend the night in his flat. Once again, he struggled to sleep. He realised it was only a matter of time before he, too, would be arrested. 'I could no longer psychologically cope with remaining hidden and waiting,' he says.

He decided to turn himself in.

On 4 June, exactly two weeks after he had left the barracks in so much pain, Francisco walked back through the main gate to the 9th Brigade. Immediately, he was confronted by a man he had never seen before. 'He was very dark,' says Francisco, 'and he did not speak.' Nervously, Francisco began to explain that he had been off sick, but the man did not appear to understand and he called another man in a language Francisco did not understand. The second man was also very dark-skinned, but silent. Again, Francisco gave his explanation and stood watching as the two men spoke to each other. 'They were Kwanhama,' says Francisco, referring to an ethnic group from the very south of Angola. Then a third man appeared. His name was Guimarães, and he was a commander of the 9th Brigade. 'He was the only one I knew,' says Francisco, who explained a third time that he had been under doctor's orders to rest for eight days. Guimarães abruptly ordered him to be locked up. Francisco was thrown into a cell that already held another man, his young neighbour, the member of the youth league who had been taken away the day before.

At this point, Francisco's story starts to get confusing. We have been talking for a couple of hours without a break. Maybe he's tired, maybe I am. But, as I understand it, for the next few days, he was held in Luanda under arrest, first in one place, then another. Sometimes he was alone, sometimes he was with others. He was interrogated and frightened, and on several occasions he was certain he was about to be executed. At one point, he was being held in what he calls 'an open prison' inside the barracks, where he was free to move around but could not leave. There, at night – I find this quite bizarre – he hid in an old Portuguese tank, abandoned at independence. 'They couldn't find me in there, *pá*,' he says, chuckling from the bottom of his throat. During the day, he heard many stories about other people who'd disappeared, including the three musicians, Zé, de Castro and Nunes.

On 7 June, he was ordered into the back of a four-by-four. 'It was a "wazz"', he says, emphatically referring to the Soviet-made UAZ-469. He lets out another one of his loud squeals, 'Eeeeeee! And they took us to the airport! *Porrrra!*' The r's roll down the roof of his mouth like a ball bouncing down steps. 'Fucking hell! There were hundreds, *pá! Centenas!*' For two days, he was held at Luanda's main airport with these other prisoners, some as young as fourteen. On the morning of 9 June, he and 158 other men were herded onto a Boeing 737. 'It was brand new,' says Francisco, 'but they'd taken all the seats out.' They were told they were being sent into the bush as military replacements for the Kwanhama combat units now controlling Luanda. 'It was a complete lie!' he shouts. 'We were prisoners. We were being banished. We didn't have buttons. We didn't have shoelaces. We didn't even have belts.'

An hour and a half after they rose into the skies above Luanda, they were touching down on the other side of the country, in Luena, Moxico province. 'It was ten minutes past one when we landed,' says Francisco, and I don't have the heart to ask him how he could possibly recall such detail. One by one, they filed onto the runway in this faraway town. The airport was completely surrounded. 'There were rows and rows of troops and rows and rows of Russian four-by-fours, and every single one was being driven by a Cuban,' says Francisco. 'I knew then that I was well and truly imprisoned.' He ends the sentence with a burst of laughter and pats me firmly on the arm.

'But we'll be here for days if I tell you any more,' he says, announcing a sudden end to the interview. 'If you want to know the rest, you must read my book.'

I'm speechless.

'You'll be able to buy it in Lisbon,' he adds cheerily.

'But it's not out yet, is it?' I say.

'It soon will be.'

I try pleading, 'But what about the concentration camp? We haven't even got there yet.'

'We were incarcerated in meat wagons,' he says. 'We could barely move. We travelled through the night, surrounded by soldiers, all the way to Calunda, 600 kilometres from Luena, to the death camp. That's where we were banished. Exiled. That's where I spent three years.' He pauses, catching the words in his mouth and repeating them softly, 'Three years... Many awful things happened there. But you will have to read the book.'

He looks at his watch and pulls himself forward, readying to leave. Then something stops him.

'Do you know the film *Escape from Sobibór*?' he asks me.

'Escape from where?'

'Sobibór,' he says impatiently. 'Sobibór.'

Sobibór was one of three German extermination camps in Poland during World War II. The others were Treblinka and Bełżec. They were established as part of Operation Reinhardt, the Nazis' 'final solution'. Sobibór was opened in 1942 and at least 250,000 Jews were killed there. The only survivors were people who could work, mending boots or coats, making shirts or tending animals. Of course I have heard of Sobibór, but I've never seen the film.

'Well, I have,' says Francisco, 'and I've also read the book, and let me tell you that apart from the gas chambers, at least the workers in Sobibór had the minimum. They had food and they even had electricity. But for us!' Francisco is suddenly much louder. 'In our camp! We had none of that. It was a camp that was built very rapidly, that was improvised purely to hold people without even the most minimum minimum minimum conditions.' He squeezes the words into each other, tightening his throat as if he's trying to suffocate them. 'And still they terrorised us. They executed teenagers, boys aged sixteen years, in a sort of satanic ritual. They were trying to inculcate a theory of fear deep in our hearts.'

Trying to stop himself from talking, he says again, 'This is all in my book. You must read my book.' But as soon as he seems to be closing the conversation, out pops a question. 'People tell me I shouldn't publish anything because I will lose everything,' he says. 'What do you think? Do you think we should sell our dignity and hide the truth just to gain cars and money?'

'Of course you should write the truth as you know it,' I say, repeating the advice João Faria gave me, but in my head I'm wondering who am I to tell Francisco what he should or should not say. I don't live here, I don't run the risks he does, I just pop in and pop out.

He responds with his own answer. 'We cannot hide the truth from one generation to the next. We cannot have this football-clubbism, this "I support Arsenal, he supports Benfica". The truth is what will give us peace and reconciliation. Only the truth.' He hesitates and I think he is about to laugh again, but instead a final trail of words tumbles out. 'You have to defend the interests of the majority. You have to change education. This is what needs to happen here, but it's not happening. But... well... oh, I don't know.'

This sudden surfacing of doubt feels like an odd tone on which to end our conversation. What I've found so compelling about Francisco is the certainty with which he speaks. I wonder if the contrast in his voice is anything to do with the way he feels about the past and the present. For it is only now, as we prepare to part, that he has referred to the present and the future and raised the complex matter of 'what needs to happen here', as he puts it, and what is not happening.

Standing up to go, he offers his hand and we shake firmly and decisively. He reminds me again to buy his book – 'It's called *Nuvem negra*' (Black cloud) – and wishes me good luck with mine. Then he turns to João and thanks him in a comradely way, pulling him close to his chest and slapping him on the back. As he swivels on his heels to leave, he releases a last shot of laughter that is so sharp it sounds like it might split him in two. It sounds, I'm thinking as he marches to the door, like the laugh of a man who has lived on his nerves for too long.

Francisco departed, João invites me for a coffee. So we walk around the corner to a restaurant that is often filled with ageing white men. Inside, a game of football is being broadcast on a flat-screen television high on the wall. The men, with moustaches so thick and long they cover their lips, are gazing upwards, grunting and cheering at the match of the day. We decide to sit outside, on the patio by the pavement. It used to be open-air, this bit, but now the space is encased in one-way glass to stop beggars badgering the clientele. Personally, I'd rather the restaurant did something about the evangelical gathering on the corner. Singing their hearts out, hundreds of people dressed in white are overflowing onto the street out of a makeshift church. Many are standing on tiptoes, necks stretched, trying to see the preacher inside, who is shouting into a microphone with such excessive amplification that I can feel his voice vibrating in my bones.

João is interested to know how my research is going, but I'm not really in the mood for talking. The conversation with Francisco has left me with more questions, not only about the *vinte e sete* but about my own approach to the subject. It's all very well my going along with the endless criticisms I've heard voiced about the *mestiço* and white minority, but I'm beginning to wonder if it isn't a bit simplistic. Shouldn't I have asked Francisco to explain his position in more detail? He simply asserted that the *mestiços* in power at the time of the *vinte e sete* were responsible for the violence that was unleashed, insisting that the blacks with equal or, in some cases, more power were mere figureheads. I didn't ask him for his thoughts on the killings of whites and *mestiços* after the uprising, such as Victor Reis, the white Portuguese man whose *mestiça* wife, Maria, has endured so much grief in her life. I, myself, know white and *mestiço* Angolans who are completely committed to this country. How useful can it be to group them all together on the basis of their epidermis? Should I have challenged Francisco more rigorously? Have I been too soft in these interviews because of my own sense of guilt about the racism that pumped the heart of European colonialism? As Francisco himself said, it is a very delicate subject – but it requires tackling nevertheless.

I look through the restaurant window at the white men inside. Some of them might be visiting Angola on business, but some will have been born here and may well have children who are, themselves, *mestiços*. Surely Angola is as much their home as it is the home of the man sitting opposite me now, himself the product of mixing between Africans and Europeans, albeit several centuries ago.

20

METAMORPHOSES OF THE ENEMY

Some say Ndunduma Wé Lépi (the Thunderer of Lépi) is a man with a lot of blood on his hands. I've even heard him compared to Jean-Bosco Barayagwiza, the founder of the Rwandan radio station Radio Télévision Libre des Mille Collines, which repeatedly broadcast an order to Hutus to 'cut down all the trees' and kill the 'cockroaches', or Tutsis, in 1993 and 1994. Ndunduma's preferred phrase was *bater no ferro quente*, which literally means to beat, or hammer, on hot iron. As director of *Jornal de Angola*, he wrote a series of inflammatory editorials under that headline in July and August 1977. They were devoted, he explained, to 'the fight against factionalism', the 'urgent task' to 'beat on iron while it is hot',[46] to 'preventing the lizards from rearing their ugly heads again, even after they had turned into vipers'.[47] Often, he ended the pieces with the imperative and an exclamation mark: '*Bater no ferro quente!*' Strike while the iron is hot!

His detractors say this rousing phrase was a provocative call to arms, a bloody message intended to stir up fear and loathing, to encourage Angolans to go out and attack anyone suspected of supporting Nito Alves. Like Barayagwiza, who was sentenced to thirty years in prison for crimes against humanity and public incitement to commit genocide, Ndunduma's critics say he holds significant responsibility for the deaths that followed the Twenty-seventh of May. A prominent journalist, William Tonet, has argued that, alongside Neto's speeches, Ndunduma's editorials 'undoubtedly contributed to the eruption of the greatest genocide of Angolans of all time, consolidating the physical elimination of cadres of great worth, largely autochthones and members of the MPLA.'[48]

Certainly, it is important to consider that *Jornal de Angola* was, at this time, the country's only daily newspaper and therefore had a dominant voice. A second daily, *Diário de Luanda*, established in 1936, was closed down in May 1977, accused by the authorities of promoting factionalism. For the majority of Angolans, who were either illiterate or unable to access the *Jornal de Angola*, or both, Ndunduma's pieces were also broadcast on national radio, thereby extending his reach across the entire country.

Bearing all this in mind, I can't help but feel trepidation about contacting the man. Apparently he doesn't trust journalists and, for years, has been resolute in his refusal to discuss the *vinte e sete*. So I'm fortunate when a friend of his agrees to call him on my behalf and, a few days later, gives me the go-ahead to call Ndunduma myself. Such is my anxiety about how to approach this grim character, it takes me nearly a day to pluck up the courage to actually dial his number. When eventually I do, I'm cut with a curious guilt: the voice that greets me down the line is thinning and frail and almost broken.

'Thank you for calling,' he says. 'But I will have nothing to do with this subject, nothing whatsoever. For ten years I have not discussed it with anyone, yet they continue to prejudice my name so it is me who is the victim. I am the victim.'

I'm not sure how to respond to this, or whether it's even worth trying to convince him to talk. His reluctance is palpable. So I end up telling him that I understand how he must feel, even though I haven't the faintest idea, and that I don't intend to cause him any more grief. As I'm saying the words, I realise that perhaps I do feel a tiny bit sorry for a man who is so hated – and to my amazement, he accepts my minimal display of empathy as sincerity.

'Since you are so polite and have come to me through a trusted friend, I will let you come to my home.' He waits as I scribble down the address. 'This is the last time I will speak on the matter, though, and it won't be for long.' I hear a scuffling sound and he hangs up. I can hardly believe my luck.

Fernando Costa Andrade was born in April 1936 in the village of Lépi in Angola's central highlands. His parents straddled the racialised divisions of colonialism: his father was a white Portuguese citizen, a man who owned a bottling factory, and his mother was an Angolan subject, a *mestiça*. Ndunduma went to school in Huambo, fifty kilometres east of Lépi, and later in Lubango in neighbouring Huíla province. There were no tertiary-education establishments in Angola at the time, so when his basic schooling ended his parents sent him to Lisbon to study architecture. Arriving in the metropole, like so many other young intellectuals coming from Portugal's African colonies, he was drawn to Casa dos Estudantes do Império (Imperial Student House). Funded by Salazar's colonial government, it offered cheap lodging to visiting students and became the main meeting point for political activists and artists. Heated discussions would continue for hours about African independence, communism and Castro, literature and love, and it was here – no doubt against the Portuguese dictator's intentions – that some of the most respected future leaders of liberation movements would develop their ideas and networks.

For Ndunduma, this period in Lisbon was critical. Here he developed a love for poetry and art, which brought him into contact with Agostinho Neto, then just a poet and medical student, and Mário Pinto de Andrade, who had gained a reputation in Paris and Lisbon as a literary critic, and was to become one of the founders of the MPLA and, later, its leader from 1960 to 1962. Involvement with these two, among others, saw Ndunduma become increasingly politically engaged throughout the 1950s, such that, at the end of the decade, he was forced to leave Portugal as 'a fugitive'. First, he went to Italy, then, briefly, Algeria, followed by Brazil, where he was imprisoned following the 1964 coup, and then, for two and a half years, Yugoslavia.[49] Despite moving from country to country, he managed to continue his studies in architecture, and he also held regular conferences and meetings to promote lusophone African literature. However, his main activity was as a representative of the MPLA, a subject he writes about with tedious self-indulgence and name-dropping in the second volume of his autobiography, *Chegadas* (Arrivals).

As the 1960s came to an end, Ndunduma was requested by Neto, now MPLA president, to leave Yugoslavia and travel to Zambia to establish the movement's Department of Information and Propaganda. But he wanted to gain experience as a liberation fighter, so, after a brief stay in Lusaka, he travelled to eastern Angola to fight as a guerrilla. It was then that he got his *nom de guerre* and confirmed his position as a devoted and loyal

MPLA member. Come independence, Neto invited him to head up *Jornal de Angola* and *Diário de Luanda*. The president wanted someone in charge whom he could trust. However, Ndunduma felt that running both papers would be too much, so he chose *Jornal de Angola* and promised Neto that he would maintain direct contact with the Ministry of Information in all matters. Thus it was, under Ndunduma's direction, that the paper became the MPLA's mouthpiece.

To meet Ndunduma, I am advised by my landlady to borrow her car. If I arrive on foot, she warned, he'll not take me seriously. So I drive to Alvalade, a wealthy middle-class Luanda neighbourhood, home to a number of prominent politicians, diplomats and a good sprinkling of wealthy businessmen. His house is opposite a building still calling itself the embassy of Yugoslavia, at the end of a long crescent-shaped road named after Comandante Nzaji, one of the men who were killed in Sambizanga. It is a rectangular concrete block – two storeys high, one room wide and two deep – typical of the modernist style built by the Portuguese during the 1960s, and surprisingly modest for a member of Angola's ruling class.

When I arrive, the garden gate is open. So I wander in, following a tidy path between waxy green bushes to the front door. I no longer remember what I was expecting, but when the Thunderer of Lépi appears, I know it was not this. A little unsteady on his feet, he is surprisingly small – he seems to be shrinking before my eyes – and his wrinkled skin is as pale as mine. Nevertheless, he is immediately welcoming, wrapping a hand around my arm and looking affectionately into my eyes. 'Thank you for coming,' he says, sincerely, I think, 'and thank you for arriving on time.' He smiles up at me, 'Of course, you're British,' and I smile down at him. I don't tell him that I was so worried about arriving late that I've been parked around the corner, outside the Karl Marx cinema, for the past half an hour.

Inside, his hallway dissolves into the sitting room, which is bordered by a short set of concrete steps running up to the first floor. Plain metal banisters are covered with pictures which spread to the surrounding walls, where shelves full of books vie for space. Ndunduma walks over to a large spongy armchair, positions himself behind it and begins fiddling nervously with the antimacassar, straightening it, pulling at the small creases, repositioning it and straightening it again, before inviting me to sit down. Then he moves around to the front, so that he's looking down at me in the chair, and with a perfectly straight face, opens our discussion with one of the more memorable gambits I've ever heard.

'I am not a necrophiliac. I do not have a particular bent for necrophilia. Nor am I a vulture, one of those birds that comes to pick over cadavers. Do you understand?'

Gobsmacked, I nod my head and, for a horrible moment, I think I might laugh, but I manage to swallow my anxiety or ridicule, I'm not sure which it is, and add, a little too emphatically, 'Totally. Of course. Yes.'

'For many years,' he continues, 'I have managed to detach myself from all of this, but for some people it has become their psychiatric disorder.' This makes him chuckle, and he relaxes a bit and sits down in the armchair beside mine. 'Fortunately, I do not have that problem.'

'You mean, with the *vinte e sete de maio*?' I ask.

'Of course!' he replies, and his short introduction suddenly gathers momentum and volume. 'Why don't I have a problem? Why aren't I ill? Eh? The reason is simple. I completely consciously, absolutely conscientiously, sincerely and truthfully have done nothing...' – he pauses to emphasise the word – 'bad...' – another pause – 'which I can be accused of. And if you have been told that I am guilty of something for the last twenty or thirty years, then you had better know that it is not true. I have nothing on my conscience. Now,' he says, heavy breathing slowing his speech, 'I will speak to you on the record for a maximum of forty-five minutes. Anything else is off. Understand?'

I understand this is not a question. 'Completely,' I say.

Spreading his elbows to the armrests, he forms a small pyramid with his fingers, into which he nestles the bottom of his chin, pushing his head back so I can see up his nostrils. I take this as my cue.

'I suggest we begin on the day of the uprising itself,' I say, 'the Twenty-seventh of May.'

'The day of the coup attempt,' he corrects me. 'The day they tried to shoot me.'

On the evening of 26 May, Ndunduma went to have supper with his friend, Augusta Conchiglia, an Italian reporter with the Paris-based journal

Afrique-Asie. She lived on the Marginal, the wide avenue lined with palm trees that runs along the bay of Luanda looking out to the Atlantic. They ate spaghetti and Ndunduma stayed over. 'Normally, I would have gone home, but my wife, who was a doctor, was on a night shift that evening.' He looks at me gravely. 'Thanks to that coincidence, I'm alive today.'

At dawn the following morning, a group of factionalists arrived at his house in Alvalade with the intention, he says, of killing him. He learned later from a neighbour that they returned two or three times that day, desperate to track him down. Apparently, the same group also went to the offices of *Jornal de Angola*. 'It was one of the first things they did, even before they went to the radio station,' says Ndunduma. 'A colleague told me they wanted to shoot me.'

Fearing for his safety, he decided to take refuge at the house of the defence minister, Iko Carreira, who was not only a close friend but was also married to Ndunduma's cousin. Conchiglia agreed to drive him there because her car was small and less conspicuous than his. 'Because I worked at the newspaper, I had a big one,' he says, a little boastfully. 'They would have noticed it.' But I'm less interested in the size of his car than why he thinks they were so intent on killing him in particular: surely Iko would have been higher up their hit list?

My question is met with incredulity. 'Why were they after me?' says Ndunduma, staring at me as if I was insane. 'Because I was important! I was the director of *Jornal de Angola*. I had instructions to write certain things, and so I wrote, always ideologically, against them. I attacked their leader, Nito Alves, and because of that, I received a series of completely anonymous letters. Death threats.'

'When?' I ask.

'During the months before the coup.'

'Can I see them?'

'You can't!' he says. 'It would take me a long time to find them and even if I kept them in a place that was easy to access, I do not want to read them again.'

'But you wouldn't have to. I would.'

'No!' he snaps. 'Anyway, they were not only aimed at me. They were also aimed at Lara, Iko and Onambwe.' He lets out a long sigh and looks at his fingernails. 'Of course, there was racism in all this,' he says, wearily. 'But their main problem was that I was not afraid, and I also knew that they didn't stand a chance. I knew the strength of the forces we could rely on.'

'The Cubans, you mean?'

He tightens his lips and points at my recorder, waggling his finger. I take it he's not going to answer that one.

'Later that day,' he continues, 'on the president's orders, we were assembled together to make certain key decisions and to be protected in a special place.'

'A special place?'

'Somewhere outside the city. Every day we came in to the Ministry of Defence – me, the director of the radio station and several others.'

'Who else?'

'I won't use names,' he says, looking away dismissively. 'We gathered every day in this small room, which became the room in which we led... we led...'

He seems to have got stuck, his jaw hanging open over the sentence as if he's forgotten how to speak.

'What?' I ask. 'The purge?'

His mouth snaps shut.

'We used to check everything with Iko,' he says. 'I received orders and I carried them out. There were people coming through the ministry every day as prisoners. I saw them. On one occasion, soon after the coup attempt, I saw the journalist who sent you here, I saw him coming in as a prisoner.'

Nobody sent me here, but I do know who he means. He's talking about Reginaldo Silva, who worked for the BBC Portuguese for Africa service for over twenty years. Without Reginaldo's advice, I probably wouldn't have survived my time as the English-language reporter here. His encyclopaedic knowledge of the country's political cast, and his ability to work out the difference between rumour, paranoia and reality, is the result of many years of news reporting, stemming all the way back to his first break as a young hack at *Jornal de Angola*. However, according to Reginaldo, that job also cost him two years of his life – and he places the blame on Ndunduma, his then boss.

On 28 May, shortly after arriving at work, Reginaldo was ordered, by Ndunduma's secretary, not to leave the building. She called the military security, who promptly turned up and arrested him. They took him to DISA's headquarters. From there, he was sent straight to São Paulo prison and held without trial until 4 February 1979. He says that during his time inside, he was told by the head of the prison, a man named Ngunga, that the authorities knew he was not guilty of factionalism. The reason he had been arrested was that they believed he would have supported the factionalists had the coup been successful. And the reason they thought that, according to Reginaldo, is that Ndunduma had told them. He bases his claim on a conversation they shared a few days before the uprising. Following a press conference at the presidential palace, Ndunduma had given Reginaldo a lift back to the office. During the short journey, he told Reginaldo that he had received information from Onambwe that the young reporter was involved with the factionalists. He advised him to exercise more '*auto-crítica*', a term which had little to do with the self-criticism it implies and much more to do with toeing the party line. But Reginaldo refused, insisting he was not guilty of any wrongdoing.

Ndunduma's version of events is a little different. He claims that he knew that some prisoners were being shot, and insists he did everything he could to help Reginaldo. 'I even managed to speak to the president and the defence minister, which is why he is alive today,' he says.

'So you mean you intervened to stop him from being executed?'

'All I'm saying,' he replies abruptly, 'is that I managed to get a letter to someone, including certain members of the army who were dealing with the case, and because of that he was not shot.'

I'm not sure how to interpret this. The man many allege to be a mass murderer is telling me he is a hero who really saved lives, while also admitting that there was a plan by the MPLA leadership to shoot Reginaldo simply because they suspected he would, in the future, have supported Alves. 'Have I understood you correctly?' I ask.

'I cannot play with state secrets,' replies Ndunduma. 'It is a subject of the past.'

You're telling me! Thirty years past. 'How long are Angolan state secrets supposed to last?'

Looking away, he says, 'Twenty-five years, and, well, I could... I cannot...'

A look of total despair has come across his face.

'What?' I ask.

'I know he went to prison and he must have suffered, but he has his life and I believe that is thanks to me. Yet for twenty-five years, I have been accused of everything. He has stirred up my name, and now they all say that I shot people, that I assassinated people, that I sent people to their deaths. Well I didn't!' he shouts, now managing to sound quite helpless. 'I didn't! I didn't! It is clear that I didn't!'

But unfortunately, it's not at all clear. He has just told me he was based at the Ministry of Defence, where, as he himself admits, people were being sent to their deaths. Moreover, I've read in a number of private Angolan newspapers that Ndunduma, the writer Artur Pestana, otherwise known as Pepetela, and Manuel Rui Monteiro, also a writer and lawyer, were on a special panel whose job it was to send people to be executed. I put this to Ndunduma and he becomes immediately defensive, shaking his head with frustration.

'This is the last detail I'm going to give you,' he says, a little bizarrely because from where I'm sitting he seems to be giving me remarkably few details. 'President Neto knew that the military and other authorities were carrying out executions by firing squad. But what you have to remember is that the factionalists had killed our comrades, burning to death our very best, in Sambizanga. As a consequence, he thought there should be a commission, so he nominated a very big one indeed, by which I mean that big figures were involved. However,' he says, swallowing a cough, 'it was a commission to hear – to hear, I say, not to judge – those who had been arrested and imprisoned. And yes, I was on that commission with Pepetela and Manuel Rui. But I repeat,' he says, almost shouting again, 'we were not there to judge. We were there simply to hear. The military chose the ones we heard and the military judged.'

I'm puzzled. What could possibly have been the point of a commission that did nothing other than hear the accused?

Ndunduma forces a smile, as if the stupidity of my question is obvious, and with a sudden burst of conceit, he explains, 'Our objective was to divulge important information to the public. We did not send anyone to their deaths. In fact, after ten or twelve days, some of us started getting rather bored.'

The image of these three men listening to the accounts of terrified prisoners through wide-mouthed yawns is not particularly appealing – but Ndunduma has moved on to a rather different train of thought.

'We were not that radical,' he insists, 'yet we got the blame. Us three. Pepetela was attacked because he was a writer. I was attacked because I was director of the *Jornal*. And Manuel Rui was attacked because he was a lawyer. Of course,' he adds, repeating an earlier phrase, 'there was also a dose of racism in all this.'

Indeed. That a tribunal could be established, less than two years into independence, comprising one white man and two *mestiços*, is nothing if not complicated, particularly given that the majority of people brought before them were black. 'Surely you can see that?' I ask.

'You misunderstand,' he replies. 'The racism was towards us.'

Oh dear. He seems to be locked in a pattern of thought in which he is always the victim. So I try another tack, pointing out that he, Pepetela and Manuel Rui sided with Neto and, in the end, that that was the side that killed thousands of people. 'Wasn't it?' I say.

But now, it seems to be me he's getting bored of. A cocky smile spreads across his face, and he responds in a voice that sounds soporific. 'Talking about the number of dead,' he says, 'is like talking about Angola's inflation rate: no one knows how many people were killed.'

For a man who says he was very close friends with the defence minister, this strikes me as a pretty shoddy answer. Surely he can be a bit more accurate than that.

'Look, with the utmost sincerity I do not believe there were many. But Iko himself told me that there were 2,000 or perhaps just over that. And yet,' his voice sharpening for attack, 'every year your journalist friends push the numbers up. It went from 20,000 to 30,000 to 50,000 and now, some of them are saying that 80,000 were killed. Not even the Angolan army had 80,000 troops! It's ridiculous!'

For all I know, these five-figure numbers might be wide of the mark. But even if, for argument's sake, we accept Carreira's figure, it remains the case that many more people were killed by the authorities than by the so-called factionalists. More to the point, 2,000 is still an awful lot of dead people. I put this to Ndunduma and watch as his eyebrows rise up in surprise and he flatly refuses to say anything. He simply sits in his chair, lips sealed, and fingers spreading over his knees like a pair of dead starfish.

Watching him now, stubbornly silent, it occurs to me that perhaps the debate about numbers has become something of a red herring, a way to avoid more serious discussions about what actually happened. 'For example, your part in the purge,' I say. 'Your editorials. How do you feel about them now?'

But he's still in a grump, and looks at me as if I'm speaking gobbledygook.

'The editorials,' I say again, a little louder. 'Why did you write them?'

He turns to face me, his eyelids narrowing to old folds of skin.

'You, of all people, must surely understand!' he says, his voice straining with tension. 'I had to use very grabbing headlines. It is journalism, no? Where do you think I first heard the phrase, *É preciso malhar o ferro enquanto está quente* (It is necessary to hammer on iron while it is still hot)? From the president, of course! They were his words, and my job was to transmit those words, yet I was the one who ended up being the scapegoat.'

In Ndunduma's view, far from provoking hatred and murder, if his editorials failed in any way at all, it was because they were too sympathetic to the *nitistas*. 'I tried to say that the coup attempt was motivated by discontent, by certain failings on the part of the government,' he explains. 'Because of that, I was accused of justifying the coup and some of them in authority were incredibly angry with me. So if anyone thinks I was calling for massacres, they must be illiterate. Either that,' he says, now starting to look exhausted from all the anger, 'or they never actually read what I wrote.'

But I have. I've read every single word of his editorials several times over. Thanks to the Colindale newspaper library in downbeat Barnet, I've also got photocopies of the lot.

To be fair, I think he has a point when he says his criticisms were not confined to the factionalists. In one piece, for example, he declares, 'to beat on hot iron is, ultimately, to hammer out our own defects'.[50] In another, 'the fight against factionalism is [...] an order that must be accomplished not only as a concerted battle against those who practise it, but equally against our errors and ideas that permit the appearance of factionalists.'[51] He also warns that mismanagement of the state, 'if done wrongly, generates discontentment and, consequently, creates internal enemies'.[52] It does not take a lot of imagination to see how some in government might have interpreted these comments as an apology for the uprising.

In fact, Ndunduma's writing shows no tolerance whatsoever for any wandering from the MPLA path. Blurring the lines around what it might mean to be a factionalist, he progressively broadens the definition of the enemy. So, for example, he homes in on 'the indecisive among us [who] camouflage their lack of courage or inability to resolve problems with a sickly bureaucratism'.[53] Those he calls 'the liberals' are no better. They 'hide their disorganisation with spur-of-the-moment improvised solutions, only to contradict them when faced with the criticism of the majority, saying that, yes, they agree with these criticisms and had done so all along'.[54] He even suggests that the attack on factionalism offers an opportunity to wipe out other approaches that the authorities dislike: 'The fight against factionalism includes the fight against bureaucratism and liberalism. Beat on hot iron so that the iron acquires the right form!'[55] An experienced poet and editor, Ndunduma must have been aware of the power of metaphor – that to encourage people 'to hammer' was to incite violence.

Alongside these attacks on deviant behaviour, he calls on the population to be on their guard for what seem to be psychological 'displays of factionalism'.[56] By this, he doesn't mean those who might march with guns to the presidential palace, or break into prisons to free the inmates. No, Ndunduma is referring to those who 'wait for the order from above',[57] who display 'a lack of courage, selfishness, deep-rooted habits, an absence of initiative, fear of doing the wrong thing or incompetency'.[58] He is referring to those who display 'sluggishness' and 'inertia'; the kind of traits, he writes, that are 'unfortunately abundant among us'[59] – the kind, one might add, commonly referred to by European colonialists seeking to promote a particular idea of the African. In fact, Ndunduma's definition of a traitor seems to refer to anyone who does not match his devotion to the movement. In other words, 'The party [...] controls the masses, not in order to make sure that they really participate in the business of governing the nation, but in order to remind them constantly that the government expects from them obedience and discipline.'[60] So wrote Frantz Fanon in his damning analysis of African national-liberation movements when they finally take power.

It is hard to see how one could live up to Ndunduma's standards of loyalty. To this end, and with a heavy dose of sarcasm, he calls on the population to look out for those cadres who are arrogant, 'the fallacious and cynical jugglers, who have learned everything in one day and already know much more than all the other cadres put together.'[61] Just as Neto did in his speech of 21 May, Ndunduma encourages the public to be on their guard for fake supporters of the ruling party, those who 'out of necessity are waving the flag and unfurling displays of indestructible faith' in the MPLA. These deceptive individuals are attempting to mask their opposition and are 'in fact the ones who are factionalists [...] and who must be fought against.'[62] Yet many Angolans felt compelled to show overt support for the ruling party, fearing that if they did not, they would be accused of factionalism. So how could one tell the difference between a genuine flag-waver and a fake? And who is to say, in an atmosphere of such fear, that the flag-waver was ever completely certain of his or her loyalty him- or herself?

Adding to this recipe for nationwide paranoia, Ndunduma calls on party militants to spy on their comrades, their friends, their neighbours and family. The obligation of militants, he writes, is 'to discover factionalists or other metamorphoses of the enemy',[63] because 'national security is an obligation of all citizens, particularly revolutionary militants.'[64] Beating on hot iron is a 'task for the entire militant base, which through the force with which it beats, will reinforce the MPLA and its true force.'[65] Just as Fanon had observed in earlier post-colonial governments, then, 'the militant is turned into an informer.'[66]

Throughout these editorials, what becomes clear is Ndunduma's outstanding concern with the power of the MPLA and its president. His rhetoric is obsessed with what 'the People' must do for the party and its leader, never the other way around. The fight against factionalism, he writes, must be 'a single-minded battle against a certain political vision that is [...] opposed to the very essence of the vanguard of the Party we seek to create.'[67] It is a fight to 'strengthen the MPLA [...] to raise the closed fists of the militants and unite around Comrade President Agostinho Neto, leader of all the Dear People.'[68] He even states, obscurely, 'it would not be possible to beat on hot iron if the MPLA did not exist.'[69]

Ndunduma's enthusiasm for MPLA discipline and power does not seem to extend to the socialist principles upon which the party was supposed to be based. He states that 'one of the most important problems in our life as an independent Nation' is 'class struggle and racism.'[70] However, contrary to what you might expect, he wanted to suppress class struggle, not promote it. And, as he makes clear during our discussion three decades later, the racism he is so concerned about is that which is focused on the whites and *mestiços*, never the blacks. In his fifteenth editorial, entitled 'Down with racism', he includes a lengthy quotation from Neto caricaturing the arguments of *nitistas* and others who wanted equality and transparency. 'We do not think,' said the president, 'that the petite bourgeoisie, simply for being petit bourgeois, should be shot down [...] We do not think that we should physically eliminate all the *mestiços* in order that Angola become a land purely of black people. This is wrong!'

Instead, Neto insisted that 'we always speak of national unity, unity that signifies several things, not only the equality of races [and] of tribes, but also the possibility of all of us, in Angola, to work together, in order to arrive at a desirable level.'[71]

It is telling that neither Neto nor Ndunduma discusses the serious frustrations of the poor, largely black population who, after independence, watched *mestiços* take many of the best jobs left vacant after the Portuguese exodus. While it is true that the MPLA faced huge challenges in finding qualified and skilled individuals to help get the country back on its feet, anger was growing among the poor towards those who had suffered less under colonialism and now appeared to be benefitting most.

Rather than acknowledging the pressing need to tackle inequalities linked to race and class, Ndunduma proposes technocratic solutions for the state's difficulties. He writes:

> [W]e need organisation, we need statistics, we need methods and systems of work, technicians, clerks, we need essential bureaucracy, we need absolute and rigid control of finances, of collectives, of firm political control of men across an ideological analysis of their activities and of militant objectives.[72]

Fanon foresaw this 'fetish of organisation',[73] and certainly, Ndunduma seems obsessed. 'To organise,' he writes, 'is to beat on hot iron and to heat up that which is cold in order to organise it better.'[74]

Less interested in the 'people power' that the MPLA had nominally embraced in the run-up to independence, he appears to be calling for an authoritarian technocracy run by a well-trained, well-controlled elite. From here, the party can start to build 'the revolutionary man, ideologically new'.[75] Indeed, it is in Ndunduma's first editorial in the series that he declares that the 'fight against factionalism' rests on the urgent requirement 'to readjust, to analyse our priorities, to restructure, to make a leap forward, a new start without compromises'.[76] This exhortation resonates strongly with the stories I've heard about the way the authorities behaved following the Twenty-seventh of May: the honeymoon of independence was over – from now on, an intolerant dictatorship would rule, without compromises, from top to bottom.

So, yes, I have seen his editorials, and I've tried hard to read them objectively. And while it is true that he did voice criticisms of the government and the management of the state, overwhelmingly the tenor of these pieces encourages hatred and violence towards a wide range of people including the so-called factionalists, but not only them. Reading through them brings to mind the hellfire-and-brimstone sermons that were common in Catholic churches prior to the 1970s. Perhaps Ndunduma's political rhetoric was influenced as much by his religious upbringing as the ideological beliefs he acquired later in life. Perhaps that is where the paranoia-inducing ideas come from: it's wrong to be disloyal and it's wrong to be disobedient, but it's also wrong to be too loyal and to sit back and do as you are told. Everything he offers seems to be a double bind designed to leave any reader feeling guilty, whatever they do. The emphasis, I notice, seems to hinge on sinfulness.

Given the very tense political atmosphere at the time, it is highly likely that these editorials would have contributed to the spiralling violence. Indeed, recent scientific research has produced empirical evidence to show that quite subtle manipulations of disgust can sway the way people think about minority groups.[77] Braving what I fear will be an angry response, I make the point to Ndunduma directly. 'After all,' I say, 'you did call on the Angolan public to "extinguish" those you called "lizards". That was a straightforward demand to kill, wasn't it?'

Calmly pointing his nose in the direction of my recorder, he blinks in steady rhythm – one, two, three, four – his face fixed on the little box on my lap. 'It's time you turned that off,' he says.

Surely he doesn't think he can get away with that. 'These articles are at the heart of the accusations against you. How do you defend them?'

'You've read them,' he replies. 'You know what is in them. And I've told you, my job was to represent President Neto. I have nothing more to say.'

'Nothing at all?'

He shakes his head.

'I'd rather leave the politics,' he says, 'and show you my artwork.'

I can see I'm not going to win this battle and, certainly, I'm interested in seeing his paintings. But there are two final questions I want to put to him, firstly his thoughts on the Soviet Union, and Moscow's role in the uprising. 'I'd really like to know whether you think they supported Nito Alves?' I say.

'Yes. Definitely,' he says, with such absolute immediacy I can only assume he's relieved we're no longer discussing him. 'They wanted someone they could control, and Nito was ambitious and vain and confused. He was also a Maoist who converted to Sovietism after visiting Moscow.'

'And what about Neto?' I ask, extending the interview for as long as I can. 'Was he converted to Sovietism too?'

He coughs up a small laugh. 'He was completely different. He was happy when a country helped Angola, but he would not do whatever they asked him. He would not do that under any circumstances.'

I've read that Neto's independence of mind is what really riled the Soviets, and that this is why they wanted to get rid of him – if, indeed, they did.

'Did they?' I ask Ndunduma.

'Yes. Exactly,' he says, now surprisingly agreeable. 'Let me give you an example.'

In 1967, the Portuguese began using exfoliants in Angola. FAPLA was struggling and the MPLA desperately needed help. Earlier in the decade, they had enjoyed support from the Soviets, but Moscow had never been very impressed by Neto. With Soviet support waning, Neto travelled to China in the hope of winning military and financial aid from this other communist giant. But Beijing did not fully trust the MPLA, suspecting it of being pro-Soviet. So they told Neto that they would help him on one condition. 'Beijing wanted him to make a declaration against Soviet revisionism,' explains Ndunduma. When Neto refused, they refused to provide any help. So Neto went on to Moscow. 'Of course,' says Ndunduma, 'these countries are full of informers and they knew where he'd been.' So now, it was Moscow's turn to lay down conditions. They told Neto they would provide support if he denounced the Chinese. Not only did he also refuse this request, but he refused their offer of a plane ride home. Instead, he bought a train ticket to Belgrade with his own money and spent three days travelling across the country. 'I was the leader of the MPLA in Yugoslavia then, so I was told to meet him at the station,' says Ndunduma, oozing pride. 'You see, Lara, Neto would never be submissive, he'd never be a lackey to anyone.'

A chubby little boy has walked into the room. He is perhaps seven or eight years old. He cuddles up to Ndunduma, leaning lovingly against his legs. Ndunduma introduces us, and his son smiles shyly into his father's knees.

'His mother is much younger than I am,' he says, 'and she's black.'

He pats the little boy on the bottom and sends him scampering out.

With his son out of earshot, he asks me to switch off the recorder. This time I do as I'm told, and he proceeds to give me a curious selection of highly personal details about his life. He talks about his marriages, explaining how each one ended. I can't for the life of me work out why he is revealing this information, recorder on or off. I'm not only a journalist, but I'm a stranger. He describes his life as having been difficult and, furnishing me with further proof, announces that his father had a moustache like Hitler's. I can't think of an appropriate response to this statement – should I be sympathetic? Should I laugh? – so I simply nod, cocking my head slightly to the side, as if to feign mild interest, which is absurd because I'm totally riveted by this stream of confession, which he now brings to an end.

'You must see my art,' he says.

I follow him obediently towards the rear of the house, through a dark kitchen, out into the yard at the back. A steep set of steps leads up to an old outhouse, a single, narrow room that might have been built for a servant but is now his studio. Inside, it is more like a small gallery than the working space for a painter: it's spotless. Sets of his oil paintings are arranged neatly on each wall, and more canvases are stacked up in the corners. He leads me from one painting to the next, looking at me expectantly but without speaking a word. Again, I'm not sure how to respond. They are colourful impressions of the sun and the sand, and of silhouetted figures carrying heavy loads on their heads. 'Clichéd' is the first adjective that comes into my head, then 'mediocre'. So I comment on the amount of work he's produced instead – 'Impressive!' – and leave it to him how he interprets it. But I'm not sure he cares what I think. 'I've sold a lot,' he says. 'People love my work.' I nod, agreeably, but the conversation has dried up.

He walks me back into the house, where he offers me what he calls 'a little gift'. He pulls a biro from his pocket and then two books from one of the shelves. In each, he writes an identical message: *Para Lara Pawson, nova Amiga, com o carinho, Costa Andrade*.[78]

'If you really want to understand me, you need to read these,' he says. He presses the two autobiographies into my hands, and I take the opportunity to tuck in one last question. I want to know if he would still describe himself as a Marxist.

'Yes,' he says instantly, 'a Titoist. Tito is the leader I've most admired.' He looks at the books in my hands and then at my face.

'And the party you still represent?' I add. 'Would you describe the MPLA as Marxist?'

'The government are a bunch of thieves,' he replies, 'and they're fast turning into a dictatorship. I am afraid that, soon, they will be completely out of control.'

Taken aback by his sudden frankness, I wonder if this is some sort of tease.

'Why would I joke?' he asks, utterly serious.

He guides me out of the front door, nudging me down the garden path towards the gate, where we kiss goodbye. As I walk away, I can feel him watching me.

'Lara!' he calls, just as I'm about to get into the car.

'Yes?' I stop, and turn.

'You won't lie, will you? My son gets awfully upset about journalists who lie about me.'

'I promise,' I say, raising a hand. 'I won't lie.'

He remains at the gate, watching as I start the car and steer it around in a clumsy three-point turn. He's still there when I swing left, back onto Rua Comandante Nzaji. I can see him in the mirror, small and sad.

21

ON THE BEACH

Only a few days left. The authorities did agree to renew my visa, but only once and only for fifteen days. I tried arguing for more, and failed. So I must accept that six weeks is better than nothing, and that I am going home on Wednesday.

For my final Sunday, I'm on the beach with friends. We're on the Ilha, a finger of land that curls into the Atlantic from the foot of the hill topped by the old slaving post, the Fortaleza de São Miguel, the place where Zé Van Dúnem was tortured. Home to a community of fishermen, the Ilha doubles as a sort of mini-resort, with expensive beach bars, restaurants and discos dotted along its shores. We're on the west side, where the ocean spreads away from the beach, glimmering gloriously until the horizon, where the view is broken by the long line of waiting cargo that only seems to grow. Today, I count sixteen ships.

The beach is packed. We're a little way beyond Miami Beach, a popular venue owned by Isabel dos Santos, not only the president's eldest child, but also the richest woman in Angola and one of the richest people on the continent. Her power stretches way beyond African borders, however, to Portugal in particular, where she holds major investments in banking and telecommunications, among others. In 2013, the US business magazine *Forbes* valued her net worth at more than a billion dollars.[79] But equally intriguing is Isabel's education: she studied at St Paul's Girls' in London, one of Britain's top private schools, followed by King's College London. If at all possible, I prefer not to give my cash to Miami Beach.

We've come to Café del Mar, a rustic parody with moments of thatched roofing that hovers above the sand on wooden decking covered in cream chairs and tables, and wicker and leather sofas, all of which remind me of an Ikea catalogue. It is frequented by the wealthy, wearing pale linen and what look like extortionately priced sunglasses. We are served by men in white, who bow down to the sand to hand us glasses of freshly squeezed *maracujá* (passion fruit), bowls of chips and, later, ice cream. We seem to be surrounded by beautiful bodies lying like cats stretched out on the hot sand. Children are playing ball games, and young men are hurling themselves up in the air into flying somersaults which take them crashing into the waves of the sea. In the distance, a slender man is running and leaping along piles of huge concrete cubes that form one of the many groynes protecting the Ilha seashore from erosion. I watch him for nearly half an hour, dashing barefoot back and forth along these high barriers, committing his body to the awkward angles and the empty spaces beneath his feet. Not once does he slow down or trip up.

Closer by, loafing on a towel so large it's more like a rug, another man is lying like a beached whale, but with hairy breasts and in a temper. A jellyfish has stung his bulging calf. He's telling anyone who'll listen to stay out of the water. I think he's Russian.

Now, I'm watching three girls, lying in a row, their round bottoms almost completely bare to the sun bar a narrow strip of cotton that disappears between their thighs. In front of them, a man with rags around his midriff is rolling in the sand talking to himself. The girls laugh at him as he stares at their bodies, fiddling with himself awkwardly somewhere below. Then two men in berets with batons appear and the writhing tramp is escorted away. Later we are entertained by buskers who come strolling along, beating rhythms into drums made from large plastic containers and aluminium cans. They are teenagers, all boys, and they make a good sound. As they walk past, one of them breaks away, weaving through the towels and the oiled bodies, shaking a rusty tin. When he's standing above me, looking hopefully at my bag, I notice his T-shirt. 'We will have revenge' printed in English, red on green. Does he know what his message means? I'm about to ask him when the berets with batons turn up, and he vanishes like magic.

I feel something on my wrist.

'I want a dragon. Do me a dragon.'

It's the son of one of my friends. He wants a tattoo on his tummy. He hands me a felt-tip pen and I start to draw. First, a large stomach, then the tail, then the nose and some big teeth. The little boy keeps asking me if I've finished. I try to work in some eyes, some fire from the nostrils, and the spikes that run down a dragon's spine. When I've finished, the child is delighted. He rushes off to show his tattoo to people around us he doesn't know. I admire him chatting so freely with complete strangers. And then he comes back, all cross and whiny.

'You forgot the wings!' he shouts.

'So I did! Get me the pen then!'

Immediately, he prostrates himself before me, an impatient finger pointing at his tummy. I begin drawing a pair of large feathery wings, but this time I'm slower. My attention has been taken by a curious sight further along the beach. A young man is kneeling down, facing the water, which is licking at his knees. His arms are stretched out to either side, like a crucifix, and his mouth is wide open as if he is about to start yelling. His entire body, including his face and hair, is covered in sand. He's also shaking manically, as if experiencing an epileptic fit. He looks as if he might suddenly fall forward onto his face and suffocate. However, another young man is standing by his side, holding one of his arms, stopping him from falling. But then he starts to vomit, the man on his knees, a thick white creamy bile at first spurting and then dribbling from his mouth. Sandy lumps slide down his chin onto his chest and then to the sand at his knees.

'What are you doing?' demands the boy beside me. 'Do my wings!'

'I'm just watching that man,' I say, quietly, concentrating.

The little boy sits up and watches with me. At that moment, the man falls forward, face down into the sand, where he lies completely still. The man who was holding his arm shouts to someone else. Now the two of them are dragging their friend forward towards the water. Perhaps they're going to wash him. But as they arrive at the water, they pull him further in, to where it is at least a foot deep. Then they pull his body up, his arms stretched back like wings, then they let him go, and he disappears into the sea. I watch him in the water, half floating, half sinking. The two other men remain standing on either side. Are they going to pull him out? They do, eventually, and his body is heavy and loose. Another friend runs down to join them, a larger man with broad shoulders. Between the three of them, they push the body onto his left shoulder until it's hanging like a towel down the front and the back, bouncing gently on each stride forward. They walk up the beach, passing a few feet in front of us. The little boy, waiting patiently now, looks at them and then at me.

'Is he dead?'

'Probably just sick,' I reply, but as we watch them walking away, I feel certain that the child is right. I think I've just watched someone being murdered. The inoffensive Brazilian music coming out of Café del Mar crescendoes in my ears. I feel sick and desperate and I wish I knew what was real and what was fiction.

22

◆

HOW OUR HEADS
ARE FORMED

I've developed a mild obsession, while working on this book, of listing other happenings from 1977. It began when I realised that I'd celebrated my father's fortieth birthday on the same day that Maria Reis flew from Luena to Luanda in search of Victor. I remember the party quite clearly. It was 10 June and lots of my parents' friends came for lunch at our home in south-west London. We squeezed together around a collection of tables arranged in a U shape in the room we called the playroom. I think my father gave a speech and my mother got cross with the dog, Franco. I was nine at the time, but when I made the connection, over thirty years later, between the birthday celebrations and Maria's journey, I felt ashamed of my English suburban childhood all tucked up in ignorance.

The list has since developed into a motley collection of more public events. For example, in the UK, on 27 May, the punk band the Sex Pistols released the single 'God Save the Queen'. A radical riff on the national anthem, the song coincided with the Silver Jubilee celebrations for Queen Elizabeth II. Particularly potent was the second line, linking Her Majesty with 'the fascist regime'. The track made it to number two in the official UK charts despite being banned by the BBC and the national broadcasting regulator, both of which deemed it too offensive to air. More significantly, 1977 was the year Steve Biko, the leader of South Africa's black consciousness movement, was killed in police custody; it was the year Elvis Presley died in his bathroom; and it was also the year that two members of the Baader-Meinhof group were found dead in their prison cells. On 2 May 1977, long before she decided to throw herself into human rights, Bianca Jagger threw a party in New York to celebrate her thirty-second birthday. Famous then for her marriage to rock star Mick Jagger, the celebrations were attended by the likes of Liza Minnelli, Truman Capote and Arnold Schwarzenegger, and photographs showed the birthday girl riding bareback among her guests on a white horse. That year, John Travolta rose to fame in the film *Saturday Night Fever*; the artists Gilbert and George hit the headlines with their Dirty Words Pictures exhibition; and Chinua Achebe, in his scathing essay examining *Heart of Darkness*, described Joseph Conrad as 'a thoroughgoing racist'.[80]

I've also included a pile of music, most of which I think I remember from watching *Top of the Pops* with my brother and sister on Thursday nights. There's the hit single, 'Yes Sir, I Can Boogie', sung by the curiously vague pair of Spanish women known as Baccara, and 'I Feel Love' by Donna Summer, the first piece of popular music to be produced with an entirely electronic backing track. Another favourite is 'I Wanna Get Next to You' by the Los Angeles soul and funk band, Rose Royce, about a cash-poor young man in love with a woman who likes hanging out in fancy places. It made it to number fourteen in the UK charts in April 1977.

In Cais de Quatro (Four Quays), one of Luanda's own fancy places, the track is trailing from the speakers right now, recovering memories I could do without, just as I'm about to embark on my final interview in Angola. This restaurant is popular with the rich and the manicured. It sits on the east side of the Ilha, so instead of looking out to the ocean, you look back across the bay, over clapping waves, towards the city that is steadily expanding, upwards and outwards, day by day. I'm here with someone I thought I'd dislike. His name is Aníbal João da Silva Melo.

In 1977, he was an editor at Rádio Nacional. Today, he holds an MPLA seat in the National Assembly and, like so many of his party forefathers, is a published poet and author of fiction. The first I knew of him was in the late 1990s when I began reading his columns in *Jornal de Angola* and occasionally the privately owned weekly *Semanário Angolense*. He struck me as jingoistic and verging on the fanatical in his unswerving support for the party. The black-and-white mugshot probably didn't help: pale cheeks bulging from either side of a moustache moulded in a downward curve around his lips, and his eyes concentrating crossly through a pair of spectacles. It all contributed in my head to a particular idea of the man.

Here, today, in the flesh, however, I'm finding him rather likeable. We choose a small table set back from the water, and sit down either side of one corner, elbows almost touching. When the waiter approaches, it is Melo who takes control, ordering our drinks and some *petiscos* (tapas) to nibble on while we talk. I'm keen to get going and as soon as the young man in white has swivelled away, I announce my intention to record the conversation.

The pause before the response is unnerving, but as I am about to learn, this is simply the way Melo talks: with studied concentration.

'*Como quiser*,' he says, at last. 'As you wish.'

I open my mouth, to ask the first question, when we are interrupted.

'*Tudo bem, João?* What's up?'

The words come from a tight pair of jeans suddenly at the side of our table. A tall woman – I guess she's in her forties – is looking down at us.

'Yah,' João half responds. '*Prima*.' He stands up, they kiss, and she returns to a packed table on the other side of the restaurant from where a few of her friends start waving. João offers them a flutter of fingers before turning back to me and launching straight in to the *vinte e sete*.

'It is important to have a serene reading of what happened,' he says, his deep voice delivering each syllable in a steady rhythm that helps control a pronounced stutter. 'In my analysis, we must distinguish between the Twenty-seventh of May and the 28th.' He half halts. 'First, the attempted military *coup d'état* of the Twenty-seventh of May. This was a great mix-up, what I am accustomed to calling *a salada russo–kim... kim...*' Melo makes several attempts to get the word out before finally succeeding. '*Kimbunda*.' The Russian–Kimbundu salad.

'By this you mean it was Soviet-sponsored?' I say.

He coughs, and a fist pops up to cover his mouth. '*Exactamente!*' The word comes out so precisely, it sounds like a military order. He continues, 'Ideologically speaking, it was a mix of Stalinist discourse from Nito Alves and some of his principal ideologues from Portugal's Communist Party. This was coupled with what I call the ideology of *nitismo*, which combined populist, demagogic and racialist appeals that were very anti-white and anti-*mestiço*. These were their two big lines, and Nito was completely wrong to wind up the masses.' Here, he stops again. The waiter is already back with a tray of drinks and saucers of food. Melo remains silent while the man places each item carefully on the table; only when the waiter is gone does he continue. 'You don't tow them along with such a base idea;

you don't appeal to the lowest common denominator; you have to explain to the *povo* the social history; you have to explain to them that this is a multi-racial country. Colonisation exaggerated the differences between races, but two years from independence was not time enough to resolve these problems. Not even today are they resolved.'

I notice, while he's speaking, that he looks sideways, his pupils straining towards the right-hand side of his eyes. It makes me think he's got something to hide; either that, or he's painfully shy.

He continues, 'Neto didn't have a lot of choice either. It was important for the white and *mestiço* cadres to be able to see whites and *mestiços* in the leadership of the movement. That's why Lara was so important. He was number two. He was the dualist.'

I know this is all important – particularly from Melo's viewpoint as a *mestiço* himself – but I feel I've discussed race with a lot of people now. What I'd really like to do is return to his Russian–Kimbundu salad, an expression I've never heard of until today.

The admission sees him smile. He takes his glass and leans back to drink, waiting for me to speak.

'Regarding the Soviet role,' I say, 'is there any proof of that?'

Labouring over the liquid, he takes his time to swallow before he speaks. But when he does, he is firm and certain: 'Their participation is unquestionable. Nito was a Russian marionette. It is clear they wanted to install him in power.'

As much as I would love something in this story to be categorical, I'm not sure it is all that clear. Recently, a number of respected historians, who've had access to either Soviet or Cuban documents, have argued that Moscow much preferred Nito to Neto and was disappointed when the alleged coup attempt failed.[81] However, like so many of the facts feeding into the *vinte e sete*, even the eminent professors' proof seems fuzzy and fragmented. Supporting information includes the length of time it took the Soviets to criticise the uprising – they waited four days before condemning the *nitistas* – and the claim that a Soviet diplomat left Luanda on 28 May in a hurry. But the bulk of evidence is interviews and documents that support the idea that Neto had always had a troubled relationship with the Soviets, culminating in the early 1970s when Moscow stopped funding him, instead throwing its weight and money behind his rival, Daniel Chipenda. This continued until the end of 1974, when Neto finally managed to regain control of the movement and, in turn, win back Soviet support. Even then, it was no easy ride. Moscow kept nudging Neto to join forces with UNITA in a bid to squeeze out the FNLA. His refusal irritated the Soviets, who remained uneasy about his single-mindedness right through to independence. They were equally wary of his two closest allies, Lara and Carreira, who they viewed as European-style social democrats and whose power within the new administration they resented. Documentary evidence suggests the Soviets continued scouting for more trustworthy partners, and popular choices were the Minister for Interior Administration, Alves, and also Prime Minister Lopo do Nascimento, both of whom made official visits to Moscow in 1976. Indeed, Alves led the Angolan delegation that attended the Communist Party's 25th Congress in February that year, and enjoyed an ovation for his speech. Even so, while all this may well add up to intrigue, none of it amounts to unambiguous proof that the Soviets provided concrete support to a *nitista* plot.

I make the point to Melo, who seems reluctant to be drawn on detail.

'Frankly speaking,' he says, 'what we can see is that Alves wanted a radicalisation of the regime and the economy, but he was very confused, very Maoist, very dangerous, *né*? Most of his ideologues were white and his speeches were all over the place. And as it became evident in the end, this great Russian–Kimbundu cocktail could never hope for a great deal!' He breaks into a snigger – at the failure of the uprising, I think – but I can't help but wonder if he knows any more of the substantial facts than I do.

Part of the problem is that Moscow has refused to give researchers access to its Angola archives dating from 1976 to 1980. Even a former desk officer in the Communist Party's International Department, the political historian Vladimir Shubin, has lamented the lack of available documents, which he insists is more a failure of administration than a political plot. In his view, claims that Alves was a Soviet favourite are baseless. He cites four main reasons for the rumours: first, the fact that Alves promoted himself as a serious socialist who defended 'people power'; second, Alves' reference to discussions with Soviet officials in his writings; third, that he enjoyed significant support from the 9th Brigade; and fourth, the success of his February 1976 visit to Moscow. However, Shubin argues that the only 'hard proof' that Nito was a Soviet favourite came from a documentary in which he featured and that was seen by a number of Angolans who were studying in Moscow in the 1980s. The students interpreted the film as proof of a Soviet-backed plot, but apparently the truth was less controversial: the film-makers had never even heard of the *vinte e sete*, let alone Alves' role.[82] His place in the film was, according to Shubin, mere coincidence.

We're interrupted again. This time it's the Angolan ambassador to Portugal, in a shimmering grey suit. Melo stands up. The two men embrace and exchange what looks like a political performance of muttering and guttural chuckle but, for all I know, might be entirely sincere. When I am introduced, I hold up a hand from across the table and His Excellency smiles in my direction. The two men embrace again and the ambassador proceeds to his table. We proceed to what Melo calls 28 May.

'We can't deny what the *nitistas* were up to,' he says. 'These *golpistas* took the initiative to carry out a coup and they were the first to kill. They killed our leaders in Sambizanga. However,' his chin retreats into his neck, sending his voice down an octave, 'the reaction of the state – this is what I mean by 28 May – was undeniably disproportionate, particularly in Luanda and in the east, in Moxico.'

I think of Victor Reis. 'Why was Moxico such a focal point?' I ask.

'Because of the death of Comandante Dangereux,' he says with a surge of frustration, his voice rising, almost melodic. 'There is no other reason than that. "They've killed our man, so we'll kill all of them." That was the mentality! This was no longer a confrontation between *nitismo* and the leadership of the MPLA: this was regionalism between people in Luanda and those of the interior.'

His candour surprises me. I'd expected him to be among those who deny the extent of violence that followed the uprising: it seems odd that such a staunch defender of the MPLA would be so prepared to admit to this, especially when the subject continues to be taboo.

'And this partly explains the whole mystification of it,' he says in response, though I'm not entirely sure what he means.

'Are you saying that the disproportionate response created the fear and that the fear led to the taboo?' I ask.

He shakes his head and I catch him looking me in the eyes, which I think might indicate a degree of trust growing between us. 'I was in Sambizanga on the evening of 26 May,' he explains. 'I was there with people who were involved. And I can tell you that from the early hours of that morning, I did not see a big demonstration of any sort. There was an attempt by the *nitistas* to persuade people to go out in the streets, but

I didn't actually see many do that. So we have to ask ourselves a question: was this because people were afraid to go out or because there was an absence of real support?'

He stops, and for an awkward moment I think he's asking me for the answer. But then he continues, animated and fluent and absolutely certain of his views.

'If there had been a mass movement onto the streets, which then disappeared as people went back home, then it would suggest that fear was a factor. But there wasn't this mass movement in the first place. There simply wasn't this support!' He laughs again, as if his reasoning is conclusive empirical evidence, but there is a tightness in his humour, an anxiety that makes it uneasy, like he's suppressing something uncomfortable in his gut.

More to the point, I'm confused. I thought we were discussing whether or not the fear that is so prevalent in Angola today resulted from the government's brutal response to the uprising, whereas Melo is talking about a pre-existing fear that influenced participation in the uprising. 'Are you suggesting,' I ask, trying to fathom his argument, 'that this is a case of faulty memory on a massive scale?'

'*Exactamente*,' he says. 'And the reason this has happened is that the leadership of the MPLA and the state – for reasons I myself cannot explain – has been unable, during all these years, to communicate with the people about the Twenty-seventh of May.'

'And why is that?'

'Because it has a guilt complex,' he replies. 'And maybe that complex results from 28 May being disproportionate. However, there is also this para...' – he takes a breath and pushes the word out hard and loud – 'paradox, which is that after *nitismo*, the regime radicalised itself. Economically, it became Marxist–Leninist; and politically, the early 1980s was the most closed period in Angola's recent history. This is the paradox – that the MPLA responded to the pressure from the *nitistas* in this way.'

In other words, despite quashing the uprising and executing its leaders, the regime proceeded to pursue the sort of leftist policies the *nitistas* had been asking for.

Melo is nodding in agreement. 'Yah,' he says. 'Exactly.'

Again, I'm surprised by his frankness, which takes us back to the role of the Soviets. Some of the old MPLA documents show that the movement didn't simply pursue so-called *nitista* policies, as Melo is suggesting, but proceeded along a path that would be more pleasing to Moscow. In December 1977, for example, the MPLA held its first Party Congress, which Moscow had been pressing for for several years. As well as confirming his decision to establish a special presidential regiment to secure his own position as leader, Neto used the occasion to announce the movement's extended title: the MPLA-Workers' Party. From now onwards, Marxism–Leninism would be the ruling ideology, and the MPLA-PT would be the vanguard of the working class, which in turn was the directing force of the nation, never mind the negligible size of Angola's urban proletariat.

'Ultimately,' I suggest, 'the MPLA felt it had to conform in order to keep the Soviets off its back.'

'That too! Yes!' he says, looking delighted. 'I agree! But it was a response to one of Nito's calls – that's my point.'

This is an unusual experience – finding a member of the MPLA in agreement with me – and I feel a rush of optimism, as if my relationship with Angola might suddenly be swerving into better times. But it doesn't last long. I can already hear the counter-arguments entering my head. For example, in October 1976, on returning home from his own trip to Moscow, Neto dismissed Nito from his ministerial post. Not only did the Soviets say nothing in response, but six months later, in March 1977, they ratified a friendship treaty with the Angolan parliament based on Marxist–Leninist principles. At the time, this was interpreted by a number of analysts as heartfelt Soviet approval of the MPLA – two months before the uprising. Moreover, even after the Twenty-seventh of May, there was no reduction in Soviet arms supplies to Angola, nor was Neto punished for executing the leading *nitistas*, including Moscow's so-called favourite, Nito Alves. How to explain this? Had Moscow finally concluded that Neto was the better bet after all? That he was the compliant African Marxist who would spread socialism across the continent? It seems unlikely. After all, throughout this entire period – before, during and after the December Congress – while the MPLA did adopt a spread of Marxist–Leninist policies, Neto continued to do his best to keep a number of leading Western companies on board, including De Beers, Cabgoc, Texaco, Petrofina, Fiat and Volvo.[83] More significantly, although I've not been able to confirm this independently, I have heard that he continued trying to strike up a fruitful political relationship with the United States.

'The trouble is,' I say, turning to Melo, 'everyone has their point of view, and each one seems to be totally different and contradictory. It's hard to come to any clear conclusions.'

Again, we're in agreement. '*Claro*,' he says, with a smile. 'For sure. And all I'm doing is telling you what I know.'

Given his amiability, I push the question of the violence of 28 May forward a little, by asking him how long it went on for.

'Oh, right up to Neto's death,' he replies. 'Or perhaps just a bit before, when he dismantled DISA.'

So the rumour goes, Neto was in a miserable state of remorse in the run-up to his death in Moscow on 10 September 1979. In a bid to put things right, he dissolved DISA, the brutal security service that had been built with the help of advisers from East Germany's Stasi, and which was blamed by so many for the purges of the *vinte e sete*.

'And what is your estimate on the number of dead?' I ask.

'It's a big confusion,' says Melo. 'I think that the numbers that are given are largely fantastical. Currently they've reached 90,000!' He laughs, loudly, and takes a swig from his glass. 'But it gets bigger every year. It started at 15,000, then the next year it was 20,000, then 30,000 and on it goes. This is where the state has some responsibility – to tell the truth.'

'Which is?'

'Well, first of all, Neto's speech on the night of the Twenty-seventh of May was really bad. You do not make that sort of statement publicly. He was very emotional, too emotional, because of what had happened to his men in Sambizanga. But politicians are also men. He was only a man. But it was a mistake.'

'And the other responsibility?'

'The state must compensate the families of the dead. Within the army, a few things have been done, but it is necessary to attend to all the families that were affected.' He breaks off. He's thinking. 'I lost many friends myself. Mbala Neto from Rádio Nacional and a nephew, Betinho, were both killed. I studied with Betinho. We were close friends. To this day, I miss him. I felt terrible afterwards. Terrible. I was clearly anti-Nito. He was clearly anti-Neto. I wrote publicly against Nito. But we were friends.'

As he speaks, the image I used to have of this man is dissolving. I'm touched by his honesty and feel foolish for having judged him so readily.

He continues, 'I lost many friends on both sides. Saydi Mingas. Helder Neto. They were also killed.'

The sadness on Melo's face is arresting. The more people I have interviewed, the more uncomfortable I feel about pushing them back into such difficult memories. So I urge the conversation on a little, by asking him what he thinks the impact was on the party. I've read that the membership dropped from 110,000 to 31,000, such that by 1980, from a population of 8 million people, just 0.4 per cent were members of the MPLA.[84]

'I don't know what the numbers are, but there is something more profound about the party that you need to consider,' he says. 'First, there were two lines within the MPLA: those who favoured a brutal repression, absolute and total, which was predominant; and those who thought the opposition could be controlled in a more subtle way, who thought that lives should be saved. Bear in mind, we are talking about a party with very strong and very old authoritarian roots.'

This is too enigmatic for me. 'Are you referring to its African heritage, or its Portuguese one?' I ask.

'Both,' says Melo. 'In actual fact, it comes from three origins. One is the traditional African culture, and I'm not romantic about that; I don't have this notion that everything in Africa is gold and beautiful.' He starts chuckling, and I laugh too, relieved that he is not among the masses who patronise the complex history of the continent. 'For many of us, however, our heads were formed by colonialism and fascism. This is obviously the Portuguese element, number two.' Again, we both laugh, perhaps at the shared point of view, I'm not sure. 'And third,' he says, cutting short the humour, 'this authoritarianism came from Marxism–Leninism, which had existed in the country for many years by the time of the Twenty-seventh of May. Together, these three created a very strong authoritarian culture, and if the *nitistas* had got power, they, too, would have killed many people.'

Oddly, given what I had been led to understand about the man, Melo seems to me to be surprisingly balanced.

'So you accept the view that Neto was a dictator?' I ask.

He looks puzzled. 'He was not a dictator, nor was he a puppet. He was a centraliser and a strong leader, but not a dictator.'

'Perhaps, had he lived longer, he would have become one,' I suggest.

Melo's eyes widen.

'As I said,' he says carefully, 'Angola has a strong, authoritarian tradition, and it is in all of our heads.'

PART III

'I believe I have said enough to make it clear that it is neither Marxism nor communism that I am renouncing, but rather the use that some have made of Marxism and communism. What I want is that Marxism and communism be placed in the service of Negro peoples, not Negro peoples in the service of Marxism and communism.'

Aimé Césaire[85]

23

◆

LOOSE ENDS

It's two minutes to five and the street lamps go out in east London. Someone across the road is awake, their front room yellow behind net curtains. I don't know anything about the couple in that house. They've lived there for ten years and like to keep to themselves. Once, I saw the woman in a t'ai chi class. She pretended she didn't recognise me, but I'm sure she knew who I was. We'd met a few months earlier when I'd gone over there to discuss plans to set up a community wireless network on the street. I knocked on the door and said hello, then I asked myself in for a coffee. She said that would be awkward. 'The kitchen's in a bit of a mess,' added the willowy male at her side. We've never spoken since.

It's windy. Outside, the hanging branches of the silver birches that line the pavement swash and sway. I can hear a dustbin truck and the occasional bus on Lower Clapton Road, but apart from that there's no traffic. I think of Luanda, of how busy it gets so early in the day, and here, where the only people who are awake are the Turkish men who run the shop on the corner. Two brothers, who never seem to sleep. I like the fatter one a great deal. He's been here twenty-one years and still can't speak a full sentence of English. Once, with his nephew interpreting, I asked him who he's been talking to for the past two decades. 'Family,' he replied gleefully, 'and Turkey friends.' I reminded him that we, too, have shared quite long conversations in what he calls 'Turkey-English'. Our chats tend to involve a lot of laughter and, often, me telling him off. 'Two decades,' I exclaimed the other day, 'and still not a word of English! You should be ashamed!' I've even offered him free language classes, but he's not interested. 'Why you no learn Turkey?' was his hilarious response.

It's twenty past five now. I've been up for over an hour, worrying about my research into the *vinte e sete*. Outside, a man is struggling to pull a large brown suitcase along the pavement. I wonder what he's up to. There's something about the way he's walking – the apparent weight of the luggage – that looks suspicious. If there's a body in the bag, it wouldn't be the first. The other week, a dead woman was found in pieces inside a rucksack in one of our local parks.

Perhaps I need some tea.

Since I've been home, I seem to have got a bit stuck. There are still so many uncertainties, so much that remains unresolved, such as whether the uprising on the Twenty-seventh of May was a coup attempt or a demonstration. Strange though it may sound, I suspect it was both. Certainly it is hard to accept that the leading *nitistas* wanted anything less than to seize power and force a change of government, which, strictly speaking, defines a coup. Why else would weapons have been distributed in Sambizanga and the entire 9th Brigade mobilised? Why else would the national radio station have been overrun, and the central Luanda jail attacked in order to liberate prisoners? And while it is probably true that Nito Alves and his crew did not want to kill, imprison or even exile the president, they absolutely did want to overthrow the most powerful men around him, primarily the three *mestiços* Lúcio Lara, Iko Carreira and Onambwe, and also the head of DISA, Ludy Kissassunda. On the other hand, I'm certain that there were many in Luanda that day who believed they were participating in a legitimate and peaceful public protest. Their desire to be heard by Agostinho Neto was probably genuine. One of the difficulties in trying to resolve the question of intention is that people who might know are either too afraid to speak or still too traumatised to revisit their memories. Another problem is that those who would have been able to shed significant light – Nito, Zé Van Dúnem, Monstro Imortal, Mbala Neto, among others – are all dead. They were killed by the state.

Thinking about the dead has piqued my insomnia. A while ago, I received an email from a young man by the name of Paulo Mungungo. He had read an article I'd published in a Portuguese academic journal, in which I had written about the death of Victor Reis, Maria's late husband. I had cited the letter Maria had shown me from the Portuguese embassy in Angola, which had stated that Reis was 'summarily executed by the son of the commander known as "Dangereux"'. Well, Mungungo informed me, he is the son in question. 'When my father died,' he wrote, 'he left behind a widow and three orphans, of whom two were little girls aged ten years and four years, and myself, the youngest, aged one year and five months.' Clearly, he could not have killed Reis. Not only that, but he wanted me to pass on to Maria his 'deep feelings of sadness' for the suffering she had endured all these years. He hoped, one day, they might meet.

Yet more unknowns.

Frankly, I cannot say I have a clue how many people were killed in the response to the uprising. I have no evidence to prove that the figure was nearer 2,000, or 25,000, or even 90,000. All I've heard are vague estimates and conjecture. Yet the more I've considered the question of numbers, the less the amount seems to matter. As the philosopher Judith Butler has observed, knowing how to count is 'not the same as figuring out how and whether a life counts'.[86] Of course, the number of dead serves different purposes to different people and groups. Those who feel aggrieved – mainly Alves' surviving supporters and the relatives and friends of those killed in the aftermath – tend to offer the higher numbers. Those accused of unleashing the killings – Ndunduma, for example – insist the figure is much lower. I've asked myself over and over whether I'd be more shocked if the number of the dead were towards the top of the scale. And if, later, the true figure were proved beyond doubt to be 'only' 2,000, would that mean they mattered less than if they were part of a far larger number? I hope not, but I don't know. What I find striking is that no matter how big the figure becomes, it doesn't seem to change anything in real terms. The steady inflation of the number has not led to an investigation by a well-funded media body like the *New Yorker*, or an international organisation like the UN, or a team of lawyers from the International Criminal Court, or an independent group of expert forensic scientists.

Recently, I read about a massacre in 1981 at El Mozote and surrounding villages in El Salvador.[87] A thorough investigation by a local human-rights organisation working with the Argentine Forensic Anthropology Team and the UN revealed that 767 people were killed. I have read the list of the names of the dead, including their age, their sex and, in some cases, their profession. Compelling for its details, that list of hundreds unsettles me more than the anonymous tens of thousands alleged to have died during the purge that followed the *vinte e sete de maio*. Occasionally, I've caught myself wondering whether those who quite rightly seek justice for the dead would be happier with a higher death count than a lower one. If the real figure turned out to be in the hundreds, say, would they be disappointed? Following this train of thought, I've asked myself whether there might be a golden figure that would spur the Angolan government to order an independent inquiry and then to make a public apology to the relatives of the dead. What number would make the *vinte e sete* matter?

Perhaps the trauma of war in Angola has desensitised the country. Is that why the estimates keep going up, and up, and up? Because those deaths must somehow compete with the millions who died during fourteen years of liberation war followed by twenty-seven years of civil war? Four decades of fighting: how can the *vinte e sete* gain any attention against that? My half answer has been to seek out individuals, to hear their distinct stories in an attempt to give some detail and human depth to the sweeping claims that surround this tragic 'post-colonial' event. But I still don't know if this will encourage people to think beyond big round numbers and consider the lives that were lost. I'm certain that what is needed is a proper inquiry, similar to the one that happened in El Mozote, so that Angolans could at least begin with some facts they could trust.

It's nearly six. A lady with a copper frying pan on her head has just walked past my front door followed by two skinheads. I recognise all three. I often see them sitting on the steps of our local church, or collapsed on one of the benches in the small park around the corner, sky-high on crack cocaine. I worry about the woman, out of control among those men. I worry about what they do to her at night.

In quiet desperation, I've been pursuing some of the British mercenaries who were held in Luanda's São Paulo prison at the time of the uprising. They were among thirteen foreigners who were paid with CIA funds to fight on behalf of the FNLA and were captured by FAPLA in the summer of 1976. Their trial in Luanda is a story of its own. Suffice to say, four were executed and nine sentenced to prison. I've managed to locate two. One is currently in prison in his own country; the other, a surprisingly obliging fellow, agreed to meet me for a drink in a north London bar.

It was a curious rendezvous. On my way from the Tube station, I brushed past Tony Benn. A part of me wanted to stop this principled, anti-war socialist and make a confession about my plans for the night, but thankfully I managed to resist the urge and let the old man alone.

I ordered a glass of wine while waiting for my ex-mercenary, who pitched up late. I must have been nervous because by the time the evening ended several hours later, I was definitely drunk. In hindsight, I had no reason to be anxious. He was incredibly easy-going. Possibly too easy-going. Everything I said made him laugh. Everything *he* said made him laugh. The king of repartee, that was my impression. Although, there were moments when his gaze looked less jubilant, when I'm sure I caught him looking back on his life, his face suddenly softer, more uncertain, his eyes yearning to start all over again.

I was surprised when he spoke of having Angolan friends: people, he said, he loved. He even spoke good Portuguese, which I suppose shouldn't have been such a surprise given all those years he had to practise in prison. As the evening ran on, he told me that the Cubans ran the prison when he was there and, later, he said they were running the whole country too. How he would have known that, from inside, is another question. He said that when the *nitistas* broke in on the morning of the Twenty-seventh of May, the majority of the Angolans who did not run away were members of the MPLA breakaway factions, known as the Active Revolt and the Eastern Revolt. They were mainly *mestiços*, he said, and a handful of blacks. 'They'd been banged up by Nito Alves when he was minister,' he said, bucketing laughter. But I found it hard to trust his account, less because of who he is – or was – than the perpetual banter that accompanied it. It's hard to take seriously someone who ends every sentence with a joke. The things we do to stay sane.

It was after this unusual encounter that I discovered that one of my relatives was also invited to go and fight for the FNLA in the mid 1970s. Uncle George, now deceased, was a bricklayer from Liverpool. He was in a pub in Slough when he was approached by the Cypriot-born Briton Costas Georgiou, better known as Colonel Callan. Like many of the men who were invited to fight in Angola, Uncle George was working class, fit from labouring on building sites, but probably a bit bored with life and certainly not well paid. This was Britain in the 1970s: many were looking for opportunities elsewhere. The other advantage of Uncle George, from Callan's point of view at least, must have been that he had done national service. He knew how to fire a gun. However, while he may have been poor and lacking in educational qualifications, Uncle George was no fool. Nor did he harbour any desire to go and kill people in a land he'd never heard of. He remained in the UK, where he lived and died a poor but honest man. The same cannot be said for Colonel Callan. He killed many, among them some of the very mercenaries he'd recruited. On 10 July 1976, he was executed by firing squad in Luanda.

By the by, I've also had a meeting with an Angolan woman who told me the tale of a boy called Augusto N'gangula. 'He was the little MPLA pioneer,' she explained, 'who gave his life to save many Angolans during the liberation struggle'. Apparently, Ndunduma even wrote a poem about this brave young fellow. Except, the woman told me, N'gangula is a myth, fabricated by the MPLA. She told me that she'd always assumed that Nito Alves was, likewise, 'just another MPLA myth', though, in his case, invented to put the fear of God into anyone considering criticising the movement. When I told her what I'd found out about the *vinte e sete*, she said it was the first time she'd ever heard any detail about that moment in her country's history. She said that listening to me was helping her make sense of certain stories in her family history, particularly regarding an aunt who had suffered from appalling mental-health problems throughout her life. The woman, who asked me not to name her in case her family in Luanda should suffer the consequences, seemed certain that her aunt's depression was wrapped up with the *vinte e sete*. As our conversation continued, and she spoke more freely about her family history, it was as if lost pieces of a puzzle were dropping into her lap from on high. Just before we left the little pub, two hours from London, she added, not unaffectionately, that after independence, 'Living in Luanda was a bit like living in Havana. At school we were made to sing the Cuban national anthem, and the Cuban flag went up alongside the Angolan flag.'

It's nearly eight now and the sun has broken through. Shining cars pour shots of light at the large bay windows across the road; slender men and women with flopped hairdos and drainpipe trousers cycle past, one leaning back a little, his hands resting on his thighs, steering with his weight, not his handlebars. Self-conscious moments of liberty.

I keep thinking about João Faria. The other day, a friend sent me some information about something called the 'flybot'. Weighing sixty milligrams and with a wingspan of three centimetres, this robotic insect was recently exhibited at the Museum of Modern Art in New York as part of the show 'Design and the Elastic Mind'. It's the work of Robert J. Wood, an assistant professor at the Harvard School of Engineering and Applied Sciences in Massachusetts. Wood believes his little robot will be able to fly independently within the next four years. So perhaps he's not aware of the mechanical *libelinhas* long ago spotted by my friend as they zigzagged happily about the buildings of Luanda.

A few weeks ago, I found a redacted CIA report, 'The Angolan leadership: Current perspectives and prospects after Neto'.[88] It was written by one Randy Pherson and published in December 1978. Now president of the lucrative Pherson Associates – which, I quote, 'specializes in providing training in advanced analytic techniques to analysts involved in basic analytic tradecraft, counterterrorism, counterintelligence, denial and deception, and homeland security'[89] – I had hoped to interview him, but after responding to my first email, Randy has remained resolutely silent.

The central concern of his report is what he calls 'the trend toward a black-dominated, more nationalist, and possibly more leftist state' in Angola. Washington, or at least the CIA, was clearly worried about Neto's impending departure. They thought it likely he might 'become seriously handicapped by a heart attack, drinking, or other health problems'. If that did occur – which indeed it did, in September 1979 – Randy predicted two possible outcomes. If Neto's exit was swift, a 'more radical, black nationalist and pro-Soviet line' would take over the regime. If it was more gradual, 'a mulato-influenced faction' was likely to retain power and to continue 'governing in much the same way as Neto'. Another possibility, Randy wrote, was a plot to overthrow Neto. If this was attempted, it would be led, he said, by 'members of a black-power faction'. Note the use of domestic US terminology here: Randy seems to be equating a black African push for power in Angola with the civil-rights movement in the US, drawing parallels with African-American leaders like Malcolm X. The so-called black-power option was not a scenario the CIA was keen on in Angola any more than it was at home. Instead, Randy's report supports a symbolic black leader in Angola – someone who could step into Neto's shoes – but with reduced presidential powers. Responsibility for running the country could then shift to the Politburo, 'where the mulatoes,' wrote Randy approvingly, 'now control about one-third of the seats'. What Randy feared most, it seems, was an end to what he describes as 'a campaign within the MPLA to improve relations with the West and reach a rapprochement with Zaire'.

Randy's report appears to clarify a number of points. First, it undermines claims made in the MPLA Politburo document about the *vinte e sete* – that Nito Alves was representing Western imperialist interests. The last thing Washington wanted was a radical, leftist black nationalist running the show in Luanda. Secondly, it supports the notion that Neto was trying to build a successful working relationship with the US. I suppose this shouldn't surprise me. After all, Ndunduma made it clear that Neto wanted to get the best deal for Angola as an independent African nation, regardless of whom the deal was with.

Although Randy has declined to talk to me, another American has been more forthcoming. Ambassador Don McHenry, an African-American, was the deputy US representative to the UN from 1977 to 1979 and the permanent representative from 1979 to 1981. During a telephone conversation from his office in Georgetown University, he said he'd enjoyed a good relationship with Neto. The pair engaged in what he described as 'productive talks' in 1977, 1978 and 1979. Throughout this period, McHenry says that Neto was 'very keen on a relationship with the US'. The president hoped it would 'help Angola's legitimacy and open doors economically'. Regarding Neto's political allegiances – 'I didn't get any ideological commitment from him' – McHenry's observations reinforce what Ndunduma and others have said. Nevertheless, I was taken aback by the ambassador's admission that senior US figures were in Luanda on the Twenty-seventh of May 1977. 'Our presence was not a secret,' he said. 'We were there for several days. We spoke with Lopo do Nascimento [the prime minister].' Concluding our conversation, he added, 'It shows you how pragmatic they – the MPLA – were.' It also shows how simplistic so many Angola observers have been. If he was a Marxist at all, Neto was never a clear-cut one, no matter how far you seek to stretch the definition.

Ironically, I've heard similar accounts from a former Soviet diplomat who worked with several African leaders during the 1970s. Like McHenry, my man in Moscow also noted Neto's lack of ideological commitment and insists this is partly what made Neto such an attractive candidate to the Soviet Union. Westerners may have imagined that the Soviets were devoted to global communism, but in fact they wanted someone who would not try to rush socialist development in Angola. They did not want a radical black nationalist like Nito Alves taking over. So the former diplomat told me, he was 'too radical, too leftist' and too much in favour of what he referred to as 'black racism'. 'Contrary to what you all seem to think,' he said, 'we didn't want leftists.'

The first of the day's emails have started coming through. One is from a US non-governmental organisation. Can I help them find a decent 'local' to head their programme in Angola? They must be bilingual and transparent, says the NGO, which has decided to stop depending on Westerners because they struggle to get visas and rarely speak Portuguese. I think of all the overqualified Angolans I know, and their views on foreign NGOs. In my reply, I tell them I might know one or two, adding unequivocally, 'But they will expect to be paid what the Westerners were paid.' Another email is from Ndunduma. He writes from Lisbon. 'I am very ill,' he says. 'I have cancer. If you can make it out here soon, I would love to see you. I don't have long to live.'

I go to the gym. Exercise helps me think. I switch the machine to gradient twelve and the conveyor belt rises beneath me. I begin walking uphill, pumping my arms like a soldier. In front of me there are four flat TV screens. A Carry On film is showing on two of them, BBC News on another. On the fourth, there's a Walt Disney film about two tigers being encouraged to kill each other by two men, who are white but whose faces are covered in brown paint – what they used to call 'blacking-up' – and who both wear turbans. No sound comes out of the televisions: we have the radio for that. Capital Breakfast with 'Johnny and Lisa', who vibrate from four speakers around the room so no matter where you are, you can hear Johnny and Lisa joshing. On the television, I watch the two men poking at the tigers, until a pretty white woman and her son – both without face paint – arrive to rescue the pair of cats. The men appear to snarl and crack their whips in anger. Over on screens one and two, Sid James is doing his own bit of snarling – at a blonde in pink feathers and pink tights and shoes.

I move on to the rowing machine. Beside me, a woman is sliding backwards and forwards in strong, vigorous strokes. Covered in a delicate grey material that floats around from her face to her feet, she's like a cutaway from a Pina Bausch production. Side by side, rowing to nowhere, our thoughts travel far from here. I think of the old woman I met in Luanda. We'd both travelled on the same coach from Malanje, 500 kilometres away. I offered to carry her belongings, but she laughed when I struggled to pick up the largest. 'It's easier like this,' she said, grabbing it and swinging it up in one tidy swoop to the crown of her head.

As soon as I get home, I check my emails again, with a compulsion I know I need to conquer. There's one from a Cuban woman living in Miami. She says she'd like to talk.

24

♦

A CUBA CONNECTION

I'm looking at a black-and-white photograph on my computer.

To the left of centre, beneath a sky thick with cloud, a man is standing, smiling broadly at the camera. His eyes are scrunched up and his teeth are just visible beneath a bushy moustache. A neat widow's peak lends height to his forehead and his face is framed by a pair of dark sideburns. He wears a pale shirt, clean stripes running from neck to hip, with a pair of spectacles tucked into the top pocket. His left arm hangs down in front of his body, forming a strong visual column to his left foot, which is pointing forwards. Around him stand a group of children. Some are looking at him; others are looking at us. In the bottom right-hand corner, two boys stare into the lens. The one with a large gap between his front teeth looks giggly, while the other's face is creased with anxiety. Opposite them, another boy peers suspiciously into the frame. Beside him, a small girl, naked beneath a woollen coat, stands – shoulders back, belly out – staring up at a woman, who is holding a toddler and beaming with joy. Around this woman's shoulders is the arm of our moustached man. Behind them all, a line of straw huts runs into the distance, where another woman and her baby stand beside a soldier in a beret.

The man who is the focus of this image is paediatrician Jorge Martínez. In 1977, at the age of twenty-six, he was one of 418 Cuban doctors and nurses sent to Angola as part of a civilian mission. We've made contact, inadvertently, through his niece, Ivette Levya Martínez. She's a Miami-based journalist who's been documenting the lives of Cuban veterans of the Angolan civil war on her blog, *La última guerra* (The last war). She came across my name while 'reaching out', as she put it, to Angolan veterans, and sent me an email. A few days later, she called me here at home. We discussed Angola's recent history and the role of Cuba, and in the course of the conversation she happened to mention her uncle. Rather vaguely, she said he'd lived in Angola during the late 1970s, possibly in the east of the country, but she wasn't sure of the facts.

Today, I've received another email from Ivette. She tells me that her uncle lived in Luena, in Moxico province, in 1977. Generously, she's asked him if he will be interviewed by me. He has agreed, on one condition: he won't talk over the phone. Instead, I am to email my questions to Ivette, who will pose them in Spanish and send me a transcript of his answers.

Dr Martínez arrived in Luena on 14 March 1977. 'It was a ghost town,' he says. Apart from the underground electricity supplies, which impressed him, his lasting memory of Luena is how ruined it was by war. He recalls seeing UNITA graffiti everywhere. Most of the shops and small businesses had been looted and damaged by the rebels shortly before they had fled advancing FAPLA and Cuban troops. As far as he can remember, there was not a single bar in which to relax and take a drink, and there was only one supermarket, which belonged to the Pintos, a pair of Portuguese brothers. 'It was located in front of the railway station, but it never had anything to buy,' says Dr Martínez. But despite Luena's rather wretched state, the young doctor was struck by its wide streets with lines of fruit trees running down the centre. 'We Cubans named it El Miramar de la Selva in reference to a beautiful neighbourhood in Havana.'

Further out, the town was surrounded by troops, mainly Cubans, who were defending it from UNITA. The rebels were still active in small pockets throughout Moxico, where more Cuban soldiers were leading a counter-insurgency campaign, dubbed Luta Contra Bandidos (Fight Against Bandits). 'Luena was under siege,' says Dr Martínez. 'It was totally controlled by the Cubans and their puppet, Armando Dembo, the provincial commissioner.'

All Cuban civilians living in Luena were based in a building in the centre of town. Eighteen of them were in the medical brigade. 'Three were black and three were *mestiços*, the rest of us were all white,' he says. The other Cubans worked in construction, education, agriculture or transport, and some were directly involved in developing the political structures of the MPLA, such as the children's and women's organisations. They performed a critical role in keeping Angola going after hundreds of thousands of Portuguese bureaucrats and technicians fled to Lisbon as independence loomed. From November 1975 to December 1977, 3,500 Cuban civilians went to Angola. Over the next twelve years that number would rise to 50,000.

But the Cubans who lived in Angola did so under strict conditions. According to Dr Martínez, 'Our medical work and our personal lives were completely controlled by the security arm of Cuba and its civil mission.' This made it very hard to socialise with people outside the residential missions. During his time in Luena, Dr Martínez made only two real Angolan friends – a woman called Guida and her husband, Nascimento. Theirs was the only home the doctor ever visited outside the Cuba mission; it was next door, so it was easy for him to drop in. 'I remember Guida with great affection and gratitude although I have not seen or heard of her since,' he says. The couple always had food and beer in the house because Nascimento drove a truck for FAPLA, transporting goods from Luanda. 'They were very respectful and discreet,' says Dr Martínez. 'Whenever I visited, no one else entered the house. We used to listen to music on the radio and on their record player. We never danced, but with them we always had a good time.' He had met Guida at the provincial hospital, where they both worked. She was one of his assistant nurses. The other was a woman called Cristina.

At eleven o'clock on the Twenty-seventh of May, Dr Martínez was doing his usual consultations at the hospital, when Cristina approached him. She told him that a coup attempt had taken place in Luanda. It had been led, she said, by a man called Nito Alves. 'I'd never heard of him before,' says Dr Martínez. Cristina advised him to stop working and return to the mission. So he walked back to the residential quarters. When he arrived, he found the building surrounded by tanks and Soviet armoured personnel carriers.

At two o'clock, a young Angolan man, also by the name of Nito, turned up at the mission. He was the head of the local branch of the MPLA youth wing. 'He was a very nice guy,' says Dr Martínez, 'a friend to many Cubans, especially his Cuban counterpart, Urbano Varela.' On this occasion, Nito had some important information to share with his Cuban friends. They gathered around and listened carefully as he explained that Nito Alves had betrayed the president and the nation. 'He passionately defended Agostinho Neto and the MPLA,' the doctor remembers. 'All of us felt very moved by his words.'

At about five o'clock, a Soviet four-by-four pulled up outside the Cuban residence. As well as the driver, there was another man whom Dr Martínez refers to as 'a bodyguard'. 'They came to our building looking for the clinical doctor and myself. They told us we were needed to carry out a special mission.' So the two doctors got into the four-by-four and were driven to the outskirts of Luena, to a spot between the airport and the Cuban military tank unit, where there was a ditch with a bulldozer parked beside it.

'In front of the ditch,' explains the doctor, 'stood seventeen Angolans. They were going to be executed for collaborating with the Nito Alves group. Among those who were about to be killed were people I knew. There was Cristina, my assistant, who was a few weeks pregnant; and David, an emergency nurse at the hospital, to whom I had given a book about paediatrics; and another, the only Angolan doctor in Luena, the director of health, whose name I cannot remember; and there was Nito, the head of the MPLA youth movement. The rest, I did not know.'

He watched as this line of Angolan men and women were shot without blindfolds. 'The only one who asked for clemency was Nito, but his pleas of innocence went unheard. The firing squad was made up of Angolan FAPLA troops. The Cubans who were present were limited to watching. I remember that Miguelito was there, the head of the Cuban civil mission. Also, Lieutenant Colonel Masso, the head of the Cuban regiment, and Colonel Eloy Bartot Bustos, adviser to the Cuban Ministry of the Interior, and Urbano Varela, the adviser to the JMPLA. The infamous Colonel Ramón Valle Lazo was also there.'

When all seventeen were dead, the two doctors were called forward. 'We were there to sign the death certificates,' says Dr Martínez, 'but they had already been completed and filled in.' In every case, the stated cause of death was *acidente da viação* – road accident. While the two medics signed the certificates, an experienced Cuban builder, Renato Rojas, started up the bulldozer and began filling the ditch with earth.

Afterwards, the doctors were driven back into town and dropped off at the mission.

Looking back, Dr Martínez remembers these killings coming almost out of nowhere. He is certain that in Luena there had been no demonstration or revolt of any kind – either before, during or after the Twenty-seventh of May. He is equally certain that senior members of the Cuban military had, in his words, 'prior information that something was going to occur'. He points to the arrival in Luena, just a few days earlier, of Colonel Valle Lazo. Often referred to in Cuba as '*ballenazo*', meaning 'big whale' or 'walloped by a whale' – a play on his name but also an indication of his physical size – Colonel Valle Lazo, says Dr Martínez, 'was in charge of the military and all the repression during that period of the attempted coup'.

Eleven days before the Nito Alves uprising, however, Fidel Castro told a US journalist that 'the only reason' for Cuban troops to be in Angola was 'to defend them from South Africa or any other imperialist'. He further explained, 'The mission is that of supporting Angola against any external attack while the Angolan army is organizing, training, and preparing.' It was all being done, he said, 'in order to save a black people of Africa'.[90] While some Angolans would certainly dispute the last part of this claim – it certainly contradicts what several have told me – what is absolutely true is that Cuba saved the MPLA.

Without the intervention of 36,000 Cuban troops between October 1975 and April 1976, it is unlikely that Neto would have been declaring independence in Luanda on 11 November 1975 and even less likely that the MPLA would have remained in power for very long afterwards. For the fact of the matter is that in the lead-up to Portugal's departure on 10 November, the MPLA controlled only pockets of the country. In Luanda, it was effectively under siege as the two other liberation movements advanced, pincer-like, towards the capital.[91] From the north came the FNLA, boosted by Zairean soldiers, Portuguese mercenaries and a handful of South African and CIA advisers; from the central highlands came UNITA, fortified by military hardware flown in from Pretoria, South African troops, and a number of Zairean and Portuguese officers; and from the south came the SADF's Zulu column, which had invaded Angola from Namibia on 14

October, and was making swift strides north. The MPLA's weaker forces did not stand a chance.

So it was that Operation Carlota[92] began on 7 November, with Castro waving off the first contingent of Cuba's Special Forces at Havana airport. Their entry onto the Angolan stage inspired Gabriel García Márquez in a stylish and rather romantic piece he penned for the London-based journal *New Left Review*. They were, the Colombian novelist wrote, of a 'high ideological and political level; some have academic degrees, read a great deal and are constantly concerned with intellectual excellence.'[93] They were also the island's elite fighters – within hours of landing in Angola they had overwhelmed the FNLA and its allies in a brilliant artillery attack to the north of Luanda.

Well aware of the enclave of Cabinda's oil wealth – it was contributing $450 million a year to government coffers – Castro had told his men that defending this Angolan province was as important as defending the Bay of Pigs had been in 1961. Once again, their superior skills paid off and, by 12 November, the enemy here had also retreated. Not only that, but the US giant Gulf Oil had continued to operate its offshore installations without interruption throughout the entire battle.

Less than a fortnight later, on 23 November, the Cubans ambushed the Zulu column, killing and injuring dozens of South African troops just 300 kilometres south of Luanda. The Battle of Ebo, as it came to be known, was a turning point in the fight for control of Angola. The SADF lost confidence, and although they kept trying to break through Cuba's defences, each week their task became harder as thousands more of Castro's troops streamed into the country, boosted by tonnes of Soviet weapons.

On 27 March, defeated and humiliated, the last South African soldiers left Angola. Four days later, the UN Security Council called on Pretoria to reimburse Angola for war damages and declared its operations 'an act of aggression committed by South Africa against the People's Republic of Angola.'[94] The symbolism was undeniable: the army of a white-minority government supported by the United States had been defeated by the troops of a small socialist island and an African liberation movement. Little wonder Castro crowned Carlota 'that glorious page in our revolutionary history'.[95]

But having consolidated the MPLA's power, Cuba's involvement in Angola soon developed into a mission whose primary purpose was to protect Neto and his immediate political circle. The experience of General

Rafael Moracén Limonta, one of Cuba's most distinguished military leaders and a man honoured as a 'Hero of the Cuban Republic', is useful here.[96] At the end of 1975, he was told by Cuba's minister of armed forces, General Raúl Castro, that he was to travel to Angola to lead a tank unit in Cabinda. He fought a few battles in Cabinda before receiving new orders from the minister to command a special unit to ensure President Neto's security.

> He explained to me how important the unit we were going to form would be, both for Angola and President Neto. He also told me that I ought to be on alert because at any time there could be an attempted *coup d'état*.

Moracén adds, 'And actually, things really did turn out as the general of the army, Raúl Castro, had predicted.'[97]

Come May 1977, when the tension between the so-called *netistas* and the *nitistas* was palpable, Moracén advised Neto to leave the presidential palace. In an interview years later, one which suggests he might have had prior knowledge of the uprising, Moracén recalls, 'I spent the whole of the night of the 26th through to the 27th without sleeping.' He says that the coup began at four o'clock in the morning: 'The *golpistas* [...] took the prison and released all the prisoners, including the mercenaries. They took over the national radio station and started to demonstrate in groups in the streets.'

Moracén's first response, when he heard shots, was to go straight to the palace. 'When I arrived, there was a demonstration of *golpistas* moving forward,' he says, 'with the aim of taking the presidency.' So he sent instructions to his Cuban unit based a few kilometres outside Luanda, giving orders to form a column and prepare to come into the city. Moracén went to meet the unit, and advanced back towards Luanda. 'Since I didn't really know who was involved in the conspiracy, when I entered the capital, I left in reserve a tank company in the neighbourhood of Sambizanga,' he says. The rest of them pushed on to the palace, which they surrounded, swiftly gaining control of the situation. 'At the palace, I received a call on behalf of Neto telling me to take the national radio station, which was in the hands of the traitors. Things were very ugly. There was no government in Luanda.'

When he reached the radio station, Moracén remembers that 'it was full of people and factionalist soldiers'. He claims that the Cubans did not have tanks here, but were in lorries and one Soviet armoured personnel carrier only. 'There was a lot of confusion. The *golpistas*, in their respective vehicles, were constantly circling around in their BRDMs [Soviet armoured personnel carriers]. We mixed ourselves in and also started circling around the National Radio.'[98] Eventually, after Moracén's men 'got muddled up with the counter-revolutionaries', fighting broke out and there was 'a tremendous exchange of gunshot'. It was at this point that Moracén took the decision to enter the building with fifteen of his men. Inside, they disarmed the *nitistas*, and Moracén spoke by telephone to the head of the Cuban mission, Abelardo Colomé, known as 'Furry'. He asked him to send tanks immediately. Moracén then entered the recording studio, snatched the microphone from the man who was already there and tried to force him to say, '*Viva Neto!*' Contradicting what Michael Wolfers told me – that the Cuban on air spoke by accident – Moracén states: 'Then I spoke some very strong words and explained to the people that the radio was in the hands of the Revolution.' Shortly after, the Cuban tanks arrived, and 'everything calmed down'. Moracén concludes, 'This counter-revolutionary attempted coup did a lot of damage to the process of development of the national Angolan society. Brave members of the MPLA and FAPLA were murdered.'

Undoubtedly, Moracén, and Cuban troops generally, played a critical role in quashing the Nito Alves uprising.[99] Nevertheless, there are big holes in his account of the *vinte e sete*. Apart from the gun battle at the radio station, he presents Cuba's role that day as purely defensive. He says nothing of the many innocent people who were killed by FAPLA and Cuban troops, including the residents in Sambizanga whose homes were crushed under Cuban tanks or who were said to have been killed because they were mistaken for the footballer Kiferro. He makes no mention of the executions witnessed by Dr Martínez in Luena either, nor the concentration camp in Moxico province where Miguel Francisco was held and where Cuban troops were allegedly active.

Moreover, Fidel Castro – who, let's remember, said that the only reason for Cuban troops to be in Angola was 'to defend them from South Africa or any other imperialist' – must have been aware of what was taking place inside Angola in May 1977 and during the following weeks and months. To return to the observations of Gabriel García Márquez, Castro's personal involvement in the military mission was obsessive. He knew the Angolan map 'by heart', wrote the Columbian author.

His absorption in the war was so intense and meticulous that he could quote any statistic relating to Angola as if it were Cuba itself, and he spoke [of] its towns, customs and peoples as if he had lived there all his life.[100]

◆

I'm looking at another photograph now. This one is in colour.

An older man is sitting on a leather sofa. He holds a sheet of yellow paper in his hands. He looks into the camera pensively. He seems resentful, possibly distrustful, yet an air of vulnerability hovers around him. The pink line of his lips holds a tension that stretches to his chin. A thin layer of silver hair is combed neatly back away from his forehead, which is clean and taut. He wears spectacles that magnify his eyes, a large watch is strapped to his wrist, and a short-sleeved shirt shows arms well toned in spite of his age. Beside him, on a small table, two festive figurines stand beside a lampshade. One is Father Christmas, the other a tiny snowman.

Dr Martínez is now in his sixties. He lives in Miami, where he joined his wife and son when he left Cuba in 2002. Until I sent him my questions, no one in his family knew what he had seen on the Twenty-seventh of May 1977. He'd never told anyone about the execution of the seventeen Angolans or about signing their falsified death certificates. To refuse would have been to risk his own life. Ivette told me that when he gave his answers he was weeping.

'Even if I saved the lives of hundreds of sick and malnourished children – and I am proud of that,' he says, 'I regret having been an accomplice in an unnecessary war. I saw too many injustices, diseases and deaths, which have marked me for the rest of my life.'

He believes that Castro did not permit the Angolans to decide their future for themselves. 'Cuba forced Angola into a war that cost thousands of lives,' he says. And although he remembers the Angolans he worked with very fondly, he's less certain of how they might remember him. '[They] always respected me and treated me well,' he says, 'but they resented the presence of Cuba in Angola. The majority saw us as new colonisers, better than the Portuguese – more generous and with greater solidarity – but colonials to the end.'

Of all the accounts I've heard since setting out to understand the *vinte e sete*, Dr Martínez's story upsets me the most. I don't understand why. In the grand scheme of the event, he's been lucky. But there is something about his unwilling collusion in the murders of those seventeen Angolans that I find profoundly disturbing. That he had to watch his colleague, Cristina, being executed, and to listen to Nito, a man he admired, screaming for mercy, is hard to contemplate. Reading through Ivette's email, her uncle's answers carefully typed in Spanish, I find myself ambushed by tears. Perhaps it's because I've always admired the Cubans so much, and this story has fuzzied my understanding. I'm also overwhelmingly disappointed that Dr Martínez has no information about Victor Reis. One of my questions was whether he can remember anything about the death of a white man that day. But he cannot. 'There was not a single Portuguese among them,' reads his reply.

This leaves me with just one final question. I have a feeling I might know the brother of one of the men who was shot at the ditch that afternoon, the one Dr Martínez describes as 'the only Angolan doctor who lived in Luena, the director of health whose name I cannot remember'. I have a feeling this was the brother of Filomeno Vieira Lopes, the politician who was dragged away by police during those small demonstrations in February 2000 when I first heard of the *vinte e sete* and this whole journey began. Although I have never discussed it with him in person, I've heard through mutual friends that Filomeno's brother was a doctor who lived and worked in Luena and was killed on the Twenty-seventh of May. So I brace myself and prepare to contact him. I take no pride in admitting this, but I don't have the nerve to telephone him and break the news directly. Instead, I contact him via Skype, typing out the information so that he can read it in real time in Luanda while I am sitting here in front of my screen in London. I quote Dr Martínez in full; I press return. Two-and-a-half minutes later, Filomeno responds.

'*O médico era meu irmão*,' he writes. 'The doctor was my brother. His name was Elisiário dos Passos Vieira Lopes. His nickname was Passinhos. He was killed with his wife while their four children remained alone at home. I was in Portugal when the Twenty-seventh of May occurred. My brother had nothing to do with that group.'

EPILOGUE

One cold but clear morning in March 2011, I sat before my laptop, my eyes fixed on a video that had just been posted on YouTube. It showed Ikonoklasta, a popular Angolan rapper whose full name is Henrique Luaty da Silva Beirão, striding about the stage waving one arm extravagantly above his head. With the microphone jammed to his lips, the twenty-nine-year-old was calling for President José Eduardo dos Santos to leave power. In response, the large audience of mainly young men chanted back in agreement, '*Fora!*' (Get out!) The video was recorded on 27 February at Cine Atlântico, a popular venue for music festivals and films in the heart of Luanda. To the delight of his fans, Ikonoklasta – who is *mestiço*, and son of the late João Beirão, who headed the president's personal charity – described the regime as 'a son of a bitch government', then held up a banner bearing a message painted in bright colours. Addressing dos Santos, it read: '*Ti Zé Tira o Pé: Tô Prazo Expirou Há Bwé!*' (Uncle Zé, get out: your time expired long ago!) The crowd erupted, whistling and cheering and clapping their hands. Ikonoklasta ended his performance with a reference to the uprising in Libya, then encouraged the crowds to join him in a protest against their own president. 'The seventh of March is our day at Independence Square,' he yelled.

A fortnight before this radical gig took place, a new website had appeared named *A nova revolução do povo Angolano* (The new revolution of the Angolan people). The first, short entry called on Angolans to take to the streets on 7 March to demand the resignation of dos Santos. Exploiting the spirit of what has come to be known as the Arab Spring, the post was titled 'First Ben Ali of Tunisia, second Hosni Mubarak of Egypt, who will be the next?' We now know that Libya's Muammar Gaddafi was next. But the message to Angola's own ageing dictator, in power since 1979, was clear.

When Monday, 7 March, came round, only seventeen people, including four journalists, gathered at Independence Square for the protest, which began in the earliest hours of the morning. They were all arrested, including Ikonoklasta.

Hearing about this in London, my first thought was just how little had changed since February 2000, when I had witnessed those three equally tiny demonstrations close to the Carmelite church. The vast majority of Angolans were obviously still too afraid to express public opposition to the regime, and perhaps the rapid arrests showed they had good reason. And yet, something had altered. Although the 7 March protest could not begin to compare with the extraordinary scenes witnessed in Cairo's Tahrir Square earlier in the year, what intrigued me was how the Angolan establishment responded.

Apparently fearful of the examples set in the north of Africa, the MPLA's first provincial secretary in Luanda, Bento Bento, gave a speech in which he stated, 'Angola is not Egypt. Angola is not Libya. Angola is not Tunisia.'[99] In discourse so dated it verged on the absurd, he accused Western intelligence agencies and pressure groups in France, Portugal, Italy, Brussels and the UK of instigating the opposition. 'They have enacted,' he said, 'a proper operation against Angola, the MPLA and especially our comrade and president, José Eduardo dos Santos.'

In a bid to show the world its popularity, the MPLA organised its own pre-emptive 'pro-peace' rallies across the country. State radio said 500,000 supporters took to the streets of Luanda on 5 March, waving MPLA flags, wearing MPLA T-shirts and drinking MPLA-funded beer and fizzy drinks. Independent media estimated the figure to be closer to 20,000. Whatever the number was, what took place was not an authentic outpouring of adoration for the regime. State employees were ordered to attend, and beyond the capital all did not go well. In the diamond-rich province of Lunda Norte, for example, MPLA supporters were attacked by other members of the public, and the provincial governor, Ernesto Muangala, fled for safety.

Ironically – and in direct contradiction of article forty-seven of the new Angolan constitution approved in 2010, which grants all citizens the right to demonstrate peacefully – Bento Bento also threatened anyone thinking of exercising their right to protest against the MPLA. 'Whoever tries to demonstrate will be neutralised,' he said, 'because Angola has laws and institutions and a good citizen understands the laws, respects the country and is a patriot.' The Secretary General of the party, Julião Mateus Paulo, known as 'Dino Matross', was only marginally more blunt, warning anyone brave enough to protest that they 'will get it'.[100]

Far from being mere rhetoric, these warnings sounded uncannily familiar and must have been frightening for many Angolans. Several opposition parties warned the public against demonstrating. Some argued it would be foolhardy to participate in a demonstration called by unknown figures. Others warned that the protest could lead to purges like those of 1977 and 1992 – when violence and, later, return to civil war followed Angola's first attempt at multiparty elections.

However, the caution displayed by the political class was criticised by a number of younger Angolans, among them Ikonoklasta. In his view, the established opposition parties were helping to maintain 'the climate of terror'. 'They are out of touch with the majority of Angolan people,' he told me in an email, 'and are either too lazy or too old-fashioned to take action for their beliefs.' Acknowledging the long-term trauma resulting from the *vinte e sete*, he nevertheless suggested that attitudes were beginning to budge. 'The world has changed a lot since 1977,' he said. 'The collective psyche, that was asleep during all these years of repression and suffering, is finally waking up.'

In the weeks and months that followed this first show of protest, anti-government blogs and Facebook and Twitter accounts proliferated, all focused on one message: dos Santos must go. I started receiving messages from people who said they were speaking in the name of Nito Alves, and I began to notice that the long-dead factionalist was now active on Facebook in several guises. More remarkably, protesters were not cowed by the state's response to the 7 March demonstration. Despite being confronted by mounted police and armed riot police, some handling aggressive police dogs, hundreds turned out in Luanda on at least six major demonstrations that year, while smaller protests took place within the *musseques* and across other parts of the country. Some people were injured, many ended up spending periods in prison, and the more vocal activists reported direct and indirect threats to themselves, their friends and family. Even so, this street-based opposition, organised by young and angry activists, continued.

Come March 2012, the state stepped up its response to the increasingly vocal minority. With parliamentary elections due in August – which would also determine who would be president – the authorities were getting worried by the rising tide of criticism. When dozens gathered in Luanda and the southern city of Benguela to demonstrate against irregularities in the electoral process, the national police were joined by plain-clothes infiltrators who attacked the protesters. Among those seriously injured were Ikonoklasta, who needed stitches for a wound to his head, and Filomeno Vieira Lopes. The injuries sustained by Lopes, now in his late fifties, were so serious that after receiving initial treatment in Angola, he travelled to Germany for an operation to his right arm and hand.

Two days after these protests had been so brutally disrupted, one of Angola's few private newspapers was temporarily closed down by police. Computers were seized from the offices of *Folha 8* (Page 8), and its editor, William Tonet – often seen wearing a T-shirt portraying Nito Alves' face above the words 'You can kill a man but never his ideas' – was arrested and taken in for questioning.

Still, the demonstrators would not be bowed. Within weeks, a group of former presidential guards and war veterans announced plans to march to the presidential palace on 27 May to demand their unpaid salaries. The symbolism of the date was lost on no one, least of all the state. On the actual day, the presidential guards decided against participating and held out for further negotiations, but many veterans took to the streets anyway. Their protest was broken up by security forces before it reached the palace, but in the days and weeks that followed more veterans gathered in public to demand their pensions and back pay. On 20 June, thousands descended upon the military signals regiment headquarters in Luanda. Many of these protesters were arrested and detained, and at least two former soldiers were reported missing by friends and family.

In the midst of so much political activity, an Angolan friend told me how his ageing mother had expressed her distress at the protests. She did not understand why the youngsters were causing so much trouble given that the president only wanted to remain in power until his seventieth birthday. Had she been right, dos Santos would have stood down on 28 August 2012. But she was wrong. Three days after becoming a septuagenarian, dos Santos, as presidential candidate of the party which took over 70 per cent of the vote, won the right to remain in position for another five years. According to the new constitution, he could enjoy yet another five-year term after this one. In other words, he may remain in power until his eightieth birthday.

EPILOGUE

As I sit at my desk, eight months later, wondering how I ought to end this book, I have just received yet another email from Luanda. Ten people were arrested yesterday during a small protest at Independence Square. One of the detained goes by the name of Nito Alves. Another demonstrator was so severely beaten by the police he was unable to move. He goes by the nickname Mandela. The purpose of their protest was simple. Yesterday was 27 May 2013. They were holding a vigil for the thousands of victims of what they refer to as 'the massacre' of 1977. They were also remembering two men who disappeared on the same day last year during a similar demonstration.

The body of the email is written in Portuguese, but the author has signed off in English. 'Thank you for your concern.' The formality of this final phrase taps at my conscience, emphasising the distance between the book I have written and these events, far away in Luanda.

I push back my chair and turn to the shelves beside me. A small paper bag lies on top of a row of books. A gift from Maria Reis. I place it on my lap and tip the contents onto my knees. Lying in white tissue paper, a pair of dolls with smiles that span their plastic cheeks. They are dressed in pink, and have blue and white ribbons in their plaited orange hair. They wear white gloves and shoes that wobble at the end of their skinny limbs of rubber, like they are holding hands and tap-dancing deliriously down my leg.

I think of Maria, pounding the pavements, trying to disappear from her grief. I remember our stroll along the beach, in the sunshine, in Cascais. Attempts to lighten the load of the day, to temper those years of silence. Again, I look at the dolls fixed in their grins. Still, I can't work out what they mean.

ACKNOWLEDGEMENTS

Above all, my thanks go to those who agreed to share their memories of the Twenty-seventh of May 1977. This extends to the people who spoke to me but do not appear in the final version of this book. The idea to write a book was conceived in London during an early conversation with João Van Dúnem, who sadly died in February 2013. It was my encounter with Maria Reis, however, that compelled me to track down more stories and to refuse to give up. I am deeply grateful to both Maria and her daughter, Vânia.

I am particularly indebted to a number of Angolan friends. Without their extraordinary generosity, courage and friendship, this book could never have come into existence. It therefore saddens me hugely that, due to the political intolerance of Angola's ruling elite, they cannot all be named here. This extends to some who currently reside in Britain, but who have asked to remain anonymous in order not to risk the well-being of their families back home.

This book took much longer than I had ever expected. That elusive visa into Angola is partly to blame. At one point, believing we would be travelling to Luanda to live for at least a year, we rented out our London flat, only to find ourselves stuck in Britain and homeless. Several friends came to the rescue with board and lodging for weeks on end. A big shout out to Freddie Boswell and Stephen O'Connor, to Phoebe Boswell, Maureen Mackintosh, Crispin Hawes, Amanda Powell-Smith and Tim Evans, and Katy Orr and Nick Pahl too.

When I finally arrived in southern Africa I was blessed to receive logistical support from many, who asked for nothing other than that they neither be identified nor implicated in my politics. Thank you, therefore, to the five truck drivers, the helicopter pilot, the policeman, the baker, the many priests and nuns, who took me in, fed me, made me laugh and ferried me about. If you ever make it to London, there is *always* a bed here. I'm very grateful to Hendrik Ehlers and the MGM team, too, for shoe-horning me in.

I am grateful to John Naughton, Bill Kirkman, Richard Synge and Hilary Pennington for a Press Fellowship at Wolfson College, Cambridge, which boosted my confidence and bought me an early trip to Portugal. Most of all, John's enthusiasm for my writing since then helped push back sudden tides of self-doubt which might otherwise have overwhelmed me.

I am also very grateful for the Writing Fellowship at the Wits Institute for Social and Economic Research, University of the Witwatersrand, Johannesburg. My former university tutor at the School of Oriental and African Studies, the brilliant Shula Marks, suggested I apply. She also put me in touch with Jon Hyslop, who encouraged me further over a few beers in London. Thank you both, and thanks to the rest of the team under Debbie Posel's leadership, especially Najibha Deshmukh, Samadia Sadouni, Josephine Mashaba, Irma du Plessis and Lara Allen for their sense of humour, their candour and their friendship.

Along the way, a number of people warned me that the Twenty-seventh of May 1977 happened too long ago and, being about Angola, would be too remote from British readers to be published here. David Godwin's faith in the book buoyed my confidence that they were wrong: I'd like to thank him and also Caitlin Ingham and Anna Watkins.

To my editor, Joanna Godfrey, it is with triumphant pleasure that I thank her for an immediate enthusiasm for the manuscript. It has been fabulous working with her, and I am more grateful than she will ever realise for her commitment to this project. Thank you also to Alexandra Higson and Alex Billington, whose efficient management of the production process was inspirational. In particular, I salute Alex Middleton, the copy-editor, who continually went the extra mile with a speed, clarity and generosity that astounded me. A true professional. Also, Sarah Terry, the eagle-eyed proofreader, who saved me from public embarrassment. For their combined energies to promote this book in all sorts of ways, thank you to Antonia Leslie and Katherine Tulloch. And to Alice Marwick, a big thumbs-up for such a terrific and intelligent cover design: you may come last in the production process, but in the reading process your cover will always come first.

In between conception and publication, a mountain of other people kept me going. If I were to thank each and every one, I'd need to write another book. So, for their considered feedback on the manuscript, warm thanks

ACKNOWLEDGEMENTS

to the one and only Mike Harrison, whose writing has been inspirational, to my lovely neighbour Anna Hope, and to Firoze Manji, the inspiring Marissa Moorman, Michael Oliva, Caryl Phillips, Jon Schubert and the late Paul Scherer. For his passionate criticism, António Tomás, and for his comradeship, Leo Zeilig. Also to Mary Harper, whose generosity has been humbling and so, so much more. For answering my endless queries on the particularities of translating Portuguese into English, Ana Naomi de Sousa is queen. For repeatedly rebooting my confidence, my dear friends David Dibosa, Anna Feldman and Miri P. For setting an example from afar, thank you to Rasna Warah, and also to Dum Spiro Spero, for top tips on texts.

For their solidarity, shared outrage, and insistence that this book needed writing, my cigar-smoking amigo from Springfield Park, and also to Master Ngola Nvunji, who, regrettably, I only met in October 2010 as a result of Jimmy Mubenga's tragic death. Huge appreciation for their pride and patience goes to my parents, Carolyn and Michael Pawson; for his prodding and pushing, my brother, Bobby Pawson; and for her early encouragement, the lovely Alicia Pawson. I'd also like to thank Tim Cotton for his empathic response to the text; and especially my sister, Xandra Cotton, whose sense of humour and abiding faith in me boosted my spirits again and again.

Finally, Julian Richards. Never once wavering, he accompanied me, step by step, on what turned out to be an incredibly difficult – at times almost impossible – journey. This book could never have been completed without his extraordinary sacrifice, profound sensitivity, intellectual integrity and boundless love. Without him, I dread to think.

NOTES

1 In order to reflect the gravity of the events of that day, I have written the date in full as 'the Twenty-seventh of May' rather than using the more conventional '27 May'.
2 Achille Mbembe, *On the Postcolony* (Berkeley, CA, and London: University of California Press, 2001), p. 14 (emphasis in the original).
3 Tony Hodges, *Angola from Afro-Stalinism to Petro-diamond Capitalism* (Bloomington, IN: Indiana University Press; Oxford: James Currey, in association with the Fridtjof Nansen Institute, 2001), p. 46.
4 Caroline Reuver-Cohen and William Jerman, eds, *Angola: Secret Government Documents on Counter-Subversion* (Rome: IDOC, 1974).
5 Bureau Político do Movimento Popular de Libertação de Angola, *Angola: A tentativa de golpe de estado de 27 de maio de 77* (Lisbon: Edições Avante!, 1977). Unless otherwise stated, all further quotations in this chapter are taken from this text, a booklet of sixty-five pages. All translations from this and other Portuguese-language sources are my own.
6 Basil Davidson, *In the Eye of the Storm: Angola's People* (London: Longman, 1972), p. 160.
7 Ibid., pp. 158–61; Marissa Moorman, *Intonations: A Social History of Music and Nation in Luanda, Angola, from 1945 to Recent Times* (Athens, OH: Ohio University Press, 2008), pp. 39–40.
8 For extensive details about Cuba's relationship with Angola and the extraordinary role Cuban troops had in defending Angola from US-backed invasions from Zaire and South Africa, see Edward George, *The Cuban Intervention in Angola, 1965–1991, from Che Guevara to Cuito Cuanavale* (London: Routledge, 2005) and Piero Gleijeses, *Conflicting Missions: Havana, Washington, and Africa, 1959–1976* (Chapel Hill, NC: University of North Carolina Press, 2002). In this book, I have depended on both as crucial sources.
9 Barbara Walters and Fidel Castro, 'An interview with Fidel Castro', *Foreign Policy* 28 (Autumn 1977), pp. 40–1.
10 Rafael del Pino, 'Inside Castro's bunker' [unpublished manuscript, 1991], p. 107. See also Rafael del Pino, *Proa a la libertad* (Mexico: Editorial Planeta, 1991).
11 In Luanda in particular, 'people power' – *poder popular* – was embraced by neighbourhood groups and committees as a central tenet in the struggle for total independence from Portuguese colonial rule, as opposed to a form of neo-colonial independence. Once independence was achieved, on 11 November 1975, the MPLA embraced it as a slogan. For a much more detailed exploration,

see Jean-Michel Mabeko Tali, *Dissidências e poder de estado: O MPLA perante si próprio (1962–1977)*, 2 vols (Luanda: Editorial Nzila, 2001).

12 James Sanders, *South Africa and the International Media 1972–79: A Struggle for Representation* (London and Portland, OR: Frank Cass, 2000), p. 150.

13 Davidson, *In the Eye of the Storm*, p. 161.

14 Stuart Hall, 'New ethnicities', in Houston A. Baker Jr, Manthia Diawara and Ruth H. Lindeborg, eds, *Black British Cultural Studies: A Reader* (Chicago, IL, and London: University of Chicago Press, 1996), p. 167.

15 Frantz Fanon, *Black Skin, White Masks* (1952; London: Pluto Press, 1986), p. 192.

16 Peter Hallward, 'Fanon and political will', *Cosmos and History: The Journal of Natural and Social Philosophy* vii/1 (2011), p. 109.

17 I have chosen to write Van Dúnem with an acute accent over the 'u', as it was requested by João.

18 David Birmingham, *Portugal and Africa* (Athens, OH: Ohio University Press, 1999), pp. 69–71.

19 During the course of my investigation, I tried to talk to Amnesty International about the events surrounding the Twenty-seventh of May 1977 in Angola. I was interested to learn how the organisation felt about Agostinho Neto, given the allegations made against him by people like João Van Dúnem. Apart from two conversations with a very amiable former Amnesty employee, I found it remarkably difficult to get a response. A second former Amnesty staffer claims to have read a letter addressed to the organisation from Lúcio Lara in which he denies allegations of mass killings taking place 'in the dead of the night'. However, it seems that the letter has been mislaid, either by Amnesty or the researcher himself.

20 David Birmingham wrote a preliminary history of the *vinte e sete*, including a thoughtful analysis of its relationship to the problem of agricultural production and food distribution, in his chapter 'The twenty-seventh of May'. See Birmingham, *Portugal and Africa*, pp. 142–54. The information in this and the following paragraph lean heavily on pp. 145–7 of this work. I only came across this article during the course of my investigation, although it was originally published in 1978 in the journal *African Affairs*.

21 Colin Legum, ed., *Africa Contemporary Record, Annual Survey and Documents 1977–78* (London: Rex Collings, 1978), p. B515.

22 See Sergei Kononov, 'Angola's "diamond mafia"', *Asia and Africa Today* 11 (2003), pp. 50–1 [Russian]. I am indebted to the Moscow-based Portuguese journalist José Milhazes, whose blog drew my attention to this article. See http://darussia.blogspot.co.uk/2007/02/contributos-para-histria-angola.html (accessed 6 September 2013).

23 Gerald Bender, *Angola under the Portuguese: The Myth and the Reality* (London: Heinemann, 1978), pp. 200–1.

24 Frantz Fanon, *The Wretched of the Earth* (1961; London: Penguin, 2001), p. 136.

25 Victoria Brittain, *Death of Dignity: Angola's Civil War* (London: Pluto Press, 1998), pp. vii, xv, xi.

26 Human Rights Watch, *Angola Unravels: The Rise and Fall of the Lusaka Peace Process* (New York, NY, Washington DC, London and Brussels: Human Rights Watch, 1999), p. 15.
27 This is a Portuguese legal expression, which refers to the customary questions asked of a witness to determine their eligibility. So a complete and longer translation of Teixeira's book title would be, 'In answer to the customary questions asked to establish eligibility to serve as a witness, he made no disqualifying statements'.
28 MPLA-PT is also said, jokingly, to mean '*Mulatos e Pulas Libertaram Angola – e Pretos Também*'. *Pulas* is a derogatory term for whites. The acronym therefore means 'Mulattoes and Whites Liberated Angola – and Blacks Too'. The implication is that black Angolans played an insignificant role in the country's liberation. It also suggests that their role was overlooked by the MPLA leadership.
29 Mbembe, *On the Postcolony*, pp. 196–7.
30 Américo Cardoso Botelho, *Holocausto em Angola: Memórias de entre o cárcere e o cemitério* (Lisbon: Nova Vega, 2008), pp. 325–7.
31 Amnesty International, *People's Republic of Angola: Background Briefing on Amnesty International's Concerns* (March 1983), p. 27.
32 Helder Neto did die during the Twenty-seventh of May, however he was not among those who died inside the vehicle in Sambizanga. It seems that Mateus may be confusing Helder Neto with António Garcia Neto, who was among those found dead inside the burned vehicle.
33 Bender, *Angola under the Portuguese*, pp. 229–30.
34 Ibid., p. 233.
35 The material in this paragraph is drawn from Moorman, *Intonations*, pp. 186–8.
36 Ibid., pp. 13–17.
37 Gleijeses, *Conflicting Missions*, pp. 338–9.
38 'Angola and Cabinda', *Africa Confidential*, 22 November 1974.
39 Much of the information in this paragraph is drawn from Ricardo Soares de Oliveira, 'Business success, Angola-style: Postcolonial politics and the rise and rise of Sonangol', *Journal of Modern African Studies* xlv/4 (2007), pp. 595–619.
40 In 1979, after Neto's death, Freudenthal lost this job, probably because he was white. He was replaced by a black Angolan, Hermínio Escórcio.
41 Gleijeses, *Conflicting Missions*, p. 343.
42 Ibid.
43 Soares de Oliveira's article expounds beautifully on the birth of Sonangol and its relationship with the Angolan state. See Soares de Oliveira, 'Business success, Angola-style'.
44 'O MPLA está unido' [The MPLA is united], *Jornal de Angola*, 22 May 1977.
45 'Liquidar o fraccionismo!' [Liquidate factionalism!], *Jornal de Angola*, 22 May 1977. It runs over four pages.
46 'Bater no ferro quente' [Beating on hot iron], *Jornal de Angola*, 10 July 1977.
47 'Bater no ferro quente: Despertar os esquecidos' [Beating on hot iron: Awakening the forgotten], *Jornal de Angola*, 28 July 1977.
48 William Tonet, 'Livro Negro do 27 de maio de 1977. O Auschwitz de África. O Stalinismo de Neto' [Black Book of 27 May 1977. The Auschwitz of Africa. The

Stalinism of Neto], *Folha 8*, 11 June 2011. Available at http://folha8.blogspot.com/2011/06/livro-negro-do-27-de-maio-de-1977-o_11.html (accessed 6 September 2013).

49 Fernando Costa Andrade, *Adobes de memória*, vol. 2: *Chegadas* (Luanda: Caxinde, 2002), p. 162.
50 'Bater no ferro quente' [Beating on hot iron], *Jornal de Angola*, 21 July 1977.
51 'Bater no ferro quente' [Beating on hot iron], *Jornal de Angola*, 10 July 1977.
52 'Bater no ferro quente' [Beating on hot iron], *Jornal de Angola*, 22 July 1977.
53 'Bater no ferro quente' [Beating on hot iron], *Jornal de Angola*, 12 July 1977.
54 Ibid.
55 Ibid.
56 'Bater no ferro quente' [Beating on hot iron], *Jornal de Angola*, 20 July 1977.
57 'Bater no ferro quente' [Beating on hot iron], *Jornal de Angola*, 12 July 1977.
58 'Bater no ferro quente: Combater o burocratismo' [Beating on hot iron: Fighting bureaucratism], *Jornal de Angola*, 29 July 1977.
59 'Bater no ferro quente' [Beating on hot iron], *Jornal de Angola*, 13 July 1977.
60 Fanon, *Wretched of the Earth*, p. 146.
61 'Bater no ferro quente' [Beating on hot iron], *Jornal de Angola*, 20 July 1977.
62 'Bater no ferro quente' [Beating on hot iron], *Jornal de Angola*, 19 July 1977.
63 'Bater no ferro quente' [Beating on hot iron], *Jornal de Angola*, 21 July 1977.
64 'Bater no ferro quente: Vitória do MPLA' [Beating on hot iron: Victory of MPLA], *Jornal de Angola*, 31 July 1977.
65 'Bater no ferro quente' [Beating on hot iron], *Jornal de Angola*, 19 July 1977.
66 Fanon, *Wretched of the Earth*, p. 146.
67 'Bater no ferro quente' [Beating on hot iron], *Jornal de Angola*, 10 July 1977.
68 Ibid.
69 'Bater no ferro quente' [Beating on hot iron], *Jornal de Angola*, 6 August 1977.
70 'Bater no ferro quente: Abaixo o racismo' [Beating on hot iron: Down with racism], *Jornal de Angola*, 3 August 1977.
71 Ibid.
72 'Bater no ferro quente' [Beating on hot iron], *Jornal de Angola*, 12 July 1977.
73 Fanon, *Wretched of the Earth*, p. 85.
74 'Bater no ferro quente' [Beating on hot iron], *Jornal de Angola*, 23 July 1977.
75 'Bater no ferro quente' [Beating on hot iron], *Jornal de Angola*, 21 July 1977.
76 'Bater no ferro quente' [Beating on hot iron], *Jornal de Angola*, 10 July 1977.
77 Alison George, 'The yuck factor: The surprising power of disgust', *New Scientist*, 20 July 2012.
78 'For Lara Pawson, my new friend, with love, Costa Andrade.'
79 Kerry A. Dolan and Rafael Marques de Morais, 'Daddy's girl: How an African "princess" banked $3 billion in a country living on $2 a day', *Forbes*, 2 September 2013.
80 Chinua Achebe, 'An image of Africa: Racism in Conrad's *Heart of Darkness*', *Massachusetts Review* xvii/4 (1977), pp. 782–94.
81 Christopher Andrew and Vasili Mitrokhin, *The KGB and the World: The Mitrokhin Archive II* (2005; London: Penguin, 2006), pp. 454–5; Odd Arne

Westad, *The Global Cold War: Third World Interventions and the Making of Our Times* (New York, NY: Cambridge University Press, 2005), pp. 239–40, 244.
82. Vladimir Shubin, *The Hot 'Cold War'* (London: Pluto Press, 2008), p. 70.
83. 'Angola: Diplomatic jigsaw', *Africa Confidential*, 17 July 1978.
84. Nuno Vidal and Patrick Chabal, eds, *Angola: The Weight of History* (New York, NY: Columbia, 2008), p. 129.
85. Césaire, then *député* for Martinique in the French national assembly, in a letter to Maurice Thorez, general secretary of the French Communist Party, 24 October 1956.
86. Judith Butler, *Frames of War: When Is Life Grievable?* (London: Verso, 87), p. xx.
88. Mark Danner, *The Massacre at El Mozote* (London: Granta, 2005).
89. Randy Pherson, 'The Angolan leadership: Current perspectives and prospects after Neto. An intelligence assessment' [report by the National Foreign Assessment Center (CIA), December 1978]. Available at http://216.12.139.91/docs/DOC_0001260311/DOC_0001260311.pdf (accessed 22 November 2013).
90. From the Pherson Associates website. Available at http://www.pherson.org/index.php/capabilities/ (accessed 6 September 2013).
91. Walters and Castro, 'An interview with Fidel Castro', pp. 39–40.
92. For much more detail on the military and political situation at independence, see the brilliantly researched accounts in John Marcum, *The Angolan Revolution*, 2 vols (Cambridge, MA: MIT Press, 1969–78) and Tali, *Dissidências e poder de estado*.
93. For superb accounts of Operation Carlota see George, *The Cuban Intervention* and Gleijeses, *Conflicting Missions*, which are relied upon here.
94. Gabriel García Márquez, 'Operation Carlota', *New Left Review* 101–2 (January–April 1977), p. 128.
95. George, *The Cuban Intervention*, p. 345.
96. Fidel Castro, 'Speech by Dr Fidel Castro Ruz, president of the Republic of Cuba, at the ceremony commemorating the 30th anniversary of the Cuban Military Mission in Angola and the 49th anniversary of the landing of the "Granma", Revolutionary Armed Forces Day, December 2, 2005'. Available at http://www.cuba.cu/gobierno/discursos/2005/ing/f021205i.html (accessed 5 September 2013).
97. The information on Moracén is taken from an interview he gave to Cuban journalist Luis Báez, later published in a book by the same reporter. See Luis Báez, *Secretos de Generales* (Havana: Editorial Si-Mar, 1996), pp. 264–7.
98. On 27 June 1966, Moracén played a pivotal role in containing what was almost a successful coup attempt against the government of Congolese president Alphonse Massamba-Débat. In an uncanny resemblance to Angola's Twenty-seventh of May, had Cuban troops not been in the country to protect the president, the challenge may well have succeeded.
99. Moracén's comment that they 'mixed in' with the crowd suggests that the Cuban troops were probably black. He himself is a black Cuban and, on his first mission to Angola in 1965, was surprised to discover that the Cuban unit

he would lead comprised only black Cubans. 'Blacks, only blacks, we were all blacks. It baffled me. I wondered, "Shit! What's going on?"' It may have been that their skin colour enabled them to move less conspicuously in Africa; however, some suggest that a certain racism may have saved white and *mestiço* Cubans from what was a highly risky (and ultimately doomed) mission.

100 Moracén was so trusted by the MPLA that after Neto's death in 1979 he was put in charge of security for the new Angolan president, a post he held until 1982. In 1995, he returned to Angola as military attaché to the Cuban embassy, a job he retains to this day.

101 García Márquez, 'Operation Carlota', p. 134.

102 Broadcast on state television, Televisão Pública de Angola, 1 March 2011.

103 'Dino Matross avisa: "Quem se manifestar vai apanhar"', *Club-K* [online newspaper], 18 February 2011. Available at http://www.club-k.net/index. php?option=com_content&view=article&id=6983:dino-matross-avisa-quem-se-manifestar-vai-apanhar (accessed 13 April 2013). His comments were also discussed at length in a column by newspaper editor William Tonet. See William Tonet, 'A descoberta do Tio Dino Matross' [The discovery of Uncle Dino Matross], *Folha 8*, 1 March 2011. Available at http://folha8.blogspot.co.uk/2011/02/descoberta-do-tio-dino-matross-angola.html (accessed 27 November 2013).

BIBLIOGRAPHY

Achebe, Chinua. 'An image of Africa: Racism in Conrad's *Heart of Darkness*', *Massachusetts Review* xvii/4 (1977), pp. 782–94.
Alves, Nito, 'Treze teses em minha defesa' [unpublished manuscript, 1976–7].
Amnesty International, *People's Republic of Angola: Background Briefing on Amnesty International's Concerns* (March 1983).
Andrade, Fernando Costa, *Adobes de memória*, vol. 2: *Chegadas* (Luanda: Caxinde, 2002).
Andrew, Christopher, and Vasili Mitrokhin, *The KGB and the World: The Mitrokhin Archive II* (2005; London: Penguin, 2006).
Báez, Luis, *Secretos de Generales* (Havana: Editorial Si-Mar, 1996).
Bender, Gerald, *Angola under the Portuguese: The Myth and the Reality* (London: Heinemann, 1978).
Birmingham, David, *Portugal and Africa* (Athens, OH: Ohio University Press, 1999).
Botelho, Américo Cardoso, *Holocausto em Angola: Memórias de entre o cárcere e o cemitério* (Lisbon: Nova Vega, 2008).
Brittain, Victoria, *Death of Dignity: Angola's Civil War* (London: Pluto Press, 1998).
Butler, Judith, *Frames of War: When Is Life Grievable?* (London: Verso, 2009).
Castro, Fidel, 'Speech by Dr Fidel Castro Ruz, president of the Republic of Cuba, at the ceremony commemorating the 30th anniversary of the Cuban Military Mission in Angola and the 49th anniversary of the landing of the "Granma", Revolutionary Armed Forces Day, December 2, 2005'. Available at http://www.cuba.cu/gobierno/discursos/2005/ing/f021205i.html (accessed 5 September 2013).
Danner, Mark, *The Massacre at El Mozote* (London: Granta, 2005).
Davidson, Basil, *In the Eye of the Storm: Angola's People* (London: Longman, 1972).
—— 'Angola since independence', *Race & Class* xix/2 (1977), pp. 133–48.
—— *The Black Man's Burden: Africa and the Curse of the Nation-state* (London: James Currey, 1992).
Dolan, Kerry A., and Rafael Marques de Morais, 'Daddy's girl: How an African "princess" banked $3 billion in a country living on $2 a day', *Forbes*, 2 September 2013.
Fanon, Frantz, *Black Skin, White Masks* (1952; London: Pluto Press, 1986).
—— *The Wretched of the Earth* (1961; London: Penguin, 2001).
Francisco, Miguel 'Michel', *Nuvem negra: O drama do 27 de Maio de 1977* (Lisbon: Clássica Editora, 2007).
García Márquez, Gabriel, 'Operation Carlota', *New Left Review* 101–2 (January–April 1977), pp. 123–37.
George, Alison, 'The yuck factor: The surprising power of disgust', *New Scientist*, 20 July 2012.
George, Edward, *The Cuban Intervention in Angola, 1965–1991, from Che Guevara to Cuito Cuanavale* (London: Routledge, 2005).
Gleijeses, Piero, *Conflicting Missions: Havana, Washington, and Africa, 1959–1976* (Chapel Hill, NC: University of North Carolina Press, 2002).
Guevara, Ernesto 'Che', *The African Dream: The Diaries of the Revolutionary War in the Congo* (1999; London: Harvill Press, 2000).

Hall, Stuart, 'New ethnicities', in Houston A. Baker Jr, Manthia Diawara and Ruth H. Lindeborg, eds, *Black British Cultural Studies: A Reader* (Chicago, IL, and London: University of Chicago Press, 1996), pp. 163–72.

Hallward, Peter, 'Fanon and political will', *Cosmos and History: The Journal of Natural and Social Philosophy* vii/1 (2011), pp. 104–27.

Hodges, Tony, *Angola from Afro-Stalinism to Petro-diamond Capitalism* (Bloomington, IN: Indiana University Press; Oxford: James Currey, in association with the Fridtjof Nansen Institute, 2001).

Human Rights Watch, *Angola Unravels: The Rise and Fall of the Lusaka Peace Process* (New York, NY, Washington DC, London and Brussels: Human Rights Watch, 1999).

Kononov, Sergei, 'Angola's "diamond mafia"', *Asia and Africa Today* 11 (2003), pp. 50–1 [Russian].

Legum, Colin, ed., *Africa Contemporary Record, Annual Survey and Documents 1977–78* (London: Rex Collings, 1978).

Marcum, John, *The Angolan Revolution*, 2 vols (Cambridge, MA: MIT Press, 1969–78).

Mateus, Dalila Cabrita, and Álvaro Mateus, *Purga em Angola: Nito Alves, Sita Valles, Zé Van Dunem o 27 de maio de 1977* (Porto: ASA Editores, 2007).

Mbembe, Achille, *On the Postcolony* (Berkeley, CA, and London: University of California Press, 2001).

Milhazes, José, *Angola: O princípio do fim da União Soviética* (Lisbon: Nova Vega, 2009).

——— *Da Rússia* [website]. Available at http://darussia.blogspot.co.uk (accessed 22 November 2013).

Moorman, Marissa, *Intonations: A Social History of Music and Nation in Luanda, Angola, from 1945 to Recent Times* (Athens, OH: Ohio University Press, 2008).

Movimento Popular de Libertação de Angola, Bureau Político do, *Angola: A tentativa de golpe de estado de 27 de maio de 77* (Lisbon: Edições Avante!, 1977).

——— *First Congress of MPLA, Luanda, 4–10 December 1977: Report of the Central Committee: Theses on Education* (London: Mozambique, Angola and Guiné Information Centre, 1977).

Neto, Agostinho, *Sagrada esperança* (Lisbon: Sá da Costa, 1974).

Pacheco, Carlos, *Repensar Angola* (Lisbon: Nova Vega, 2000).

Pherson, Randy, 'The Angolan leadership: Current perspectives and prospects after Neto. An intelligence assessment' [report by the National Foreign Assessment Center (CIA), December 1978]. Available at http://216.12.139.91/docs/DOC_0001260311/DOC_0001260311.pdf (accessed 22 November 2013).

Pino, Rafael del, 'Inside Castro's bunker' [unpublished manuscript, 1991].

——— *Proa a la libertad* (Mexico: Editorial Planeta, 1991).

Reuver-Cohen, Caroline, and William Jerman, eds, *Angola: Secret Government Documents on Counter-Subversion* (Rome: IDOC, 1974).

Said, Edward, *Culture and Imperialism* (1993; London: Vintage, 1994).

Sanders, James, *South Africa and the International Media 1972–79: A Struggle for Representation* (London and Portland, OR: Frank Cass, 2000).

Shevchenko, Arkady Nikolaevich, *Breaking with Moscow* (London: Jonathan Cape, 1985).

Shubin, Vladimir, *The Hot 'Cold War'* (London: Pluto Press, 2008).

Soares de Oliveira, Ricardo, 'Business success, Angola-style: Postcolonial politics and the rise and rise of Sonangol', *Journal of Modern African Studies* xlv/4 (2007), pp. 595–619.

Somerville, Keith, *Southern Africa and the Soviet Union* (London: Macmillan Press, 1993).

Tali, Jean-Michel Mabeko, *Dissidências e poder de estado: O MPLA perante si próprio (1962–1977)*, 2 vols (Luanda: Editorial Nzila, 2001).

Teixeira, Ildeberto, *E aos costumes disse nada* [self-published memoir, 1988].

Thornton, John K., *The Kongolese Saint Anthony: Dona Beatriz Kimpa Vita and the Antonian Movement, 1684–1706* (Cambridge, Melbourne and New York, NY: Cambridge University Press, 1998).

Tonet, William, 'A descoberta do Tio Dino Matross' [The discovery of Uncle Dino Matross], *Folha 8*, 1 March 2011. Available at http://folha8.blogspot.co.uk/2011/02/descoberta-do-tio-dino-matross-angola.html (accessed 27 November 2013).

—— 'Livro Negro do 27 de maio de 1977. O Auschwitz de África. O Stalinismo de Neto' [Black Book of 27 May 1977. The Auschwitz of Africa. The Stalinism of Neto], *Folha 8*, 11 June 2011. Available at http://folha8.blogspot.com/2011/06/livro-negro-do-27-de-maio-de-1977-o_11.html (accessed 6 September 2013).

Vidal, Nuno, and Patrick Chabal, eds, *Angola: The Weight of History* (New York, NY: Columbia, 2008).

Walters, Barbara, and Fidel Castro, 'An interview with Fidel Castro', *Foreign Policy* 28 (Autumn 1977), pp. 22–51.

Westad, Odd Arne, *The Global Cold War: Third World Interventions and the Making of Our Times* (New York, NY: Cambridge University Press, 2005).

Wolfers, Michael, and Jane Bergerol, *Angola in the Frontline* (London: Zed Books, 1983).

Wright, George, *The Destruction of a Nation: United States' Policy Toward Angola since 1945* (London and Chicago, IL: Pluto Press, 1997).

OTHER SOURCES

Africa Confidential [fortnightly newspaper]
Club-K [online newspaper]
Folha 8 [weekly newspaper]
Jornal de Angola [daily newspaper]

INDEX

Achebe, Chinua, 214
Active Revolt, 104, 229
Afghanistan, 85
African National Congress, 48, 150
Agora (newspaper), 113, 122
agriculture, 68–9, 120, 236, 256n20
Algeria, 193
Aljube prison, 118
Alvalade, 194, 196
Alves, Nito, xii, 4–5, 16, 23, 31–7, 42, 49–55, 61, 69–72, 75, 79, 91, 95, 104, 106, 115, 130, 138, 140–2, 146, 150, 159, 161, 172, 175, 179–80, 182, 185, 191, 196, 198, 206, 215, 217–18, 220, 226–7, 229–30, 232–3, 237–9, 242, 247–9
Amílcar Cabral Committee, 73
Amin, Samir, 47
Amnesty International, 66, 115, 118, 256n19
Andrade, Mário Pinto de, 193
Angodiplo, 106
Angolan civil war, 1, 4, 13, 17, 31, 40, 43, 66, 68, 82, 86–7, 107, 120, 128, 151, 165, 172, 175, 178, 228, 236, 243, 247–8
angolanidade, 34
Arab Spring, 245
assimilado, assimilação (*see also* colonialism) ix, 33–4, 62

Baader-Meinhof group, 213
Baccara (band), 214
Bairro Indígena, 175
Bairro Operário, 138
Bairro Rangel, 160, 168
Bakongo, 152
Banco Africano de Investimentos, 47

Banco Pinto e Sotto Mayor, 13, 19–20
Barayagwiza, Jean-Bosco, 191
BBC (British Broadcasting Corporation), i, 1, 4, 11, 64–5, 127–8, 178, 197, 213, 233
Beckett, Samuel, 122
Beijing, 118, 206
Beirão, João, 245
Belgians, 102
Belgrade, 206
Bełżec, 188
Bender, Gerald, 80
Benenson, Peter, 66
Benguela, 40, 69, 106, 248
Benn, Tony, 229
Bento Bento, 246
Bergerol, Jane, 49, 54, 63
Biko, Steve, 213
Blair, Tony, 44–5, 172
Bloom, Bridget, 49
Boa Vista, 156
Botelho, Américo Cardoso, 115–16
BP, 47
Brazil, Brazilian, 120, 130, 132, 166, 193, 212
Britain, British, i, ii, xvii, 5, 13, 34, 44, 46–7, 49, 52–3, 56, 57, 62, 64, 66, 77, 82, 85, 89, 94, 99, 121, 128–9, 156, 194, 209, 230
 mercenaries, 228–9
 political culture ('English'), 128
British Library, 39
 Colindale newspaper library, 78
Brittain, Victoria, 5, 83–7, 138
bufo, bufos, ix, 121, 155, 167
Bula, José Manuel Paiva, 141, 150, 167, 182
Bustos, Eloy Bartot, 238
Butler, Judith, 227

Cabgoc (Cabinda Gulf, *see also* Chevron), 164–6, 220
Cabinda, 52, 164–6, 240–1
Cabral, Amílcar, 47
Calunda concentration camp, 187
Campo de São Nicolau (prison), 107, 168
Cape Verde, Cape Verdean, 64, 169
Capote, Truman, 214
Carnation Revolution, 68, 70, 95, 166, 179
Carreira, Henrique Teles Iko, xii, 58, 70–1, 84, 93, 100, 140–1, 148–9, 151, 163–4, 176, 196–7, 200, 217, 226
Carreira, Ilda, 58–9, 71
Casa dos Estudantes do Império, 53, 193
Casa de Reclusão (prison), 74
Castelo de São Jorge, 110
Castro, Fidel, 37, 45, 74, 78, 161, 165, 193, 239–40, 242–3
Castro, Raúl, 241
Castro, Urbano de, 148–9, 159, 181–2, 186
Cazenga, 139
Césaire, Aimé, 223
Chatham House, 47, 49
Chávez, Hugo, 45
Chevron (*see also* Cabgoc), 47, 166
Chile, 5
China, Chinese, 117, 118, 120, 145, 147, 206
Chipenda, Daniel, 216
Christian, Christianity, ix, 29, 55
  Capuchin missionaries, 41
  Carmelite church, 1, 132, 246
  Catholic, 10, 44, 126, 176, 205
  Protestants, 44, 176
CIA, ix, xi, 3, 11, 36, 161, 228, 231–2, 239
Cidadela (stadium), 51, 175, 177
class, class struggle, 5, 33, 52, 61, 73, 79–81, 104–5, 106, 119, 157, 176, 179, 194, 203–4, 220, 229, 247
Clifford Chance, 88
Coelho, Rui, 159
coffee production, 68, 102, 164
Cohen, Teresa, 34
Cold War, 36–7, 43, 55, 66, 83, 160, 165
colonialism, 4, 46–7, 52, 61, 111, 190, 202, 243

colonialism, Portuguese, ix, 1, 13, 14, 52, 72, 79–80, 109–10, 123, 131, 146–7, 163, 166, 172, 175, 192–3, 204, 222
  repression exercised by, 33, 61–2, 80, 102–3
  resistance to, ix, xi, 75, 87, 92, 105, 149, 180, 255n11
communism, communist, 37, 43, 52–3, 66, 117–19, 193, 206, 223, 233
  anti-communist, 33
  French Communist Party, 259n85
Conchigilia, Augusta, 195–6
Congo (*see also* Zaire), 37, 102, 132
Congo-Brazzaville, 51, 66, 95, 117, 259n98
Conrad, Joseph, 214
Cruz, Viriato da, 117–18
Cuba, Cuban, i, x, 3–4, 26, 70, 90, 165, 197, 216, 229, 230, 243–4
  civilian mission in Angola, 177, 235–7
  Communist Party, 73
  Granma (newspaper), 73–4
  Havana, 37, 73, 165, 230, 236, 240
  military in Angola, i, 36–7, 42, 60, 94, 106, 140–1, 143, 150, 161, 165–7, 182–4, 187, 235–6, 238–43, 255n8, 259n98–260n100
  military in Congo-Brazzaville, 259n98
  training of Angolans in, 73–4, 147

Dangereux, Paulo da Silva Mungungo, 19, 22–4, 35, 167, 218
  son of, 35–6, 227
Daniels, Paul, 131
Davidson, Basil, 5, 34, 42, 47, 49–50, 53, 60, 66, 82–3
De Beers, 47, 220
Dembo, Armando, 236
demonstrations, demonstrators (political protest), 1–3, 4, 23, 42, 49, 53–4, 70, 92–4, 128–9, 132, 140, 149–50, 182, 218, 226, 241, 244–9
diamonds, x, 47, 246
  theft and trafficking of, 70, 103, 163
Diário de Luanda (newspaper), 31, 50, 192, 194
Diário da República (MPLA gazette), 103

INDEX

Dino Matross, Julião Mateus Paulo, 247
DISA, ix, 74, 91, 100, 103–4, 106–7, 116, 121, 141, 166, 169, 176, 180, 197, 221, 226
Dubai, 124

Eastern Revolt, 229
Ebo, the Battle of, 240
economic, economy, 3, 119, 217, 219, 232
   collapse, 'strangulation' of, 32, 68–9, 107
   growth, 103, 120, 123–4
education, 46, 80, 91, 147, 150, 189, 230, 236
   of Angolan majority under Portuguese rule, 80, 193
   of MPLA elite, 34, 209
   of Portuguese immigrants to Angola, 147–8
elections, 47, 94, 247
   1992 post-election violence, 100, 247
Elizabeth II, Queen, 213
El Mozote, 227–8
El Salvador, 227
employment, ix, 68, 120
Engels, Friedrich, 30, 105
exfoliants (*see also* napalm), 206
Exxon, 47

factionalism, factionalist, ix, x, xii, 16, 31–3, 35–8, 49–50, 54–5, 57–8, 59–62, 68, 71, 75, 79, 105–6, 138, 149, 151, 166, 175, 177, 191–2, 196, 198–205, 241, 247
Fanon, Frantz, 47, 61, 81, 202–4
FAPLA, ix, xii, 23, 48, 54, 71, 94, 148, 161–2, 179, 206, 228, 236–8, 242
   9th Brigade, 35, 93, 149, 161–2, 167–8, 177, 181–4, 186, 217, 226
Faria, João, 114–23
fascism, fascist, 4, 10, 45, 48, 213, 222
fear, culture of (*cultura do medo*), i, 3, 4, 21, 35, 42, 151, 188, 191, 203, 218–19, 230
Fiat, 220
Financial Times (newspaper), 49
Flores, Paulo, 123
Flynn, John, 47

FNLA, ix, 3, 36, 68, 73, 81, 105, 117–18, 161–2, 176, 217, 228–9, 239–40
   Revolutionary Government of Angola in Exile (GRAE), 117–18
Folha 8 (newspaper), 113, 248
food, shortage of, 15–16, 68–9, 106–7, 131, 162–3, 256n20
Forbes (magazine), 209
Fortaleza de São Miguel, 72, 168, 209
Francisco, Miguel 'Michel', 177–90, 242
Freud, Sigmund, 114
Freudenthal, Percy, 164–5, 257n40
Frutuoso, Virgílio, 50
funje, 114
Furry, Abelardo Colomé, 242
Futungo de Belas, 107

Galloway, George, 44–5
García Márquez, Gabriel, 240, 242
Gaster, Polly, 57, 61
Gato, Ciel da Conceição, 141
George, Gilbert and, 214
Georgiou, Costas 'Colonel Callan', 229–30
Germany, German, 65, 83, 188, 248
   Berlin wall, fall of the, 3
   Hitler, 207
   Stasi and East, x, 221
Ginwala, Frene, 48
Goa, Goan, 52, 182
Guantanamo Bay, 85
Guardian (newspaper), 5, 85
Guevara, Che, 25–6, 46, 73
Guinea-Bissau, 13, 47, 64
Gulf of Guinea, 135

Heart of Darkness, 214
Henda Committee, 73
Hodgkin, Thomas, 46–7, 57
Hoxha, Enver, 33
Huambo, 40, 86, 93, 106, 193
Huíla, 86, 104, 193
Hutus, 191

Ikonoklasta, Henrique Luaty da Silva Beirão, 245–8
Ilha, 25, 209–10, 214

independence, African, 81, 193
  Angolan, ii, x, xii, 1, 3–4, 13–14, 23, 31, 56, 62, 70, 72, 90, 92, 95, 103, 117, 120, 139, 150, 161–2, 175, 186, 194, 200, 204–5, 216, 217, 230, 237, 239, 255*n*11
  Congo, 102
  Mozambican, 48
International Criminal Court, 169, 227
Iraq war, 44–5, 85, 128–9

Jagger, Bianca, 214
Jagger, Mick, 214
Jaime, Aguinaldo, 88
James, Sid, 234
Jehovah's Witness, 176
Jews, 188
JMPLA (*see* MPLA)
Jornal de Angola (newspaper), 70, 78–80, 87, 124, 175, 177, 178, 191–2, 194, 196–7, 214

Kant, Immanuel, 180
KGB, 121
Kiferro, 137–9, 141–2, 167, 242
Kikongo, 144
Kimbundu, x, 34, 144, 148
  Russian-Kimbundu salad, 215–16, 217
Kinaxixi, 127
King's College London, 209
Kinshasa, 37, 132
Kissanguela (band), 182
Kissassunda, Ludy, xii, 100, 180, 226
Kissinger, Henry, 165
Kongo, kingdom of, 41
Kopelipa, Hélder Manuel Vieira Dias Júnior, 114–15
Kudibanguela, x, 50, 93, 101, 181
Kwanhama, 186–7

labour, 147
  contract, forced, 23, 102
Labour Party, 44, 45
Lara, Lúcio, xii, 34, 57, 58, 59, 70, 72, 79, 83, 84, 104–5, 117, 128, 140, 148, 151, 163, 164, 176, 196, 216, 217, 226, 256*n*19
Latão, Tony, 166, 167

Lazo, Ramón Valle, 238–9
Lello bookshop, 53, 131
Lenin, Vladimir, 30, 33, 78, 105
Leninism, Leninist, 118, 119
  Marxism-Leninism, Marxist-Leninist, 3, 31, 33, 74, 147, 165, 219–20, 222
Lépi, 192–3
Little, Arthur D., 165
Liverpool, 229
Lobito, 40
Lopes, Elisário dos Passos Vieira, 244
Lopes, Francisco Filomeno Vieira, 2, 244, 248
Lubango, 104–7, 193
Luena, 13–18, 22, 23–4, 25, 106, 187, 213, 236–9, 242, 244
Lumumba, Patrice, 102
Lynch, David, 78

Machel, Samora, 47
maize, supply of, 68–9
Malanje, 86, 106, 132, 234
Malaquias, Rui, 58–9
Maldoror, Sarah, 135
Mao Zedong, 25, 33, 118, 147, 151
Maoism, Maoist, 31, 117, 118, 119, 147, 206, 217
Marathon Oil, 47
Marx, Karl, 30, 78, 105, 113
  cinema, 194
Marxism, Marxist, xii, 29, 33, 46, 47, 53, 55, 57, 70, 71, 83, 105, 164, 166, 208, 220, 223, 232
  (*see also* Leninism)
Masso, Lieutenant Colonel, 238
Matabeleland massacres, 5, 42
Matamba, kingdom of, 127
M'banza Kongo, 41, 88
Mbembe, Achille, 4, 111
Mbundu, x, 100
Melo, Aníbal João da Silva, 214–22
mercenaries, 36, 105, 228–30, 239, 241
Mfulumpinga, Nlandu Victor, 152
McHenry, Don, 232–3
Miami, 234–5, 243
Miguéis, Matias, 117–18
Miguel, José, 117–18
Mingas, Saydi, xii, 36, 48, 62, 69, 141, 182, 221

INDEX

Minnelli, Liza, 214
Monstro Imortal, Jacob João Caetano, xii, 70, 72, 159, 185, 226
Monteiro, Manuel Rui, 199–200
Moracén, Rafael Limonta, 241–2, 259*n*97–100
Morning Star (newspaper), 47
Morro da Luz, 168
Moxico, 13, 86, 168, 187, 218, 236, 242
   1974 Inter-Regional Conference of, 67
   (*see also* Calunda; Luena)
Mozambique, 9, 29, 47, 48, 64
MPLA, ix, x, xii, 1, 3–5, 13, 17, 21–2, 30–8, 42–3, 44, 48–9, 52–5, 58, 60–2, 65–6, 67–8, 72–3, 78–81, 83, 86–7, 90–5, 100, 103–7, 109, 115–18, 125, 131, 135, 138, 141, 144, 150, 152, 161–5, 175–6, 179, 182, 185, 192, 193–4, 198, 201, 203–4, 206, 208, 214, 218–19, 229, 230, 232, 237–8, 239–40, 242, 246, 255*n*11
   1977 Congress, 38, 74, 220
   children's wing (OPA), 31
   membership, drop in, 222
   MPLA-PT (Workers' Party), 74, 106, 220, 257*n*28
   women's wing (OMA), 31, 91, 106, 168, 237
   youth wing (JMPLA), 31, 65, 106, 138, 148, 168, 185, 186, 238
Mugabe, Robert, 5, 42
Mulemba (cemetery), 151, 153, 157–9

Namibe, 107, 168
Namibia, 49, 239
napalm (*see also* exfoliants), 23, 103, 110
Nascimento, Lopo do, 104, 217, 232
Nasrallah, Hassan, 45
nationalism, national-liberation, 5, 44, 46, 56, 202
   Angolan war for, 23, 74–5, 102–3, 135, 176
Ndongo, kingdom of, 127
Ndunduma Wé Lépi, Fernando Costa Andrade, 191–208, 227, 230, 232, 233
   editorials written by, 191, 201–5
Negage, 101–3
netista, x, 241

Neto, Agostinho, x, xii, 3, 5, 23, 32–7, 43, 48, 52–3, 54, 55, 61, 64, 66–7, 69–70, 71–2, 74, 78, 83, 93, 95, 101, 103, 105, 106, 107, 117–18, 127, 139, 140, 141, 148, 151, 164, 165, 166, 180, 182, 193–4, 200, 206–7, 216–17, 220, 222, 226, 233, 238, 239, 240–1, 256*n*19
   death of, 75–6, 231–2, 257*n*40, 260*n*100
   speeches by, 79–81, 105–6, 147, 175–7, 185, 191, 202–3, 204, 205, 221
Neto, António Garcia, 257*n*32
Neto, Helder, 141, 221, 257*n*32
Neto, Maria Eugénia, 23, 80, 175, 176
Neto, Mbala, 221, 226
New Left Review, 240
N'gangula, Augusto, 230
Ngola Ritmos (band), 149
nitista, ix, x, 4–5, 24, 55, 67, 68, 70, 72, 79, 105, 106, 126, 166, 173, 181, 201, 203, 216, 217, 218, 219, 220, 222, 226, 229, 241, 242
Nunes, Artur, 148–9, 182, 186
Nzaji, Eugénio Veríssimo da Costa, 194

OCA (Communist Organisation of Angola), x, 73, 79, 104
oil, sector, 47, 88, 99, 120, 164–6, 172, 240
Onambwe, Henrique de Carvalho Santos, xii, 35, 74, 100, 116, 148, 151, 163, 180, 196, 198, 226
Operation Carlota, 240
Operation Reinhardt, 188
Operation Sirocco, 66
Organisation of African Unity, 118
Organisation of Asian and African Writers, 118
Ovimbundu, x, 29, 68, 100

PADEPA, x, 1–2
Papa Kitoko, 132
Paris, 193, 195
paternalism, 33, 102
PCP (Portuguese Communist Party), x, 30, 52–3, 215
Pepetela, Artur Pestana, 47, 199–200
Petrofina, 220
Pherson, Randy, 231–2

PIDE, x, 14, 22, 75
Pinochet, Augusto, 5, 42
Poland, 188
Portugal, Portuguese
  (*see* Carnation Revolution; colonialism; education; employment; napalm; PCP; PIDE; race, etc.)
  embassy in Luanda, 17–20, 23, 227
portugalidade, 34
Presley, Elvis, 213
Pretoria, 37, 239, 240

Quibala concentration camp, 91
Quifangondo, the Battle of, 161

race, racism, i, 22, 33–4, 41, 51–2, 61–2, 68, 79–80, 85, 100, 101–4, 139, 147, 150, 152, 163, 166, 176, 179–81, 190, 200, 203–4, 207, 213, 216, 229, 231–3, 236, 239, 257n40, 259n99
  Race & Class (journal), 5
Rádio Nacional, x, 14, 31, 35, 48, 50, 57–61, 62, 71, 93–4, 101, 140, 149, 167, 181–2, 185, 192, 196, 197, 214, 221, 226, 241–2, 246
Radio Télévision Libre des Mille Collines, 191
Rainha Nzinga, 127
Reagan, Ronald, 86
reconciliation, truth and, 44, 188–9
Respect Party, 44–5
revolution, revolutionary, 29, 30–1, 33, 43, 46, 52, 53, 55, 57, 58, 62, 68, 70, 74, 75, 79, 81, 92, 95, 101, 103, 104, 105, 117, 152, 162, 166, 175, 176, 179, 182, 203, 204, 240, 242
  anti-revolutionary, counter-revolutionary, 4, 90–1
Rhodesia, Rhodesians, 163
Risquet, Jorge, 165
Romania, 165
Rose Royce (band), 214
Rousseau, Jean-Jacques, 180
Russia, Russian (*see also* Soviet Union, Soviet), 70, 147, 187, 210, 215–17
Rwanda genocide, 191

SADF (*see* South Africa)
Said, Edward, 47

St Paul's Girls' school, 209
Salazar, António de Oliveira, x, 10, 27, 37, 72, 79–80, 193
Sambizanga, xii, 24, 35, 55, 69, 71, 106, 134
  Progresso do (football), 31, 150
  Sambizanga (film), 135–44
Santos, Eduardo Macedo dos, 67
Santos, Isabel dos, 209
Santos, José Eduardo dos, x, 3, 28, 75–6, 135, 245–6, 248
São Nicolau prison, 107, 168
São Paulo prison, 71, 115, 119, 149, 167, 182, 197–8, 228–9, 241
São Tomé and Príncipe, 64, 135, 169
Saturday Night Fever, 214
Savimbi, Jonas, xi, 11, 21, 36, 86, 144
School of Oriental and African Studies, xviii, 29
Schwarzenegger, Arnold, 214
Seko, Mobutu Sese, ix, 36–7, 107
Semanário Angolense (newspaper), 214
Sex Pistols (band), 213
Shaba (*see also* Congo; Zaire), 36
Shubin, Vladimir, 217–18
Sianuk, Anselmo Mesquita, 50
Silva, Baltazar Rodrigues da, 22–3
Silva, Reginaldo, 197–9
slavery, 4, 23, 41, 56, 62, 64, 72, 102, 132, 172
Smith, Ian, 163
Sobibór, 188
socialism, socialist, x, 3, 5, 36, 44, 48, 50, 52, 55, 57, 60, 62, 73, 150, 164, 165, 176, 203, 217, 220, 229, 233, 237, 240
  Socialist Worker (newspaper), 29
Sonangol, 47, 165, 257n39, 257n43
South Africa, South African, 3, 11, 44, 80, 132, 164, 213
  National Party, 37, 150
  SADF, troops in Angola, xi, 36, 37, 73, 150, 161, 166, 239–40, 242
  Soweto, Soweto uprising, 150
Soviet Union, Soviet (*see also* Russia, Russian), x, 3–4, 26, 31, 42, 76, 78, 105, 117, 165, 206, 215–18, 219–20, 231, 233
  anti-Soviet, 33
  Communist Party, 79, 217

military equipment and weapons in
Angola, 23, 165–6, 187, 237–8, 240, 242
Moscow, 52, 76, 79, 107, 206, 216–17, 220–1, 233
Soyo, 88
Stalin, Stalinist, 43, 105, 215
Grupo Joséf Stálin, 115, 118
Standard Chartered Bank, 47
Statoil, 47
Straw, Jack, 45
Summer, Donna, 214

Texaco, 165, 220
The Times (newspaper), 47, 48
Tito, Titoist, 208
Tocoists, Simão Toco, 176
Tonet, William, 191, 248, 260n103
Top of the Pops, 214
torture, torturer, 72, 75, 103, 104, 106, 115–16, 119, 159, 168–9, 209
chinkwalia, 116
n'guelelo, 72, 115
Travolta, John, 214
Treblinka, 188
Tundavala, 104, 106
Tutsis, 191

Uíge, 4, 101
Umbundu, x, 29, 144
UNITA, x, xi, 3, 4, 10, 17, 36, 43, 47, 65, 68, 70, 73, 81, 83, 86, 132, 136–7, 141, 144, 152, 162, 166, 176, 217, 236, 239

United Nations, 131
Security Council, 240
World Food Programme, 68
United States, 11, 36, 37, 64, 85, 164, 220, 240
Clark Amendment, 86
(*see also* Cabgoc; Chevron; CIA; oil; Reagan, etc.)

Valles, Sita, xii, 52, 54, 75
Van Dúnem, Balthasar, 64–5
Van Dúnem, João, xvii, 64–76, 87, 178
Van Dúnem, José 'Zé', xii, 31, 33, 35, 51, 52, 54–5, 65, 70–3, 75, 168, 175, 182, 185, 209, 226
Varela, Urbano, 238
Vieira, José Luandino, 47
Vita, Dona Beatriz Kimpa, 41
Volvo, 220

West Africa (magazine), 47
Wolfers, Michael, 46–55, 57–62
World War II, 56

Yugoslavia, 193, 194, 206

Zaire (*see also* Congo; Mobutu, etc.), ix, 36–7, 73, 161, 232, 239, 255n8
Zambia, 193
Zé, David, 148–9, 181, 182, 186